Twayne's English Authors Series

EDITOR OF THIS VOLUME

Sylvia E. Bowman
Indiana University

Robert Southey

TEAS 223

Robert Southey

ROBERT SOUTHEY

By ERNEST BERNHARDT-KABISCH
Indiana University

TWAYNE PUBLISHERS
A DIVISION OF G. K. HALL & CO., BOSTON

Library of Congress Cataloging in Publication Data

Bernhardt-Kabisch, Ernest, 1934 -
    Robert Southey.

    (Twayne's English authors series ; TEAS 223)
    Bibliography: p. 189 - 91
    Includes index.
    1.   Southey, Robert, 1774 - 1843—Criticism and interpretation.
PR5467.B4   821'.7   77-13098
ISBN 0-8057-6692-8

For my parents

Contents

About the Author

Preface

Chronology

1. Et in Utopia Ego: Early Life   13

2. Arms and a Maid: *Joan of Arc*   29

3. Idols of the Cave: The Man and the Poet   50

4. Mythopoesis: *Thalaba* and *Kehama*   81

5. The Course of Empire: *Madoc*   109

6. Lucifer in Spain: *Roderick* and the Laureate Verse   128

7. Days Among the Dead: Prose Writings   158

   Notes and References   181

   Selected Bibliography   189

   Index   193

About the Author

Ernest Bernhardt-Kabisch is an associate professor at Indiana University, Bloomington, where he teaches English and Comparative Literature. He was born in Germany in 1934 and attended the Eberhard-Ludwigs-Gymnasium, Stuttgart, the University of Stuttgart, and the University of Tuebingen before coming to the United States. He earned his doctorate at the University of California in Berkeley. He has been a Fulbright Fellow. His publications include articles on Wordsworth, Southey, Romanticism, and Joyce. He is currently engaged in a study of religious thought in Romantic poetry.

Preface

The twofold aim of this study of Robert Southey is to provide an overview of one of the best known of the unread poets and to show that his work has at least a lively historical interest. Southey once remarked that he was "well pleased to be abused with Wordsworth and Coleridge: it is the best omen that I shall be remembered with them." The omen has been fulfilled with the usual ironic twist, and Southey is remembered to this day as the associate of Coleridge and Wordsworth—and as the target of Byron's satire—rather than as the bard he strove to be. The present study will not greatly alter his reputation. Rather than trying to claim for his work a timeless relevance that it does not possess, I have kept in mind its contingent appeal. I have thus not scrupled to include a good deal of paraphrase and synopsis, admittedly a lowly form of criticism, but here, I believe, often the most immediately useful one.

Beyond that, however, the heroic magnitude of Southey's poetic quest must command both attention and admiration. Moreover, while a study of that quest is largely a study in failure, Southey's grand failures are more interesting than his modest successes and far more illuminative of Romanticism and Romantic myth-making generally. I have therefore concentrated on Southey's poetry, especially the long poems. I have devoted individual chapters to each of the three major epics, one to the romances, and one to the lyrical verse, and have confined the prose, which has hitherto received the principal share of critical attention, to a summary final chapter. Chapters One and Three provide perspective by dealing with Southey's early life and personality. My thesis, if I have one, is that, while an heir of the Enlightenment like his fellow Romantics, Southey was unable to break through to the new consciousness that we call "Romantic," a consciousness frankly introspective, skeptical, and symbolistic, but halted in a limbo between reason and imagination.

My debt to Southey scholarship is indicated in the notes and the bibliography. I would like to thank Indiana University for its support in the form of a research grant, Sylvia Bowman and Therese

Pol for expert editorial advice, and my wife Eva for unfailing counsel, encouragement, and patience.

ERNEST BERNHARDT-KABISCH

Indiana University.

Chronology

1774   Robert Southey born on August 12 in Bristol.

1788   Enters Westminster School.

1792   Expelled from Westminster for contumacious writing. Father dies.

1793   Enters Balliol College, Oxford; attends only two terms.

1794   Meeting with S. T. Coleridge; Pantisocracy planned. Leaves Oxford.

1795   Quarrel with Coleridge. Marries Edith Fricker. Leaves for Portugal. *Poems by Robert Lovell and Robert Southey* published.

1796   *Joan of Arc* published. Returns from Portugal.

1797   Begins study of law. *Poems* published.

1798   Resides at Westbury near Bristol; period of great poetic productivity.

1799   *Poems,* Volume II, and *Annual Anthology* published. Reconciliation with Coleridge; friendship with scientist Humphry Davy.

1800   Returns to Portugal.

1801   *Thalaba* published. Returns from Portugal. Secretary to Isaac Corry.

1802   Mother dies. Birth of Southey's first child, Margaret.

1803   Death of daughter Margaret. The Southeys move to Greta Hall, Keswick.

1805   *Madoc* published; *Metrical Tales* published.

1808   *Letters from England* published; *The Chronicle of the Cid* published.

1809   Begins to write for the *Quarterly Review.*

1810   *Curse of Kehama* published.

1813   *Life of Nelson* published. Appointed Poet Laureate.

1814   *Roderick* published.

1816   Death of son Herbert (aged ten).

1817   *Wat Tyler* published surreptitiously.

1821   *Vision of Judgment* published; controversy with Bryon.

1829   *Colloquies* published.

1834   *The Doctor,* Volumes I, II, published.

1837   Death of Edith Southey after three years of lunacy.
1838   Marries Caroline Bowles. His mind begins to fail.
1843   Dies March 21. Buried in Crosthwaite Churchyard, Keswick.

CHAPTER 1

Et in Utopia Ego: Early Life

I *Childhood*

IN his late forties, Robert Southey set out to write his own life in a series of letters addressed to his friend John May. The letters, of which he finished seventeen, are sprightly and informative; but they are also as prolix and garrulous as the anecdotes of Juliet's nurse, and they break off when their subject has barely reached puberty.[1] Though Southey lived in an age of great autobiography—and, indeed, seems to have coined the word—he left no distinct specimen of the genre. The fact is symptomatic: Southey was incapable of introspection. He could either recall reality in its surface minutiae or reduce it to poetic schemata of myth and allegory; but he could not alchemize personal fact into autonomous image and symbol. If he thereby appears at first to be more objective than his fellow Romantics, it is not because he is less in the grip of his past than they but because he is more so. More than most poets, Southey needs to be approached in terms of his past. His story is the story of an unfinished life.

His background is one of exile and frustration. His father, Robert, a draper in Wine Street, Bristol, had grown up in the country and had no love for his trade. A frustrated farmer, he was injudicious in his business—he eventually went bankrupt—and a feckless parent: Southey inherited little more from him than his name. From his mother, he had at least his good looks and his steely cheerfulness. But, although Margaret Hill Southey seems to have been a fine woman, affectionate, sweet-tempered, and sensible, she was not only uneducated but evidently incapable of asserting herself in her own or in her childrens' behalf.

The paramount influence in Southey's childhood, for both good and evil, was in fact not his parents but his mother's older half-sister, the formidable Miss Tyler, to whose house at fashionable

13

Bath little Robert was sent when he was two. One of four children whom Margaret's mother had brought into her second marriage with Edward Hill of Bedminster, Elizabeth Tyler had grown up with a clergyman uncle, whose household and parish she had eventually managed and where she had acquired a taste for high life by hobnobbing with the local gentry. At the uncle's death she had inherited most of his estate and was living on it, rather beyond her means, when Robert came to stay with her. She was by now a tempestuous beauty in her middle thirties. The daughter of an alcoholic—Mr. Tyler had drunk himself to death—and victim of parental neglect; a spinster who had been repeatedly disappointed in her expectations; a would-be society woman, a bluestocking, and an emotional recluse, she loathed most people, adulated some, and bullied the rest—especially her half-sister, Southey's mother—and was eccentric and compulsive in her ways. She dressed expensively when she went out or received visitors but otherwise lived in bedclothes and rags. She surrounded herself with elegant furnishings, including a portrait of herself by Gainsborough; but since she had a horror of dirt, she kept most of the house shut and her portrait curtained. Callers of whom she was not fond were regarded as unclean, and whatever they had touched had to be elaborately purified.

In this neurotic and stifling atmosphere young Robert spent most of his time between two and thirteen suffering the two-fold evil of over-protection and lack of nurture. While he was little, Miss Tyler had him sleep with her; but since she rose late, he would have to lie awake for hours in the morning without moving, lest he disturb her, and while away the time as best he could. Though the house stood at the outskirts of Bath overlooking fields and woods and was surrounded by a garden and orchard, Robert was kept indoors and away from boyish games, lest he soil himself, and was set to pin-pricking the lettering on old playbills.

Fortunately, Miss Tyler had some interests that the child could share. She was personally acquainted with the son of John Newbery, the "father of children's literature"; and from him little Robert, an early reader, received a whole set of Newbery's quaint six-penny books for children. Southey's fanatical love of books began here where so little else could be loved. Another advantage was that he could benefit from his aunt's passion for and patronage of the theater, which was then in its heyday at Bath. Robert saw his first play at four; and, while he lived with his aunt or when he visited from school, he was regularly taken to performances and heard much stage talk from actors and playwrights. Before he was eight, he read Shakespeare, particularly the histories, and Beaumont and Fletcher; and he soon afterwards tried his own hand at playwriting.

For these formative experiences Southey was grateful to his aunt, and she no doubt did far more for his intellectual development than either of his parents could have done. But his being made to live with her probably did him lasting harm in more vital respects. We cannot know what his feelings about his aunt were at the time; but we do note that in the earliest of Southey's remembered dreams the devil called upon one of Miss Tyler's bosom friends and victims, Miss Palmer, who was delighted with her dear Mr. Devil's presence, while terrified little Robert "sat and looked at his cloven foot, and perspired at every pore."[2] The cloven hoof, whatever its precise original significance might have been in Southey's mind, continued to pursue him all his life.

Although Southey enjoyed intervals of gaiety and freedom especially when he could stay at his grandmother's farm in Bedminster, "the very paradise of my childhood," his recollections convey considerable alienation and resentment. Death, known early and intimately to the sensitive boy, could only intensify his existential anxiety. Of his numerous siblings, only three brothers survived; all three of his sisters and two brothers died in childhood or infancy before Robert had turned fourteen—hence Southey's lifelong obsession with death and personal immortality, his need to dream of Thalaba, the destroyer of the powers of destruction. He was to lose four children of his own, including his first child and his passionately loved son Herbert.

Desolation and trauma also color Southey's school memories. At six, he entered a Latin grammar school, whose master, a hoary Baptist minister, was tyrannical and incompetent, and where the boys were a constant menace. Robert was too terrified to learn anything and was punished with incarceration and once with a severe caning. He was even more miserable at Corston, a boarding school located between Bristol and Bath, where he was sent the following year. Unlike Miss Tyler's house, Corston offered opportunity for play and fellowship in the decayed gardens of the former manor house in which the school was lodged. But the diet was lean; hygiene was all but non-existent; the headmaster's wife drank; and there was little teaching. Above all, the boy had no home to escape to at the end of the day.

Southey's early poems repeatedly allude to the year he spent at Corston as a period of exile under petty tyranny and loveless discipline. In the poem "Remembrance" (1798), he parodies the nostalgic idealization of school life of Thomas Gray's Eton Ode with a Rousseauistic sketch of his own dismal experience. The earlier "Retrospect" (1794) is more ambiguous; but here, too, the conventional nostalgia for the ignorant bliss of childhood is undercut by a sense of betrayal. In truth, Southey writes, "The days of childhood are but days of woe; / Some rude restraint, some petty tyrant sours, / What else should be our sweetest, blithest hours." If childhood memories are nevertheless sweet to him, they are so only because "two small acres bounded all my fears" and "ignorance itself was happiness."[3] The appended sonnet "Corston" is equally ambivalent.

He later recalled as particularly painful his "being kept up every night . . . when I was dying with sleepiness"—the converse of his early ordeals in his aunt's bed. The worst instances of this torment were the endless devotional readings on Sunday evenings: "Here I sat at the end of a long form, in sight but not within feeling of the fire, my feet cold, my eyelids heavy as lead, and yet not daring to close them, kept awake by fear alone, in total inaction, and under the operation of a lecture more soporific than the strongest sleeping dose" (*Life*, I, 57). Here, perhaps, is the germ of *The Curse of Kehama*: "Thou shalt live in thy pain . . . With a fire in thy . . . brain; / And Sleep shall obey me, / And visit thee never; / And the Curse shall be on thee / For ever and ever."

Robert was happier at the Bristol school which he attended for the next four years. The headmaster, William Williams, a moody Welsh pedant, was not a tyrant. But the curriculum offered little beyond writing, ciphering, Latin, and catechism. One of Southey's schoolmates, a Creole planter's son, "the most thoroughly fiendish being that I have ever known," whose eyes often burned with "devilish malignity," became the prototype for the diabolic Arvalan in *Kehama* (*Life*, I, 95). In 1784, moreover, Miss Tyler decided to move to Bristol, and Robert was promptly again commandeered by her and discouraged from visiting his own home. Hostile toward the Southeys and full of snobbish contempt for Bristol society, Miss Tyler now became a virtual recluse and increasingly hysterical in her "dustophobia." Fortunately, Robert found a playmate in Shadrach Weeks, the brother of Miss Tyler's maid, with whom he could build puppet theaters or roam through the rocks and woods

along the Avon. The school routine was now and then enlivened by
visits from Williams' cronies, like the merry madcap Dr. Jones, who
entertained the boys with improvised nonsense doggerels. Robert
was also cheered by yet another halfwit in those years: his aunt's
"half-saved" brother William Tyler, whom she had taken into her
house after their mother's death. Southey spent much time in the
company of the "Squire," as the family called him; and he later
depicted him affectionately in his Shandean swansong, *The Doctor*,
as William Dove, "who was not so wise as his friends could have
wished and yet quite as happy as if he had been wiser," half shrewd
jester, half guileless child, and as full of saws and stories as the
Brothers Grimm.[4] The euphoria of nonsense which these men ex-
emplified remained a psychic refuge for Southey throughout his
adult life.

II   *Westminster and Literary Beginnings*

A bright and precocious boy, Southey learned to compensate for
the dearth of emotional and scholastic nurture by exploring in-
dependently the world of poetry. His father's book-case contained
little besides *The Spectator*, Solomon Gesner's *Death of Abel*, and
miscellaneous plays. At his aunt's, he encountered Shakespeare and
other dramatists. But the decisive event was his chance discovery of
Tasso's *Jerusalem Delivered* in Hoole's translation, which in turn
led him to Ariosto's *Orlando Furioso* and to Spenser's *Faerie
Queene*. Almost at once Southey conceived his lifelong passion for
epic and romance. He read and reread Tasso's poem so often that
he had large portions by heart; and Spenser's magic verse and moral
idealism so enchanted the boy that Spenser thenceforth became his
supreme "master," whom he worshipped with the "reverence of
idolatrous love." By the time Robert was twelve, he had also read
Milton's *Paradise Lost*, Camoens' *Lusiad*, in Mickle's translation,
and Pope's Homer, as well as Philip Sidney's *Arcadia*, and the
Rowley Poems of his fellow Bristowan Thomas Chatterton. Ovid's
Metamorphoses, Greek and Roman mythology and history, the *Ara-
bian Tales*, and a good many current novels followed, as did
Chaucer and Bishop Percy's epoch-making *Reliques of Ancient
English Poetry*.
  Fired by these examples, and by Thomas Warton's pioneering
History of English Poetry, Southey began to project various epics of
his own, mostly on British subjects, all of them headlong and abor-

tive, but all of them diligently researched. There were numerous other poetic trials: dream visions, satires, genre pieces, heroic epistles on Classical and Biblical topics, and translations from Virgil, Ovid, and Horace. Southey's versatility and his reckless productiveness appeared from the start.

When Robert was thirteen, his uncle, the Reverend Herbert Hill, decided to have his promising nephew educated at his expense; so on April 1, 1788, Southey was entered at Westminster, which Mr. Hill chose as the gateway to Christ Church College at Oxford. Westminster was then still one of the two leading public schools in England, rivaled only by Eton, and proud of a long line of famous pupils. But its curriculum, consisting almost wholly of Latin and Greek, was obsolete—Robert was put back a whole year because he could not make Latin verses—the instruction was routine, the discipline, fitful and desultory. Bullying and fagging were as common as elsewhere, and Robert got his share of both—his first roommate, for example, was a brute given to maniacal fits of savagery. Among the nightmares which Southey had all his life, Westminster was one that haunted him regularly even in his mid-forties.

Besides nightmares, Westminster bestowed two lasting gifts upon Southey: friendship and renewed exile. His second roommate was Charles W. W. Wynn, the son of a prominent Welsh Whig family and the nephew of Lord Grenville. Eventually a Member of Parliament for the rotten borough of Old Sarum and a cabinet minister, Wynn advanced Southey's career with an annuity in 1797 and with a government pension in 1808. He shared many of Southey's interests; and, although, as a staunch Whig, he was in later years repeatedly critical of Southey's deepening conservatism, he loyally defended him in Parliament against the cry of apostasy in the *Wat Tyler* affair (see below, p. 46). A second and even more intimate friendship was that with Grosvenor Charles Bedford. Bedford, who was as solidly middleclass as Wynn was patrician, had the plodding mind and the conventional outlook of the civil servant. Although himself an occasional poet and reviewer, he did not greatly influence Southey's career—except to introduce him to William Gifford, the editor of the *Quarterly Review*—and repeated attempts at literary collaboration between the two men remained unfruitful. But he served as a lifelong confidant and sounding-board to the otherwise reserved Southey. Periodically, also, Bedford's stuffiness gave way to buffoonery; and then Southey, who always loved to talk nonsense, thought him another Rabelais.

Ironically, it was these very friendships that led to trouble. The Bedfords lived in London, and in their library Southey would put aside the stultifying task of Latin versification to feed a nascent radicalism and emotionalism by reading Voltaire, Rousseau, "Ossian," and Goethe's *Sorrows of Werther*. Here Bernard Picart's sumptuous and voluminous *Religious Ceremonies* first roused Southey's lifelong fascination with myth and inspired his ambition to exhibit the world's leading mythologies in poetry. Here, also, Southey read Edward Gibbon's *Decline and Fall of the Roman Empire* and acquired not only his lasting penchant for historical study from it but also a measure of religiuos doubt. His discipleship of these writers presently proved his undoing. In the spring of 1792, Bedford and Wynn had founded a school periodical, *The Flagellant*, which Southey joined and eventually co-edited. In the fifth number, Southey published, under the pseudonym "Gualbertus," a satirical essay about corporal punishment, in which he used the knowledge and manner recently acquired from his reading to hurl anathema at flogging as a heathenish custom and as a form of Satanism unbecoming to an institution of Christian learning.

It was Southey's first literary skirmish with the legions of the devil, and it was as luckless as his attack on the Satanic School three decades later. Mild and clerkly as the satire was, it roused the ire of the headmaster, Dr. Vincent. Southey had already offended by "abusing Burke" in one of his prose themes; he may even have participated in a school rebellion. Fear of subversion was generally in the air—the King would soon issue his proclamation against "Wicked and Seditious Writings." At all events, Vincent discovered the identity of "Gualbertus" and promptly expelled the boy.

Southey was never a Promethean rebel like Shelley. His revolutionary sympathies, at their most ardent, were qualified and bourgeois even for his time. In one of his earliest nightmares, he had dreamed that "my head was cut off for cursing the King—and after it was done I laid my head down in my mothers lap—and every now and then looked up and cursed him." The peculiar mixture of defiance and impotence in this dream typifies the very core of Southey's nature. His immediate response to his expulsion was an oddly half-hearted satirical allegory, at once blunt and double-edged, about Pedantry, the offspring of Commonsense and Ignorance, and Presumption, the child of Philosophy and Freedom, and how Jupiter, provoked by the folly of the one and by the arrogance of the other, punished both by dooming "the latter to become the pupil of the former" (*New Letters*, I, 150, 4). Even so, Southey's sense of injured merit and of arbitrary persecution was acute, particularly when he discovered that Vincent, contrary to earlier assurances, had also barred his access to Christ Church by warning the college officials against the young anarchist. "God forgive him," the eighteen-year-old boy exclaimed; "I never can."

Soon humiliated again by his father's bankruptcy, Southey spent the remainder of the year at loose ends and in a troubled condition; now reading and copiously imitating Gray and other poets of melancholy, now trying to "starve" his "mimosa sensibility" (as he later put it) by "dieting upon" the *Manual* of the Stoic Epictetus, forever after his favorite philosopher; now hailing the French Revolution and the fall of "Louis the Last," now appalled by the September Massacres: "Everything that is respectable, every barrier that is sacred, is swept away." Shortly before Christmas, Southey's father died. In January, 1793, Southey went up to Balliol College, Oxford, "a Stoic and a Republican."[5]

III Oxford

If Southey had thought that Oxford would redeem his previous scholastic experiences, he was quickly disillusioned. Oxford was "Stupidity Town," a place of "great wigs and little wisdom," of pedantry among the masters, and of licentiousness and snobbery among the scholars. Monkish in its all-male character, the university seemed but the corpse of monasticism, soulless, rotten with vices, and periodically galvanized into a ghastly semblance of life by empty rituals like the daily chapel service. The exasperated ex-Flagellant promptly wrote a poem called "The Chapel Bell," in which he jeered at the "tedious herald of more tedious . . . prayer that trembles on a yawn to heaven / . . . The snuffling, snaffling Fellow's nasal tone, / And Romish rites retained, though Romish faith be flown" (II, 150).

Amid such encircling gloom, Southey resolved to be a paragon of republican virtue, temperance, and chastity. He set a precedent by refusing to wear his hair powdered. His closest friend at Oxford, besides Wynn, was Edmund Seward, his senior by three years and a man of such "unbending morals and iron rectitude" that Southey called him "Talus." Seward was evidently something of a prig; but Southey revered him as his "moral father," and his death in 1795 shook him as his own father's death never had. Years later, he would still "dream of him, and wake myself by weeping, because even in my dreams I remember that he is dead" (*Life*, IV, 320). Seward's stern regard for duty and self-discipline strongly reinforced the lessons that Southey had already derived from Epictetus.

For all that, Southey's spirits refused to be silenced. During Easter vacation, he dragged Seward through a walking tour in search of picturesque landscapes and Gothic abbey ruins. In his second year at Balliol, when Southey was relieved of Seward's awesome presence, he defied not only the chapel bell but also his Euclid. Heaven forbid that he should "discompose / That spider's excellent geometry" or panegyrize the new university chancellor in antiquated meters. He would rather study the "College Cat" and laud her republican virtues in good modern blank verse. "Ay, stretch thy claws, thou democratic beast; / I like thine independence!" Would that spaniel Man, who "licks his tyrant's hand / And courts oppression," were like her: "Wiser animal, / I look at thee, familiarized, yet free; / And, thinking that a child with gentle hand / Leads by a string the large-limbed Elephant, / With mingled indignation and contempt / Behold his drivers goad the biped beast" (III, 56-8).[6] He loved cats all his life.

Philosophically speaking, Southey was trying to mediate between Epictetus and Epicurus's "system of ethics and pleasure combined." In religion, he was already the Deist and Pelagian that he was essentially to be throughout his life. The cardinal religious virtues to him were "meekness, humility and temperance"; "morose austerity and stern enthusiasm" he disparaged as superstitious. The crucial message of Christianity was not the atonement but the consoling prospect of a personal immortality that was to compensate for the ills of life and disarm the nihilism of "shakespeares fearfully beautiful passage—Ay, but to die and go we know not whither." To undermine this "true Xian" faith was wicked, not so much because it was presumptuous toward God, but because it was cruel toward man in that, as Southey later put it, it "restores the sting to Death and gives again the victory to the Grave."[7]

Unorthodox views like these were bound to bring Southey in conflict with his educational objectives. Mr. Hill intended him for the Anglican Church, and Southey, anxious not to disappoint his benefactor again, was resolved to bend himself to the yoke. But his resolve did not last, and the prospect of ordination soon became a sword of Damocles. Skeptical about Church dogma, Southey opposed the very idea of priesthood and denounced both the

Establishment and the Test Acts. Besides, he had no taste for "starving in creditable celibacy upon 40 pounds a year."

He tried to stall the issue by spending the term after the Long Vacation at home. But the boardinghouse his mother was keeping to maintain herself and her younger children depressed him; and the temper of his aunt, with whom he stayed as usual, was sourer than ever. Southey found some solace in the company of "some young women, sisters, with whom I was partly educated and whose histories are as melancholy as my own." But his visits were few and surreptitious, for Sarah, Edith, and Mary Fricker, though handsome and fairly well educated girls, were daughters of an impoverished, school-keeping tradesman's widow who worked as seamstresses and who were, therefore, socially unacceptable to the snobbish Miss Tyler (*New Letters*, I, 54, 37).

As usual, Southey fled into hectic literary production. Already he could look back on some "10,000 verses . . . burnt and lost, the same number preserved, and 15,000 worthless" (*Life*, I, 197). Among those preserved and not counted worthless was his first epic, *Joan of Arc*, whose over six thousand lines were mostly written during the Long Vacation at the Bedford home. The stirring legend of the "missioned maid" of Orleans helped Southey to forget his anxieties about his own impending "mission" and enabled him to disburden his heart of its disaffection and Republican fervor.

It was, as Southey felt even thirty years later, a time of apocalyptic expectation: "Old things seemed passing away, and nothing was dreamt of but the regeneration of the human race."[8] Like most young idealists, Southey was now firmly on the side of the French; and he was appalled by England's entrance into the war against the nascent republic. The execution of the Girondists and the Reign of Terror inevitably shook his confidence. But his reading of William Godwin's *Political Justice* revived his sinking trust in human nature and in the possibility of radical regeneration through political reform: "I read and all but worshipped" (*Life*, I, 247). The true causes of crime, Godwin convinced him, were poverty and social and economic privilege: "We are born in sin and the children of wrath—says the catechism. It is absolutely false. Sin is artificial—it is the monstrous offspring of government and property" (*New Letters*, I, 40).

The thought of emigration now presented itself to Southey as a final panacea. Europe was perhaps too deeply immersed in wealth and corruption, in prejudice and superstition, to be reformed. If

Democracy and Godwinism were to prevail, they would have to do
so in the New World where one could make a fresh start. Southey
had been dreaming of Utopia for some time, stimulated by examples as diverse as the sober exploits of St. John de Crèvecoeur
and the adventures of the *Bounty* mutineers. His mind needed only
the catalytic meeting with Coleridge to produce the idea of "Pantisocracy."

Early in 1794, Southey returned to Oxford, happily in love with
Edith Fricker and resolved not to take holy orders but to study
medicine instead. His enthusiasm was short-lived. His "mimosa
sensibility" could not endure the dissecting room, and the consequent abandonment of medicine brought back all the old problems.
His second term at the university was in fact his last. He never took
a degree.

IV   *Coleridge and Pantisocracy*

The decision to leave the university was precipitated by the
fateful meeting with Coleridge. It occurred at the end of the spring
term, when Coleridge, on his way from Cambridge to Wales,
stopped at Oxford for a visit and was introduced to Southey.
Although the differences between the two men in both character
and talent would appear only too soon, they found, for the moment,
much that they had in common. Both were discontented university
men; both were nascent poets; both, above all, were
radicals—Deists or Socinians in religion and Jacobins in politics. For
Southey in particular, the meeting was a cataclysmic event that dis-
pelled his uncertainty and his cautious reserve; and an enthusiastic
friendship quickly developed. Coleridge's stopover grew into a
three-week stay; and during that time, the two enthusiasts, in concert with Coleridge's friends, Robert Allen and Joseph Hucks, and
two of Southey's friends, Seward and the neurotic George Burnett,
developed the idea of "Pantisocracy." Southey evidently fathered
the idea and, after Coleridge's departure, "talked [it] into shape"
with Burnett; Coleridge gave it its name and, later, its local habitation.

In essence, Pantisocracy, "equal rule of all," proposed to bring
about in the New World, and on a small scale, what the French
Revolution was failing to achieve in the Old: the restoration of the
primordial social contract and, thereby, of the moral and cultural conditions of the Golden Age as the Enlightenment dreamed of it. A

party of twelve young men—among them Southey, Coleridge, Burnett, Allen, Seward, and Robert Lovell, the husband of the third of the Fricker sisters—were to found a settlement in the upper Susquehanna Valley where, as American Farmers à la Crèvecoeur, they would cultivate both their gardens and their minds. The leading idea was derived from Godwin—"to make men *necesarily* virtuous by removing all Motives to Evil." Private property, the root of all social and most moral evil, would be abolished—"aspheterism" was Coleridge's coinage for this feature—and all were to live and work in absolute *egalité* and *fraternité*, free from the vicious cycle of "Fear and Selfishness".[9]

The principle of equality and fraternity was to extend to men and women alike—not to mention animals. The Pantisocrats only stopped short of following either Plato or Godwin into abolishing the institution of matrimony, though the possibility of divorce by mutual consent was discussed. In fact, matrimony was a key element in the mythus underlying Pantisocracy. All of the twelve patriarchal peers were to be married to intelligent and liberal but withal docile and decorous young women who would tend the kitchen and the nursery before joining the men in the rustic parlor for joint study and conversation.

As is well known, this dream of domestic bliss was the sole item in the scheme that ever materialized—only to turn into a nightmare for the most brilliant of the Pantisocrats. Since Lovell was already married to Mary Fricker and since Southey was engaged to Edith, it seemed logical that Coleridge should be introduced to Sarah, the oldest of the five sisters. Returned from Wales to help Southey preach the new gospel in Bristol, Coleridge, though still in love with one Mary Evans, zealously mistook "the ebullience of *schematism* for affection" as he put it afterwards; and by the end of the summer found himself committed to the pleasant, practical, and very pretty, but unimaginative, parochial, and somewhat frigid Sarah.

Four months of being back in Cambridge and in London sufficed to convince the young schematist that he had made a mistake. His letters to Southey are hardly ambiguous. Despite formal protestations that he would do his "duty," he was plainly appealing to Southey, as the father of Pantisocracy, to release him from his commitment to Sarah. But Southey, too obtuse, inflexible, or both to see anything more than lack of resoluteness in his friend's palpitations, merely lectured him and, finally, went to look for him in London and persuaded him to return to Bristol and to Sarah. We should not make Southey wholly responsible for the older man's marital mistake. But we must regret his officiousness and impercipience. Before the end of 1795, both men were married; but, ironically, their friendship was at an end, at least temporarily, and Pantisocracy had died a slow death.

A major cause of that demise was simply lack of funds. The assumption that the needed capital could be earned by the pen proved illusory. Even the series of lectures on political, religious, and historical subjects which Coleridge and Southey gave at Bristol in the spring yielded little more than the young lecturers' daily bread. Southey's personal expectations, moreover, suffered a severe blow when his aunt, who had been assisting his family financially, learned of her nephew's Utopian plans and of his engagement to Edith Fricker. Miss Tyler's reaction was swift and stunning: she turned him out of doors, penniless. He never saw her again.

More telling, however, than these practical difficulties were the ideological differences that began to develop between the leaders of the group. For Southey, Pantisocracy, with its apocalyptic aura of purpose and mission, had been a sudden liberation from much anxiety and frustration. As he described it, it was at once the Ark and the Promised Land, and he himself was Noah and Moses, preparing an exodus from a world steeped in corruption and threatened with a deluge of blood. But when the prudent Edmund Seward withdrew from the scheme because of religious scruples, he took with him all the prestige he had lent to the idea in Southey's eyes. His death not long afterwards had an even more dispiriting effect. Moreover, Southey's own sense of family soon proved too strong for a full apostolic commitment, and he proposed to include both his mother and Mrs. Fricker and their younger children among the emigrants. But to Coleridge, such a compromise with the past was highly unphilosophical. The children, already mistaught, would not be able to keep "silence concerning God &c," and "*that* Mrs. Fricker—we shall have her teaching the Infants *Christianity* . . . in some aguefit of Superstition!" Worse, Southey now planned not only to hire day laborers for the more arduous pioneer tasks but to let his former playmate Shadrach Weeks and his wife accompany the Pantisocrats as servants. Coleridge was appalled at the idea of such "Helot-Egalités." And when, with America plainly out of reach, Southey at last proposed Wales as an alternative location, Coleridge saw only a further hedging of the original principles: Pantisocracy was about to dwindle into a "petty Farming Trade."

The relationship of the two men thus became more and more strained. Several months of actually housing together, moreover, revealed the real incompatibility between the prodigal and dilatory genius and the thrifty but narrow talent and the strain such differences would inevitably exert on a system of "aspheterism." Southey felt that he was doing most of the work and that his bedfellow was taking advantage of him. If he was to support anyone, it would be his wife. He finally moved out.

Southey, in fact, began to doubt the utility of abstract social theories and Utopian experiments of the sort promulgated by Godwin. From the beginning, the domestic aspect of Pantisocracy had held the greatest attraction for him; it now began to blot out all other considerations. When Wynn offered him an annuity of a hundred and sixty pounds if he were to study law, Southey accepted it as a refuge alike from Utopia and from ordination. To Coleridge, naturally, this was the final blow, and his resentment and sense of betrayal were keen and outspoken. To escape the Great Whore, Southey had thrown himself into the arms of "that low, dirty, gutter-grubbing Trull, Worldly Prudence"; and instead of sailing to the Fortunate Isles, he had scuttled the ship of Pantisocracy for a handful of silver and had left Coleridge marooned on the barren promontory of an uncongenial marriage. The breach between the erstwhile friends was complete.[10]

Meantime, Southey had been persuaded to accompany his uncle to Portugal, where the latter was chaplain to the British Factory at Oporto. The Reverend Hill hoped to save his nephew from his "imprudent attachment" to the seamstress. But he found himself outmaneuvered. Five days before departure, on November 14, 1795, Southey and Edith were secretly married. Southey's reasons for this evasion were charitable rather than romantic: he wanted to provide for Edith in case he should die abroad.

Southey's departure for Portugal signaled the end of his adolescence. In some respects, he was as desolate and as frustrated as ever. But he was at least happily married and had laid the foundations for a literary reputation. He had published, together with Lovell, a slim volume of poetry. He had, besides, written two political plays: *The Fall of Robespierre*, in concert with Coleridge, and *Wat Tyler*. Above all, he had published an epic, *Joan of Arc*, which was well received. His boldest enterprise, the pursuit of Pantisocracy, had of necessity come to nothing. But its underlying ideals remained, in one form or another, the foundation of his poetic and political thought.

V *Southey and Coleridge in Later Years*

Another equally weighty legacy of these adolescent years that is less easily assessed is Southey's friendship with Coleridge. Temperamentally unsuited to each other but linked together by family, by vocation, and, above all, by a lingering sense of joint vision and dedication, they alternately attracted and repelled each other like mismatched and jealous lovers until time and temper prevailed and their estrangement became permanent.

They did not speak for nearly a year after Southey's return from Portugal, until Southey seems to have broken the ice by sending Coleridge a quotation from Friedrich Schiller: "Fiesco! Fiesco! thou leavest a void in my bosom, which the human race, thrice told, will never fill up." But their quarrel eventually revived and deepened. Southey felt attacked by Coleridge's "Higginbottom" sonnet on "Simplicity," and he was infuriated by certain things Coleridge had supposedly said about him. Coleridge, in turn, suspected that Southey had had a part in the indiscretion of *Edmund Oliver*, the novel by Charles Lloyd, whose frantic protagonist was palpably modeled on Coleridge. Southey's harsh review of "The Rime of the Ancient Mariner" did not improve matters.

Eventually, a genuine reconciliation did come about. While Coleridge was away in Germany, his infant son Berkeley died, and Southey hastened to comfort the bereaved mother—a role he was afterward to play for life. Coleridge was grateful for this aid and, after his return, urged his brother-in-law to visit him and to remit his animosity and unjust suspicion. Southey at first responded with self-righteous recriminations, but he eventually relented. The driving force in this reconciliation was evidently Coleridge. Time and again he appealed to Southey in the name of the time "when we dreamt one Dream, & that a glorious one—when we eat together & . . . were bed fellows." His letters after Southey's return from his second stay in Portugal are full of yearning for his friend, and he repeatedly begged Southey to come and live with him in Keswick so that "the Blessed Dreams, we dreamt some 6 years ago may be auguries of something really noble which we may yet perform together."[11]

By then, Southey commanded far less of Coleridge's affection than Wordsworth did. But he represented a carefree past; and it is possible that Coleridge, increasingly unhappy in his domestic life, thought that by again living with Southey he could in some sense regain his past freedom. Ironically, of course, that is precisely what happened. When Southey, in 1803, lost a child of his own, Coleridge renewed his invitation, and the bereaved parents accepted. All went well for a while. Inevitably, however, the Southey of Coleridge's nostalgic dream faded in the presence of the earth-bound "Australis," the ostrich who could not fly, though he had "such other qualities that he needs it not." Was it not because of "unthinking Southey" that Coleridge had "married for honor & not for love"? The presence of two additional Fricker sisters (for Southey had brought both his wife and the now widowed Mrs. Lovell) did not improve matters, nor did Mrs. Coleridge's open and, Coleridge thought, invidious admiration of her brother-in-law.[12] In short, Coleridge eventually decamped, leaving his brother-in-law in charge of the "aunt-hill" at Greta Hall, a post Southey dutifully kept to the end of his life.

Coleridge always admired "dear Southey's" sterling qualities—his self-discipline; his learning; his facile, unflagging industry; his unstinting, if somewhat heavy-handed generosity; even his poetry—and he always defended him to the public. But he was hurt by what he called Southey's "unthinkingness" and "bluntness of conscience" and in the end had to admit that, while he had great "esteem" for Southey, he could not love him enough. Southey, on his part, "at first . . . loved Coleridge, then pitied him, came to condemn him, and finally, as far as he was able, tried to forget him."[13] There can be no doubt that he was genuinely and even jealously fond of Coleridge, anxious about his infirmities, and profoundly disturbed by his absence. Moreover, although he disliked metaphysics and frequently scoffed at Coleridge's "metapothecary" labors, he greatly admired Coleridge's intellectual powers and considered him "infinitely . . . the mightiest of his generation." By the same token, however, he increasingly decried Coleridge's "total want of moral strength," his "perpetual St. Vitus dance—eternal activity without action." He prided himself on his angelic patience. But he was in fact maddened by what he regarded as dereliction in one who was his intellectual superior; and his "mimosa sensibility" was no doubt deeply threatened by the spectacle of moral disintegration that Coleridge's opium addiction presented. His heart might cling to his friend, but his "meddling intellect," as he put it, could not; unlike Coleridge, he could feel love but not esteem. When, many years later, news of Coleridge's decease reached him, he wrote: "STC's death . . . will not intrude much upon my waking thoughts, but I expect to feel it for some time to come in my dreams."[14]

CHAPTER 2

Arms and a Maid: Joan of Arc

I *Epic Revival in an Age of Revolution*

IT is generally thought that, with the subsiding of the
great ground-swell of Renaissance epic into the glittering ripples
of the eighteenth-century mock-epic, the epic impulse died or passed to the novel. If so, the poets of the Romantic period were not
aware of it. For all their devotion to the lyric, they continued to
regard the long poem and the epic in particular as the queen of
poetic genres and wrote, or dreamed of writing, epic poems.[1] Epic
seemed, in fact, to be on the verge of a renascence. Primitivism, the
cult of the sublime, the growing interest in non-Classical material,
whether native or exotic, all conspired to give the definition of the
epic a new latitude and to encourage experimentation with new
forms and themes. In 1765, Richard Hurd in his *Letters on Chivalry
and Romance* accorded epic status to Ariosto and Spenser and
pronounced Gothic Romance or "romantic epic" as superior to the
Classical epic. His views were echoed by most critics. Romances
were still regarded as "wild," "irregular," and "extravagant," but
regularity and verisimilitude were no longer *de rigueur*. Bishop
Lowth's *De Sacra Poesia Hebraeorum* (1753, tr. 1793) even brought
Biblical poetry within the purlieus of the genre and fostered an interest in Biblical epic. The study of Celtic and Teutonic lore and an-
tiquity, of Oriental and primitive religions, and of comparative
mythology uncovered additional resources of epic themes and
"machinery." It was, so to say, the "Hundred Days" of the English
epic. Its Waterloo was the publication of Byron's *Don Juan*; but its
"grand Napoleon," as Byron saw, was, in every respect, Southey.
The enormous fecundity of Southey's heroic muse and his long-
lived ambition to devote an epic to each of the major religions were
not just products of an impulsive and headlong nature but the
single most voluminous precipitation of what was generally in the
air.

More immediately, of course, the Romantic and Southeyan epic got its impetus from the revolutionary fervor of the period. Great ages had always demanded great song to embody their spirit. What, then, could be plainer than the duty of a poet, especially a young one, to officiate as the bard of democracy, to sing the wrath of the People, to depict in epic form the fall of Louis the Last, the advent of the Millennium, and the regeneration of the human race? There was only one difficulty: the traditional epic had rested heavily on the very concepts of hierarchy, aristocracy, and precedent which the Revolution attacked. The feudal pomp of "pennons rolling their long waves / Before the gale, and banners broad and bright / Tossing their blazonry, and high-plumed chiefs, / Vidames and seneschals and chastellains, / Gay with their bucklers' gorgeous heraldry / And silken surcoats" (I, 209) was obviously out of keeping with Republican austerity. It is a measure of William Blake's genius to have recognized this dilemma and to have consequently rejected the entire Classical epic tradition for the apocalyptic mode of Biblical prophecy—historical analogue for timeless myth. Southey sensed the problem and planned at one time an apocalyptic poem about the story of Noah and the destruction of "universal monarchy" through the Deluge; but he never quite made the break with Classicism.

As it happened, the millennial dream quickly faded; the Armageddon for Liberty assumed the poetically more manageable proportions of a war of defense against the reactionary powers of the First Coalition; but, even with this nationalist turn of events, esthetic problems remained. The great historical and symbolic event of the era was taking place primarily in France; therefore an English poem on the subject would not be the national one that tradition prescribed. Worse still, England had joined the enemies of France and Freedom. An Arthuriad was hence as much out of the question as it had been for Milton after the Restoration. Short of writing a "para-epic," or modern *Pharsalia*, about the fall of Albion, or of withdrawing into remote historical analogues, the English bard had no alternative but the unheard-of one of hymning the cause of the national enemy.

II   *The Heroine*

In choosing the legend of Jeanne d'Arc for his subject, Southey compounded the problem, for the complex historical figure whom

we know today hardly existed then. The pioneering study of Clement L'Averdy (1790) was unknown at the time even to
Southey—the work of Jules Quicherat was still half a century
away—and the reputation of the Maid, never very savory in
England, had been tarnished even in France by the iconoclastic
ribaldry of Voltaire's *Pucelle*. Since Joan's heroic appeal would
therefore be almost exclusively polemical, her story was a precarious
base for the colossus of epic. A great poem, of course, creates its
own reason for being and does not depend, as Southey later
thought, on appeals to partisan feeling. But Southey himself ceased
to believe in his heroine, although he continued to work on the
poem at intervals all his life.

In other respects, Southey's choice of subject was brilliant, and it
anticipated by a whole decade the Maid's promotion to the rank of
national heroine under Napoleon as well as Schiller's treatment of
her legend in *Die Jungfrau von Orleans*. In accordance with
Classical precedent, Joan lent Southey's theme the authority of age.
At the same time, she was a radically modern protagonist. For,
although there had been a long line of literary Amazons—Virgil's
Camilla, Tasso's Clorinda, Spenser's Britomart—the theory that a
woman could be the hero of an epic had not hitherto been put to a
serious test. Southey's poem would boldly oppose the spirit of
equality to the tyranny of decorum and the humane commonsense
of Mary Wollstonecraft to the "despotism of Aristotle" and Le
Bossu.

What is more, Jeanne d'Arc was a peasant girl. She was thus not
only one of the people (unlike the feudal barons of traditional epic)
but a child and pupil of nature who, uncorrupted by "civilization,"
was guided in her work by "natural" inspiration. Although
Wordsworth early complained "that Southey writes *too much at his
ease*—that he seldom 'feels his burthened breast / Heaving beneath
th'incumbent Deity,'"[2] Southey's account of Joan's childhood (to
which the quoted lines allude) strikingly anticipate Wordsworth's
own nature mysticism. Joan's soul, we are told, was nursed in the
"solitude and peace" of nature's "loveliest scenes." While herding
her flocks in the "woodland wilds" of Domremi, the girl would lie
down beside a stream "glittering in the noontide sun" and listen to
its murmur "Till all was hushed and tranquil in my soul, / Filled
with a strange and undefined delight / That passed across the mind
like Summer clouds / Across a lake at eve" (I, 33 - 4).[3] In this forest
solitude, she first became aware of "strange voices in the evening

wind: strange forms / Dimly discovered through the twilight air";
and here her mission at length came upon her in one of those
visionary moments when, as she says, "every bodily sense is as it
slept, / And the mind alone is wakeful."

She was sitting alone on a rock one evening, she says, under the
ancient oak by the holy "Fountain of the Fairies," where lank
adder's tongue, "rich with the wrinkle of its glossy green," dipped
into the silently welling water, and "marked the deep red
clouds / Gather before the wind,—the rising wind, / Whose sudden
gusts, each wilder than the last, / Appeared to rock my senses." A
storm presently broke loose; and, with darkness falling around her,
the girl yielded herself to the rain and to the "wild music" of wind
and water. "The glory of the tempest filled my soul; / And when
the thunder peeled, and the long flash / Hung durable in heaven,
and on my sight / Spread the gray forest, memory, thought were
gone, / All sense of self annihilate, I seemed / Diffused into the
scene" (42 - 4).[4] Joan's prophetic authority is thus closely akin to
that of Wordsworth's Poet and Wanderer; and it is as a worshipper
of the God of Nature in the temple of His creation and as a believer
in Nature's sacramental beauty and in man's original goodness that
she confronts the doctors of the Church in Book III and categorical-
ly rejects their dogma of original sin, mortification, and "artificial
awe" before a "God of terrors."

The naturalism of the poem is somewhat blurred in the first edition by the Christian "machinery" which Southey had originally introduced in a juvenile effort to be "correct." In revising the poem
in 1798, Southey joined the critical opposition to machinery in the
epic: he eliminated the supernatural element and, at about the
same time that Wordsworth passed Milton's angel-thronged cosmos
for the vaster and more awesome regions within the Mind of Man,
inserted the following palinode into his preface: "The aid of angels
and devils is not necessary to raise [Joan] above mankind; she has
no gods to lackey her. . . . [She] acts wholly from the workings of
her own mind. . . . The palpable agency of superior powers would
destroy the obscurity of her character" (15). Machinery, Southey
now realized, was the badge and sanction of feudalism; the piety of
Aeneas, a cloak for the will to power. The true voice of God was the
voice of the people and their dreams, or else the still small voice of
the individual conscience, especially as redefined by Rousseau and
the Earl of Shaftesbury: " 'There are feelings, chief, / Which cannot lie; and I have oftentimes / Felt in the midnight and silence of

my soul / The voice of God' " (28). In later years Southey came to
think that *vox populi* had never been *vox Dei*; but he never changed his mind about the still small voice.

In this sense, Joan *is* a republican heroine, in spite of the
awkward fact that her heroic exploit results in the coronation of a
worthless king. "Vive la Republique!" Southey wrote on July 14,
1793; "my Joan is a great democrat or rather will be." Like her
humble sister, the College Cat, she stands at once for domestic
tranquility and for the will to independence. She discredits, if not
feudalism as such, at least the feudal pastime of war and the feudal
gods who sanction it. Her code is not honor but love; her aim, not
empire but peace; her deed of delivery, genuine in contrast to the
bogus liberation that Tasso had glorified. In the "Verses Intended
to have been Addressed to His Grace the Duke of Portland" on his
installation at Oxford (1793), Southey had decried those
"unhallowed" poets who had caused untold misery by singing
"Of arms, and combats, and the proud array / Of warriors" and
thus adding the promise of renown to the hope for spoils. In the
preface to *Joan*, he did not scruple to call Aeneas a villain. Joan
would, so to speak, side with Turnus and Camilla against Aeneas
and the "robber fugitives of Troy," with Hector against Agamemnon, and with Jericho against the hordes of Joshua. The poem
would show war as it appeared to the victims of war.[5] It would sing
the sorrows of Eumaeus, "worth a thousand heroes" (I, 16), rather
than the pique and fury of Achilles. Of war it must treat, but it
would be a war against war.

III   *The Poem*

The poem was conceived and outlined in the summer of 1793 at
Oxford, and a first draft was completed in the course of a mere six
weeks during the Long Vacation when Southey had just turned
nineteen. Crude as this mushroom product must have been,
Southey was elated. During the ensuing winter of dejection and
anxiety, he let the poem lie. But then Pantisocracy raised his spirits,
and a month after the meeting with Coleridge, he set out to find a
publisher and to revise the poem. At the close of the year, the young
Bristol bookseller Joseph Cottle offered to publish the revised poem
in a handsome quarto format. Printing began, but the sight of the
first galley so awed the young bard that during the next six
months—and while the printing went on—he "recast and recom-

posed" virtually the entire work. At this time, Coleridge con-
tributed to the second book what was afterwards removed and
became Coleridge's "Destiny of Nations." In this form, *Joan of Arc*
appeared in 1795.

Even now the poem did not satisfy Southey for long. Its texture,
he discovered, was marred by tedious rhetoric and artificial diction;
its structure was encumbered by "machinery" including not only
the Coleridgean "vision" in Book II but an underworld journey in
the ninth book. In 1798, at the height of his productiveness as a
lyrical poet, Southey again reworked the poem for its second edition. He rewrote most of Book I, removing all of its miracle-
mongering and substituting the present opening—one of the best
things, he thought, that he ever produced. He took out all of the
overt machinery, including the two visions (a version of the second
of these reappeared as an appendix to the third edition, under the
title "The Vision of the Maid of Orleans"). He also pruned the diction considerably by "squeezing out the whey," as he later called it.
The result was essentially the poem as it now stands, though some
passages owe their present form to revisions for subsequent editions
(1806, 1812, 1837). Only in the last one, however, did Southey
replace the most flagrant of Joan's republican harangues with tamer
sentiments. Because of these last changes, the 1798 version is
preferable to that in the *Poetical Works*.

The poem narrates the career of Jeanne d'Arc from her
appearance at Vaucouleurs to the coronation, five months later, of
the Dauphin at Rheims. Other matters, notably the childhood of
Joan and the fortunes of the war since the battle of Agincourt fourteen years earlier, are incorporated in a number of flashbacks that
occur mostly in the first half of the poem. Southey takes some liber-
ties with history by telescoping or rearranging events and by invent-
ing fictional movements and motives for historical characters; but in
the handling of detail he adheres closely to his sources.

The poem opens at Vaucouleurs, the seat of Robert de
Baudricourt, where Charles Dunois, the noble Bastard of Orleans, is
trying, without much success, to recruit fresh troops for his besieged
city. When Joan arrives, accompanied by her good uncle Claude,
and begs to be taken to the Dauphin, Dunois quickly accedes to her
entreaties. Pale, beautiful, and eighteen, she impresses him as a psychological weapon. On their way through idyllic, summer-warm
Lorraine towards the increasingly desolate and war-ravaged country
around Chinon, Joan tells Dunois about her childhood, her loveless

parents, her kind uncle Claude, her beloved friend Madelon; about
Madelon's becoming widowed by the war and dying of grief; about
her love for Madelon's brother Theodore; about the soldier whose
"fierce and terrible benevolence" first opened her eyes to her country's plight; and about her forest reveries that brought her to full
awareness of her mission.[6] A veteran, at whose hut they spend the
night, provides additional background by describing the sufferings
of the French under the "warrior-scourge" Henry V, especially at
the Battle of Agincourt, with its notorious massacre of French
prisoners, and at the siege of Rouen, when famine filled the streets
with dead and dying women and children.

Dunois and Joan reach Chinon, where the Dauphin, shut out
from Paris and contemplating flight, resides in virtual bankruptcy
with his corrupt and parasitical court, his favorites, his wife, and his
mistress, the haughty Agnes Sorel. In the famous recognition scene
that follows, Charles mingles with the crowd while a courtier imper-
sonates the Dauphin. Joan instantly recognizes the king "like one
inspired" and proclaims her mission to crown him at Rheims.
Charles—more to silence unbelief than to stifle personal
doubts—decides to have her examined by a convocation of
"prelates and priests / And doctors; teachers grave, and with great
names, / Seraphic, Subtle, or Irrefragable," who, with their strew-
ing and blessing, are derisively compared to necromancers and
Thessalian "hell-hags."

Called before this somber college, Joan invokes her own feelings,
voices, and midnight visions as indubitable revelations of "the God
within me" (70); and, when she is catechized about her state of
grace, she relates her conversion from a religion of fear and trembling to the more cheerful nature worship of eighteenth-century
Deism.[7] For, when she "saw the eternal energy pervade / The
boundless range of nature, with the sun / Pour life and radiance
from his flamy path, / And on the lowliest floweret of the
field / The kindly dewdrops shed," she could not but feel that "He
who formed this goodly frame of things / Must needs be good, and
with a Father's name / I called on him, and from my burdened
heart / Poured out the yearnings of unmingled love." Was it
therefore strange that she "fled / The house of prayer, and made
the lonely grove / [her] temple . . . had no thought of sin, / And
did not need forgiveness?" (72 - 4). The doctors, appalled by such
heresy, propose to subject the Maid to ordeals by water and fire.
But the debate is cut short when a flash of blue flame from a tomb

in the cathedral where the trial is taking place and a sound "as if below / A warrior, buried in his armor, stirred" (77) reveal to Joan the presence of sacred arms reserved for her. The prodigy convinces the doctors; the ancient armor is unearthed in solemn procession; and Joan, having donned it, proclaims her new kind of crusade: "God of peace! preserve / Those whom no lust of glory leads to arms" (83).

As if to show the futility of her prayer, Joan is promptly hailed by a somber figure in the crowd as an ill-starred "victim [of] this king-curst realm of France." The same prophetic figure soon afterwards interrupts a banquet given by the frivolous Dauphin to denounce the court's feasting while the country bleeds and starves. A messenger from besieged Orleans, Conrade, the speaker, is revealed as the warrior who had first aroused Joan's political conscience and as the one-time betrothed of the "polluted" Agnes Sorel.[8] Made cynical by loss and half crazed with grief, Conrade now bitterly regrets that he caused Joan to leave her peaceful life and the youth who loved her for the sake of a dissolute king, especially when she tells him of a vision she has had of being burned at the stake. But Joan reminds him that the cause is that of the people and declares that she has renounced all desire for "selfish happiness" and the "joys of life." She remains unshaken even when her lover Theodore appears on the scene to follow and protect her. After a moment of rapture, she sends the youth away, mindful of her "holy cause" and destined martyrdom.

In the meantime, men have begun to flock to her standard. At break of day, twelve hundred gather ceremoniously around the maid's white banner, "woven by virgin hands"; and, after a six-day march, they encamp in the forests surrounding Orleans. Here Joan encounters yet another eyewitness to the events of the war, Isabel, a country girl and war orphan from Orleans, whom she finds in the company of the melancholy Conrade, and who proceeds to give an account of the siege and of the sufferings of the city.

As night falls, Conrade returns to Orleans to carry a report about Joan's arrival. At the same time, Joan dispatches a herald with an offer of peace to the English. But he earns only derision from Salisbury, Talbot, and the other British chiefs and is led away to be burned at the stake. The French thereupon advance, aided by Conrade, who charges from the city into the English camp to rescue the herald. As the battle is joined, a thunderstorm erupts overhead, and lightning plays about the virgin's banner. The English panic and flee to their beaconed forts, and Joan enters Orleans in torchlit triumph.

The relief of Orleans constitutes an effective climax in the action—the second after the recognition and ratification in Book III. Joan's nocturnal entry into the besieged city is "historical," as Southey's own note indicates, but Southey has heightened it dramatically by means of the storm-swept battle and its sound and light effects. Thereafter, there is a falling off in the poem. Like the *Aeneid, Joan of Arc* is divided into two distinct halves: five (originally six) books deal with "wanderings"; five (six), with "war." Part one is marred by an excess of flash-backs and by a cumbersome manner of introducing them; but, since its romantic and sentimental subject was close to Southey's heart, the narrative and the rhetoric have moments that compel interest and admiration.

Part two is more uniform, swifter, and more direct in its narrative; at the same time, it savors of task work. Having once gotten his heroine successfully and dramatically into the city, Southey has the uncongenial task of chronicling military activities—not only those of raising the siege of Orleans but also those leading to the final climax of the action, the coronation at Rheims. Warfare cannot but be distasteful to a poet who not only entertains pacifist sentiments but also shrinks from representing artistically what he condemns on moral grounds. The battle scenes are worked up with a great display of Medieval armor, fortification, and ballistic arsenal—"archery must be attended to," reads a Notebook entry (IV, 202)—but the blank verse is at times monotonous, the language is disfigured by superficial Miltonisms, and the narrative is undynamic and short-winded despite a good deal of gore and occasional vivid touches ("The cold air rushed upon his heaving heart").

The action of the remaining books is briefly as follows. On the day after Joan's and Dunois' arrival, the French begin their attack on the English forts and quickly gain one position after another. They are inspired by the heroic Maid and her two desperate companions-in-arms, Conrade and the almost-martyred herald. Conrade in particular performs Homeric feats with his deadly battleaxe by almost single-handedly driving the terrified English from one of their forts. Salisbury tries to rally his troops by reminding them of Agincourt and of other instances of British prowess, but Talbot finally counsels retreat to the strongest of the forts, the

Tourelles. On their way there, the English chiefs encounter the
Maid and her companions; and Joan is wounded by Salisbury. The
herald, who is in fact the faithful Theodore in disguise, interposes,
kills Salisbury, but is in turn slain by Talbot.

The following day brings the decisive engagement: the capture of
the stronghold of the Tourelles, the key position of the English.
After much bloody fighting, the French gain the outer courts and
capture a large contingent of the enemy. Joan staunchly resists the
captains who urge that the prisoners be executed for the sake of ex-
pedience; God's cause, she assures them, does not require such extreme measures. Her faith is promptly rewarded when a bridge and
tower to which Dunois is driving the enemy collapses into the river
and the English drown in great numbers.

Their fortifications burned and their morale shaken, the English
decide to retire to the coast to await reinforcements. When news
arrives in the French camp that the Burgundians are approaching to
succor their English allies, Joan pays a night visit to the Duke of
Burgundy in order to warn him and kills an attendant knight who
attacks her. Returned to camp, she orders the dead to be buried and
delivers a funeral oration about the glory of dying in defense of
freedom. Meanwhile, the English rally around the standards of
young Talbot, who is arriving from England with fresh troops; and
the combined forces meet the French in the decisive battle of Patay.
Joan spreads terror among the English and succeeds in killing
young Talbot. Old Talbot, still raging in the field, encounters
Conrade; both are killed; the English fly. Eventually, Charles
arrives and recaptures Rheims and other towns. Joan completes her
mission by anointing and crowning the king and by admonishing
him to be a just and responsible ruler.

IV Structure, Style, and Theme

Inevitably, the reader's interest flags in these last books. The victory at Orleans constituted a natural climax for the action. The shift
from siege and countersiege to pitched battle creates some novelty;
but the issue is decided, morally as well as militarily, with the
collapse of the bridge over the Loire; and, since no significant new
issues are generated, the reader balks at having to sit through
another phase of the campaign before he is allowed to witness the
crowning event at Rheims. Moreover, Southey fails to make the
military action interesting by integrating it fully with the personal

level of the narrative. The moment of Joan's realization that the dying herald at her side is Theodore is said to be a "miserable" one,
but Joan herself appears entirely unconcerned; only in the next
book, when the military episode is concluded, do we learn of her
feelings as she looks for the corpse under cover of night. Even then
her passion is checked as soon as vented, as Joan welcomes her impending martyrdom as the gateway to reunion with her beloved.
For all of Southey's rhetorical intentions, no compelling pathos is allowed to grow; private and public spheres remain discrete, each
with its separate rhetoric; and, since personal loss is explained away
in religious and stoic-sentimental terms, the public indictment
against war remains frigid and academic.

In part, the conspicuous emotional void in this episode is due to
the omission, from the second and subsequent editions, of the
quasi-Dantean dream vision that originally followed here. But even
a restoration of the deleted episode would not substantially alter the
case. In it, the spirit of the bereaved Joan is conducted by Sorrow,
an old woman at whose heart a serpent is gnawing, across a barren
waste and a reedy lake to a Gothic *mise-en-scène* that represents the
realm of death. Here the grisly specter of Despair tempts Joan to
commit suicide to escape her martyrdom, her remorse over
Theodore's death, and the futility of a life beset by pain and ending
in corruption ("where thou seest the pampered flesh-worm
trail, / Once the white bosom heaved"). Joan is naturally un-
daunted by these insinuations: life, she knows, is livable because
duty exists while it lasts and *reward* comes when it has ended. The
scene thereupon changes abruptly to celestial radiance, and
Theodore appears as an angel to conduct her on a tour of the
afterworld. We are shown the furnaces of Greed, where the
worshippers of Mammon must drink molten gold; the dome of
Gluttony, where monk and master, prince and parish warden must
submit to monstrous deformations of the "human form divine"; the
"house of Penitence," where morose fanatics must fall to endless
prayers; cruel husbands, slave traders, and animal tormentors are
scorched and lacerated; and so on.

Having modestly declined to tour the "Palaces of Futurity," Joan
is transported to an earthly paradise in the evening star where the
blessed prepare for, or rest from, "infinite progressiveness" and
where she has a tearful reunion with Madelon and her husband in
their bower of bliss. Earth, we learn, was such an Eden "in the first
era of its innocence, / Ere man had learnt to bow the knee to man,"

before vice had divided man from man and "Cain's true son / Delved in the bowels of earth for gold." But, though betrayed by ignorance, man may acquire wisdom through experience, and thus, through progress, "earth shall once again be paradise" (358 - 60). Joan is assured of her own prospective reunion with Theodore beyond the fiery stake; and, led to the Palace of Love, a straw-roofed hut surrounded by Labor, Health, Hope, Pity, and Chastity, she listens to a hymn to Love, the Creator and Preserver.

The vision is a mine of traditional and Romantic emblems and commonplaces, and some of it makes effective undergirding for the poem's main themes. In the Hall of the Kings, for example, where "Enthroned around, the murderers of mankind . . . Each bearing on his brow a crown of fire, / Sat stern and silent," Henry V, the prime instigator of France's suffering, addresses the Maid to reproach himself for sowing "Murder and Rape" rather than peace and plenty. His and his fellow penitents' ultimate salvation, he adds, depends on the realization of the political millennium on earth—"one brotherhood, / One universal family of love" (349 - 51). On the whole, however, the vision is a shallow and lifeless affair despite some fine writing and some spirited satire. With characteristic sentimental eclecticism, Southey rejects the eternity of hell only to retain its punitiveness: his hell is merely a superlative house of correction where souls are tortured into repentance and nursed into beatitude by pain. In principle, he applies the Dantean conversion of sin into its own punishment; but frequently the torment is merely randomly vindictive. And when it comes to rendering carnality imaginatively, Southey flinches in vague horror: the punishment of seducers who "pollute" innocent maidens and force them into prostitution is said to be "long and dreadful" (344) but remains unspecified. The dearth of individual sinners makes for colorless abstraction. Above all, the sentimental pie-in-the-sky of Southey's Eden diminishes the problem of suffering and undermines the poem's political message.

Such evidence of a fractured sensibility that shrinks from contact with total experience and can take on only one thing at a time—and then only when armed with a panoply of compensating rationalizations—meets us in all of Southey; and it has a fatal effect in preventing complex and concentrated narrative thrusts. In Book VII of *Joan*, for example, Southey breaks the account of Conrade's raging on the ramparts of the English forts and suddenly has him brood about his lost happiness with Agnes Sorel. The tumult and the shouting of the battle simply stop while Conrade laments the passing of an unspecified past of pastoral peace and domestic contentment and then all too quickly consoles himself with Southey's grand panacea for every evil—the faith "in that better world of peace and love, / Where evil is not" (152). A similar patchwork is the absurd Ariostan pastiche that introduces Isabel as singing dolefully, with Conrade's head in her lap, while crowning herself and him with willow wreaths. Isabel herself, in fact, is fairly superfluous since most of her story could have been told by Conrade himself, as well as by Dunois, who in fact supplements her narrative. Her only justification is that she exhibits war from a purely civilian and feminine standpoint.

Southey achieves some complexity of vision when he uses the omniscient author's privilege to intersperse generalized domestic images that set off the action without interrupting its flow; to contrast a soldier's beastly and senseless death on the battlefield with the peaceful life he led before the war (142f., 167f.); or to evoke the plight of the widow pining away in vain hope for her husband's return (146)—a passage he thought among the best of the entire poem. But, since these reflections are confined to the "enemy," their pathos remains largely rhetorical.

Similarly, Southey sometimes employs the Homeric device of the contrapuntal simile to comment indirectly on the horror of war. Joan's midnight search for the body of Theodore among the "carcasses and broken arms" of the blood-soaked field and the groans of dying men takes place under a sky as serene and brilliant as that which "canopied / Chaldaea, while the watchful shepherd's eye / Surveyed the host of heaven" (159). Too often, however, even Southey's similes are merely inapt, as when he compares flying arrows to wind-blown leaves (149). Moreover, while at times sadly conventional in his use of oak and lion similes, Southey at other times strains too obviously after novelty by adducing more or less tenuous comparisons not only from Greek, Roman, and British history, but from Biblical, Hindu, Moslem, Mexican, Norse, and Celtic myth and legend.[9]

Throughout, Southey neglects to integrate and relate events organically. Joan's midnight escapade to the Duke of Burgundy's tent in Book IX replaces the dream journey of the first edition but serves otherwise no discernible purpose. Joan hints that, by her appearance, she has sent the fear of God into the Duke that would turn him from his treasonous ways; that it was the Burgundian who eventually captured the Maid and delivered her to her martyrdom is an irony that is never realized. Similarly, we hear much about the siege of Rouen in Book II, but nothing is said to remind us that Joan's career would find its terrible end there. Joan's refusal to permit the execution of the inconvenient prisoners stands in striking contrast to the fate of the French prisoners at Agincourt related earlier, but Southey seems unaware of the parallel. "I *think* too much for a Poet," Coleridge once remarked; "he too little for a *great* Poet." With an encyclopedic bent similar to that of his fellow poet, Southey seems interested only in fact, not in pattern. As a result, his narrative, despite its large accretion of detail, is wearyingly linear and lacking in texture.

Again, descriptive passages, while sometimes vivid, tend to be too short-winded or too uncertain in metaphor to impress the imagination strongly, as these lines describing the burning of the English forts: "Far through the shadowy sky the ascending flames / Streamed their fierce torrents, by the gales of night / Now curled, now flashing their long lightnings up / That made the stars seem pale: less frequent now / Through the red volumes briefer splendors shot, / And blacker waves rolled o'er the darkened heaven" (183). Southey is at his best in passages of straight rhetoric when these are written in a plain middle style that anticipates, though it cannot rival, that of Coleridge and Wordsworth, and which, like theirs, derives largely from the blank verse of Mark Akenside and William Cowper. Southey's style is not even. Particularly in the battle scenes of the last books, he sometimes feels compelled to put on the epic manner, and then his language is painfully Miltonic. "He the brute vastness held aloft, and bore, / And headlong hurled . . . Down from the rock's high summit, since that day, / Him, hugest of the giants, chronicling, / Called Languemagog" (173). In principle, however, Southey subscribed fully to the Romantic revolt against ornate "poetic diction," especially with respect to epic.

We have already seen an example of the poem's oratory in Joan's defense of her natural religion against the orthodoxy of the doctors. Book IX opens with an indictment of the English cause by one of their own men which, though pat and theatrical, creates some emotional impact by its sonorous iterations (*groan* | *groan, unheard* | *heard, obedience / disobey*) and alliterations (*domestic life / desolate land, crimes / cry, chance / chiefs*):

> "I marvel not that the Most High
> Hath hid his face from England. Wherefore thus
> Quitting the comforts of domestic life,
> Came we to desolate this goodly land,
> Making the drenched earth rank with human blood,
> Scatter pollution on the winds of heaven? . . .
> For thousands and ten thousands, by the sword
> Cut off, and sent before the eternal Judge,
> With all their unrepented crime upon them,
> Cry out for vengeance; for the widow's groan,
> Though here she groan unpitied or unheard,
> Is heard in heaven against us. . . .
> The wrath of God is on us . . . who dared to risk
> The life his goodness gave us, on the chance
> Of war, and in obedience to our chiefs
> Durst disobey our God." (184f.)

Or we might quote at the end of the same book, Joan's complementary speech about the worth and sufficiency of patriotic devotion:

> For easier it were
> To move the ancient mountains from their base,
> Than on a nation knowing its own strength
> To force a foreign yoke. . . . Remember . . .
> That a great people, wrongfully assailed,
> If faithful to themselves, and resolute . . .
> Although no signs be given, no miracles
> Vouchsafed, as now, no Prophetess ordained,—
> May yet with hope invincible hold on,
> Relying on their courage and their cause,
> And the sure course of righteous Providence. (198f.)

The stateliness and measured sonority of these lines make up for the bleak abstraction of the language and the vague tautology of the sentiment.

This speech, we should add, with its patriotic note and its emphasis on national integrity rather than on political liberty, is one of the notable instances of the ideological revision that the poem underwent in its last recension. Until 1837, it was addressed to "Citizens" rather than to "Countrymen"; and its rhetoric, partly borrowed from Act III of *The Fall of Robespierre*, was aimed at "tyrants" and "despot foes" rather than at "foreign masters," at the "yoke of slavery" rather than the "foreign yoke," and so on.

Similarly, the lines which now conclude Joan's coronation speech, as well as the whole poem—"Thus spake the Maid of Orleans, solemnly / Accomplishing her marvellous mission here"—read until 1837: "Thus the Maid / Redeemed her country. Ever may the All-just / Give to the arms of freedom such success." In the 1837 text, the entire coronation speech is altered from a pseudo-democratic into a royalist one. Charles is now "king over this great nation," the "legitimate lord" ordained by God (110), rather than the "chief servant of the people," whom "the people choose." Though he is still warned of the way of the tyrant, Joan's admonitions no longer include veiled threats of revolution but invoke solely the divine sanction of "judgment-day." Moreover, the Jacobin cry against tyranny is now amended by a warning against a policy of *laissez-faire* that echoes Southey's prose Philippics against conditions of Regency England in the *Quarterly Review*.[10] Ironically, of course, the new text is not only less crudely polemical but also more nearly reconcilable with history: Southey's politics had at last caught up with the politics of epic.

Such need for revisionism is symptomatic of the poem's principal failing as a narrative: its humorless didacticism and its lack of character. For all his boasted disregard of rules and precedent, Southey chose his subject for purely ideological reasons, in complete agreement with neo-Classical theory. At the same time, he lacked the sensuous and imaginative warmth that enabled a Virgil, a Spenser, or a Milton to soften their didactic rigor. Characteristically, Southey not only shared the Enlightenment's contempt for Virgil but also its admiration for Lucan's *Pharsalia*, a poem remarkable for its tendentiousness and its histrionic Stoicism. *Joan of Arc* reflects this preference as well as Southey's similar enthusiasm at this time for the *Leonidas* of Lucan's disciple Richard Glover. As the first substantial epic since *Leonidas* half a century before, *Joan* was the literary event of the year and received considerable *eclat*[11]—so much, in fact, that Southey later boasted that it had set off the "epomania" of his time. For all that, it represents no real breakthrough. Southey himself described it as the joint product of Republicanism, Stoicism derived from Epictetus, and "admiration, almost adoration, of Leonidas" (*Memoir*, II, 82). Southey's is a better poem than Glover's, but both are tertiary epics that are narrowly rhetorical in intention.

The poet is always partisan. The protagonists are permitted only those feelings which the poet himself feels and approves. All lower impulses are filtered out or else relegated to the enemy. We are thus rarely able to admire the enemy as we admire a Hector or a Turnus. Conversely, the heroine is impervious to vice and superior to weakness. Where outright idealization is not possible for historical reasons, as in the case of the Dauphin, no real synthesis is attempted. Charles is now the arch-villain of bourgeois morality, the blue-blooded seducer, now merely an awkward but indispensable chessboard king who is to be protected, lectured, and crowned—he is not a powerfully ambiguous personality like Agamemnon, nor is he the pusillanimous degenerate of history and of Shaw's ironic art. Psychological realism is foreign to Southey's narrative, and internal conflict is virtually nonexistent.

In a number of respects, Southey's later poems represent advances over *Joan*; but all of them share the same paradoxical flaw. On the one hand, their plots are elaborately "worked up" with regard to setting, incident, and "manners," and are buttressed by numerous, often lengthy, and sometimes barely relevant footnotes—"that happy *olla podrida* dish of literature, in which all heterogeneous materials may be served up" (*Letters*, I, 134). On the other hand, their characters are psychologically underdeveloped, without attaining a compensatory symbolic stature.

Sprung from a narrowly secular and rationalistic sensibility, they moreover, lack the compelling sense of a perilous universal order (or at least its absence) that the great epic has always conveyed either by symbolic implication or by explicit myth. This is true even of Southey's mythic romances, for the impulse that gives rise to them is the bookish one of antiquarianism and *Religionswissenschaft*, and their moral ideas are mostly cardinal points on the narrative compass rather than imperious regions beyond the ken of official beliefs. Unlike Coleridge's Ancient Mariner, the Southeyan hero is never "all alone" in an alien world. Physically, he may be at the bottom of the Arabian hell or in the topmost Hindu heaven; spiritually, he never drops "below the kirk" and the "lighthouse top." Like character, myth is absorbed into rhetoric or else objectified into stage effects ("machinery") and into examples of "manners." "That she believed herself inspired," Southey wrote of his heroine, "few will deny; that she was inspired, no one will venture to assert" (I, 14).

Coleridge put the problem one way when, in 1814, he scoffed at the "transmogrification of the fanatic Virago into a . . . Proselyte of the Age of Reason, a Tom Paine in Petticoats." De Quincey made the related observation that Southey's heroine is a Joan stripped of all that makes her momentous, namely, her martyrdom. Southey touches on the martyrdom, but only to sentimentalize it. He could understand the heroism of Leonidas, of doing one's duty toward one's country; but he had no patience with martyrs. He was never in that sense a Christian.[12]

He was even less a pagan. He abhorred the keen zest and the frank carnality of the Homeric heroes or of Camoens' Island of Venus. Thus, with all the *pietas* of an Aeneas, Joan has neither his passion nor the fanaticism of her prototype; she has only what Southey in the 1798 Preface called "the remembrance of subdued affection, a lingering of human feeling not inconsistent with the . . . holiness of her character" (17). In order to give her some sentimental "interest," Southey has her squired about the battlefield, not by brothers as was the historical Joan, but by an anemic young lover who predictably dies in her defense. The motif is interesting as an inversion of the old romance motif of the lady who follows her knight in disguise, but the compromise does not work well. Better a Clorinda tragically in love with her mortal enemy, or else a "Virago" impervious to romantic sentiments. But Southey was put off as much by the passion of the one as by the "enthusiasm" of the other. His imagination could not surrender to *this* world, nor create another out of itself. That is his tragedy.

V   Wat Tyler

We cannot conclude this chapter without glancing at a slight but very telling by-product of the poem just discussed. *Wat Tyler* is remembered today chiefly because of the *succès de scandale* of its belated publication. The play had been dashed off in a week in the wake of *Joan of Arc*. Attempts to get it into print had failed, and the manuscript had disappeared from sight. But in 1817 it was somehow unearthed and published surreptitiously by Southey's political enemies who were delighted by this chance to confront the "renegade" laureate with the ghost of his Jacobin past. Southey tried to stop the publishers in court; but the case was ruled against him by, of all people, the "arch-reactionary of England," Lord Chancellor Eldon, and he had to stand idly by as some sixty thousand copies in diverse editions were printed and sold as pamphlets in the streets of London. Eventually, however, a liberal Member of Parliament was foolish enough to use contrasting passages from the play and from a recent *Quarterly* article thought to be by Southey to illustrate what he was pleased to call the "malignity of a renegade." The speech drew sharp rejoinders from Wynn in the House, from Coleridge in *The Courier*, and from Southey himself in "A Letter to William Smith." Unlike his enemies, Southey wrote, he had changed with the times, but he was still a lover of liberty and a foe to tyranny. His early Republicanism had been erroneous and immature, but it had also been high-minded and courageous in its time and untainted by atheism and immorality. As for *Wat Tyler*, it was the mischievous but well-meant product of a youthful mind nourished upon Greek and Roman history and of a youthful heart "full of poetry and romance"—in short, nothing to be ashamed of (*Essays*, II, 7-21).

The play expresses Southey's early Republican fervor at its fullest. The subject could not but appeal strongly to the young poet. For one thing, its hero bore the name Tyler; and, while Southey was not actually related by blood to the Tylers, he liked to fancy himself a descendant of the old rebel, to refer to him as his dear "Uncle Wat," and even to identify with him by using the initials "W. T." as a *nom de plume*. Besides, Wat Tyler, whose story was still alive in popular chapbooks, had recently been hailed by Tom Paine as a Medieval "jacobin" and champion of the people.[13] He thus fit Southey's heroic formula even better than Joan. Like her, he represented an historical precedent for democratic principles; but he was also an Englishman with whom both the poet and his audience could identify. The play has little intrinsic appeal and no dramatic force: the action is at once meager and melodramatic; the rhetoric, too obvious and repetitive. Its saving grace is its spontaneity, the "glee" with which Southey said the play was written and which is not entirely lost on the reader.

Act I opens upon a May Day scene. Wat Tyler is gloomily watching the thoughtless gaiety of a morris dance from his blacksmith shop; and he complains at length about the people's sufferings under the grinding taxation that is imposed by "legal robbers" to pay for the "luxuries and riots of the court" and for a war that serves only the vanity of king and priest, the parasites of society. The birds have it better, for they are without the original sin of avarice. "No fancied boundaries of mine and thine / Restrain their wanderings. Nature gives enough / For all." But selfish man robs, hoards, and at best "gives to pity what he owes to justice."

These reflections, largely derived from Paine and Godwin, are interrupted by the arrival of tax-gatherers. One of them predictably insults Tyler's fifteen-year-old daughter and is brained by the incensed blacksmith. This deed triggers the rebellion: a mob quickly gathers and with cries of "liberty," "no poll-tax," "no war," chooses Tyler as its leader.

Act II opens with a song whose tetrameter trochaics faintly anticipate the throb of Shelley's "Song to the Men of England": "While the peasant works,—to sleep; / What the peasant sows,—to reap; . . . / Trampling on his slaves with scorn,— / This is to be nobly born." The crowd is assembled to hear John Ball, just delivered from prison, preach a sermon on liberty and Christian Communism and denounce the "blasphemies" of feudalism. The good priest exhorts his listeners to be bold and resolute but to temper justice with mercy. By contrast, the Archbishop of Canterbury counsels King Richard to use treachery against the rebels, assuring him that divine right and ecclesiastic sanction override all moral obligation. The scene then shifts to Smithfield: Tyler presents the people's grievances to the king and is stabbed in the back by one of Richard's ministers.

In spite of John Ball's remonstrances, the rebels now resort to terror. Wat Tyler, whose "stern rectitude" had awed the mob, is replaced by Jack Straw, the poor man's Robespierre. Ball realizes that brutality and hatred are the inevitable effects of a tyrannical rule intent on "degrading every faculty" and "repressing all the energy of mind." But he also knows that revenge, like punishment, perpetuates the evil it pretends to cure and that man's hope for betterment can lie only in reformation. Unfortunately, he finds that tyranny does not surrender to mere civil protest. The people, fooled by Richard's facile promises, are promptly massacred by his soldiers; and Ball is taken prisoner. In the final scene, Ball is arraigned at Westminster; but he fearlessly denounces hereditary privilege, private property, and all hierarchical government: "Would not the sun shine and the dews descend, / Though neither king nor parliament existed?" Condemned to be hanged, disembowelled, quartered, and beheaded, he exits prophesying a day of truth, justice, and liberty to come. The king orders "the law" to "take vengeance on the rebels," and the curtain falls.

It will be evident from the foregoing that for all of his early familiarity with plays and the theater, Southey is least adept in this genre. Even *The Fall of Robespierre*—the three-act historical "drama" for which Coleridge wrote the first act and Southey the remaining two—made that clear, done in haste as it was (though that is a standing excuse with Southey). While Coleridge manages at least to hint at the ambiguity of human motives and to touch upon the psychology of guilt, Southey's part is unrelieved rant; the trial of Robespierre is a mere shouting match in which both parties engage in tedious rounds of name calling. No character has any depth, and even the rhetoric is not engaging since the issues are not clear to the reader without the aid of a history book. *Wat Tyler* represents an advance in both clarity and restraint; but the characters are still flat and bloodless; and only John Ball has some moments of doubt and bewilderment that raise him above the level of an orator's dummy. Southey attempted the drama again in subsequent years, beginning with a "refaccimento" of *Wat Tyler* that was to have resulted in a full-fledged historical drama. "Had it been continued," he wrote later, "it might have stood beside *Joan of Arc*, and perhaps I should have become a dramatic writer" (*Life*, IV, 258). Scarcely. He could succeed well enough with spacious and episodic narrative; but, as he admitted himself, he lacked the ability to converge a great deal of feeling, observation, and thought into a single, sustained, and concentrated dramatic action; and his various dramatic plans came to nothing.[14]

CHAPTER 3

Idols of the Cave:
The Man and the Poet

I Changes in Outlook; Law; Literature

S OUTHEY'S sojourn abroad in 1795/6, though relatively
brief and uneventful, had a lasting effect on his outlook and on
his literary preoccupations. For one thing, it kindled his lifelong interest in Spanish and Portuguese literature and history. For another,
it aroused his fanatical concern with Catholic beliefs and institutions. More immediately, however, it altered his political
stance. The blatant spectacle of royal extravagance and debauchery
in the midst of poverty, disease, and ignorance which met him both
in Spain and in Portugal revived at first his already cooling
revolutionary and emancipatory ardor; but it also gave him a new
appreciation of the relatively superior conditions in England; and
he soon announced that, upon his return there, he would quit
politics and write a hymn to the *Dii Penates*—which he did.

In principle, Southey remained a Republican, or thought he did,
until about 1812. Between 1806 and 1810, he could still call himself
a Jacobin, sympathize with a radical like the young Shelley, feel
that "old governments must be cut up and put into Medea's
cauldron," and remark that most of England's problems would be
solved by transporting the royal family to Botany Bay. He always
detested William Pitt, denounced the slave-trade, and opposed
capital punishment. At the same time, however, Southey now rapidly lost his enthusiasm for radical "man-mending," as he called it.
Revolutionary positivism had never penetrated very deeply into his
basically conservative nature; and, though he still believed in
reform, he was becoming discouraged by the distance and
magnitude of its objectives. "A little candle," he observed, "will
give light enough to a moderate-sized room . . . in the street, the

first wind extinguishes it." He would, therefore, take his tea without sugar to express his abhorrence of slavery, and he might write polemical stories about various oppressed peoples—the Jews, the Albigenses, or the Helots; but otherwise he would bury the axe of the partisan in exchange for the bays of the poet and for domestic contentment, the true philosopher's stone. If governments must be "cut up," let it be hereafter: *après nous le déluge;* if it must be now, he would wisely retire into an ark, "like Noah, to preserve a remnant which may become the whole."[1]

Such ideological withdrawal from political controversy into the hurricane eye of a poetic and meditative domesticity was, of course, not unique with Southey. A literary commonplace, it had already informed the test-tube revolution of Pantisocracy, as expressed in Southey's sonnet on the subject—"Ah that my lot / Might be with peace and Solitude assigned, / Where I might from some little cot / Sigh for the crimes and miseries of mankind!" (II, 104)—and it is basic to Wordsworth's self-image as "Recluse." Coleridge, at first full of praise for Southey's sonnet, subsequently denounced—in the "Reflections on Having Left a Place of Retirement"—the selfishness of visionaries who "sigh for wretchedness, yet shun the wretched." For all three "Lake poets," however, poetry now became their politics; domestic reclusion, their ark and commonwealth. Southey merely stated the matter more baldly: "in a little sphere, / The little circle of domestic life, / I would be known and loved; the world beyond is not for me" (232).

The period between Southey's return from Portugal in the summer of 1796 and his second, longer visit there in 1800 was in fact one of rootlessness and uncertainty; though also one of poetic fulfillment. Southey now determined to read for the law and was admitted to Gray's Inn in February, 1797. But, though he formally "kept" a number of terms there during the next several years, he did little actual studying. Law repelled him, and he disliked London, in spite of the opportunities it offered of foregathering with intellectuals like Mary Wollstonecraft. He was only too glad to quit the metropolis when it appeared that Edith was made ill by its climate. During the next three years the Southeys lived in various southern towns, never really settled except for a period between June, 1798, and the midsummer of 1799 when they leased a house outside Bristol at Westbury—"Martin Hall," as they called it, because of its many swallows. At length, they resolved to return to Portugal.

The main reason for this decision was the sudden fear that Southey, who was plagued by ill-health during much of this migratory period, might be suffering from consumption. His real problem was no doubt intense anxiety rather than physical illness. He detested the law; he felt he lacked the necessary quickness of mind for a barrister—"a blockhead who speaks boldly can baffle me"; and he was unable to remember anything he had read in his books. At the same time, Wynn's annuity—that "millstone of dependence hanging round my neck"—obligated him to continue. As usual, he sought escape in literature; but such tactics could only add to his burden. Finally, there remained only flight into disease—and to Portugal.

Thus, while ostensibly studying law, Southey was in fact primarily engaged in literary labors. "This morning I began the study of law," he wrote in his notebook on February 22, 1797; "this evening I began Madoc." Early the same year, he published *Letters Written during a Short Residence in Spain and Portugal*, a book that proved popular and went through several editions. At about the same time, he began, like Coleridge, to write verses for the *Morning Post*—at a guinea a week—and to contribute to the two leading literary periodicals, the *Monthly Magazine* and the *Critical Review*; for the latter of which he wrote, in October, 1798, the somewhat jaundiced review of Wordsworth's and Coleridge's *Lyrical Ballads*. The year at Westbury, in particular, was memorable to Southey for its productivity. *Madoc*, begun in 1794 but then put aside, was now recommenced and finished in draft form by mid-summer of 1799. At the same time, the plan for *Thalaba* took shape, and its composition began the day after the completion of *Madoc*. Moreover, the year was for Southey, as for Wordsworth, one of lyrical flowering. In May, 1798, he had met William Taylor, a frequent contributor to the *Monthly Magazine* and the leading transmitter of contemporary German literature to England. Animated by the contact with Taylor, whose acquaintance grew into a fast friendship, Southey wrote numerous ballads, experimented with new poetic forms, and in 1799 and 1800 published a volume of poems and two volumes of an *Annual Anthology* of minor verse, the bulk written by himself.

The period was also auspicious in personal ways. After several years of strained relations, Southey had become reconciled with Coleridge. During an extended visit in August, 1799, the two poets traveled to the romantic Valley of the Rocks at Lynmouth, wrote the notorious "Devil's Walk" together,[2] and planned an epic on

Mohammed. Besides, there was Humphry Davy, the brilliant young Bristol scientist and amateur poet whom both Coleridge and Southey had befriended. Southey saw much of him, and when Davy, that "miraculous young man," regaled him with exhilarating whiffs of the laughing gas he had discovered, it seemed a foretaste of paradise.

II *Southey's Personality*

Although we now tend to think of Southey as the comical butt of Byron's abrasive satire, as the mouthey laureate and bathetic dry-Bob of *Don Juan* and the *Vision of Judgment*, he was, at least in his pre-laureate years, an impressive figure. A "lean, lank, greyhound-like creature" by his own confession, he was for a long time very handsome and looked very much like a poet. "Tall, dignified, possessing great suavity of manners; an eye piercing, with a countenance full of genius, kindliness, and intelligence"—so the genial Joseph Cottle remembered him; and even Byron snidely admitted after their only meeting: "To have that poet's head and shoulders, I would almost have written his Sapphics."[3] Existing portraits show us a fine oval face framed by rich, curling auburn hair; a prominent but finely aquiline nose; arched eyebrows; a dimpled chin; and a mouth whose full lips have a hint of childish mirth playing about them.

At the same time, however, there was even in Southey's outward appearance something that belied the image of the poet. "A hectic flush upon his cheek, a roving fire in his eye . . . a look at once aspiring and dejected"—so William Hazlitt saw him; as a man racked by fantastic and unresolved contradictions; as a "poetic libertine" in revolt against all literary decorum, yet a moral and religious bigot; kind of heart, yet cold in manner; a libertarian turned legitimatist; a quester who "missed his way in Utopia [and] has found it in Old Sarum."[4]

Hazlitt was too much the political partisan not to caricature what he portrayed; but his insight was keen. Especially Southey's frigid exterior was frequently remarked upon by all but his closest friends, and by no one more often than Southey himself. Except for the brief period of Pantisocratic fervor, he confessed in 1797, he had always been "silent and self-centering" even in childhood, "shelter[ing] myself in my own thoughts" as "a hedgehog rolls himself up when noticed. . . . God never intended that I should

make myself agreeable to any body." The same prickly image
recurs thirty-three years later: toward most people, Southey says, he
is "cold and courteous"; some "make me draw into myself like a
tortoise, or roll myself up in prickles, like a hedgehog; and
sometimes . . . I bristle like a porcupine at an odious presence."
Elsewhere Southey compares himself to a holly tree; and the motif
of holing and rolling up like an animal appears again and again. A
sonnet was to extol "the happiness of a toad in a stone." In the half-
humorous conversation poem "The Filbert," he muses about the
bliss of being a maggot and passing his days in the snug simplicity
of a nutshell, untouched by wars and taxes and by the aches and
fears of man, and feeling "no motion but the wind that shook / The
Filbert-tree, and rocked us to our rest" (III, 68). One of his favorite
legends was that of the Seven Sleepers; and he wished that man
could hibernate like bears. "I should roll myself up at the end of
October," he muses wistfully, "and give orders to be awakened by
the chimney-sweeper on May-day."[5]

Remarks like these gain perspective when we recall Southey's
loneliness and his painful sensitivity to cold and to late hours in
childhood. His stoic reserve was a way of taking arms against a sea
of lovelessness; his coldness and silence, a defense against a cold
and silent world. Southey often brooded about his isolation. The
only person, he said, with whom he could be wholly intimate, was
Coleridge. Yet the very thing that made such intimacy possible,
Coleridge's outgoing nature, was also a threat to Southey and an
object at once of longing for what he could not have and of contempt for what he insisted he did not want. "Your feelings go naked, I cover mine with bear-skin; I will not say you harden yours by
your mode, but I am sure that mine are the warmer for their
clothing." "If Momus had made a window in my breast," he told
himself, "I should have made a shutter to it." And then again, with
the mixture of sadness and complacency that is the twin-birth of
isolation, "I have a trick of thinking too well of those I love, better
than they generally deserve, and better than my cold and con-
taining manners ever let them know."[6]

Probably no one of woman born and of sound mind is cold and
unfeeling by nature alone; but Southey had, in fact, a more than ordinary share of feeling, as well as an acute sensorium, even in later
life. "How has this man contrived," Thomas Carlyle exclaimed,
"with such a nervous-system, to keep alive, for nearly sixty years?
Now blushing under his grey hairs, rosy like a maiden of fifteen;

now slaty almost, like a rattlesnake, or fiery serpent? How has he not been torn to pieces long since, under such furious pulling this way and that? He must have somewhere a great deal of methodic virtue."[7] Southey himself once compared himself to the Boiling Well near Bristol—seething at the bottom, though smooth on the surface—and he frequently spoke of his prolonged struggle to root out his "mimosa sensibility," to subdue his feelings, and to keep them, like "Helots," under a "most Spartan despotism." Rendered explosive by early frustration, his feelings had to be repressed and could not be set free.

Southey's inability to harmonize the opposites within him could only cripple his artistic endeavor. In 1811, he told the tempestuous Walter Savage Landor that he must always work on two or more projects at once in order to avoid the "continuous excitement" and the haunting dreams produced by work on a single poem: "The tears would flow while in the act of composition, and would leave [the] whole system in the highest state of nervous excitability, which would soon induce disease in one of its most fearful forms. From this state I recovered in 1800 by going to Portugal . . . and I have kept it off since by a good intellectual regimen" (*Life*, III, 300). He could let himself be overwhelmed by his feelings or he could divide and conquer them by "intellectual regimen"—Carlyle's "methodic virtue"—but he could not harness them creatively. His poetic vision therefore never attains the intensity of the tragic. He spoke of the "Pains of Imagination" (*Life*, I, 288); and as his earliest memory was of being tormented by "sad songs and dismal stories," so as a grown man he lectured his friend Caroline Bowles on her "cruel" preoccupation with suffering. Literature, he felt, should not add to the heartache of life but should cheer and comfort. His own works are full of sentimental pathos, but they consistently evade the problem of suffering by rationalizations.

Southey's tenuous hold on a painful present is complemented by his obsession with the afterlife as the only future entirely worth hoping for, as well as by his periodic indulgence in a childish jocularity which he thought Rabelaisian but which is actually regressive—an attempt to compensate for the mirthlessness of his early years. Southey was happy enough in his tranquil domesticity, surrounded by his children, his books, and his cats. The best life, he remarked, was that of a hermit who had "a good Mrs. Hermit," a "due number of young Hermits playing about his hermitage," and a few

other such hermitages within reach (*Commonplace Books*, IV, 494);
and the best maxim in the Catechism was contentment with one's
appointed lot. Perhaps so; but great poetry will scarcely grow in
such a tepid climate. A different orientation might have turned him
into a kind of Regency Lewis Carroll; but, if Southey lost his way in
Utopia, he did not find it in Wonderland.

Southey's dread of strong feeling accounts, in turn, for his
Puritanical moral rigor. "There is the same excuse for drunkenness
and debauchery as for oversensibility," he once wrote. At times, he
could affect a rakish mood; but to most of his contemporaries he
was a Malvolio critical of cakes and ale. "He is a young man of the
most rigidly virtuous habits," Dorothy Wordsworth observed in
1798. Shelley, less sympathetic, wrote, "You are such a pure one as
Jesus Christ found not in all Judea." Most telling, perhaps, are
Coleridge's comments. In public he praised his brother-in-law for
having "passed from innocence into virtue" untainted; but his
private view was less simplistic. There is, he wrote, "a bluntness of
Conscience superinduced by a very unusual Infrequency as well as
by Habit & Frequency, of wrong Actions." Southey, who has "from
earliest childhood preserved himself immaculate from all the common faults and weaknesses of human nature," has that kind of
moral insensitivity. "Sunt, quibus cecidisse prodesset, says St.
Augustine." At once too weak and too strong for such a fortunate
fall, Southey had only the "colossal virtue" of the Pharisee. "The
smiles, the emanations, the perpetual Sea-like Sound and Motion of
Virtuousness, which is Love, is wanting—He is . . . at best, a
smooth stream with one current, & tideless."[8]

Southey's moral sentiments often appear sensible enough. He disparaged the bigotry of the Society for the Suppression of Vice and
vigorously condemned the repressiveness of monastic celibacy as
unnatural and exacerbating: "God wisely gave us passions, and it is
society that has made the indulgence of them vicious."[9] In general,
however, he was concerned more to disarm passion than to cultivate
it, he had been something of a prude even at twenty when he had
joined in burning a fellow-student's erotica; and, as the years
progressed, an authoritarian fear of passion gained the upper hand,
often in the form of a somewhat prurient obsession with sexual
license. A professed proto-Victorian champion of "Household Virtue" and "Domestic Purity," Southey saw himself from early youth
as an embattled and lonely contender against the forces of vice and
dissipation. Life in Spain and Portugal he found "depraved beyond

all my ideas of licentiousness." The eroticism of romances like *Amadis of Gaul* and *Palmerin of England* scandalized him, and his own translations of these poems are duly purged of carnal detail. In his notorious attack on the "Satanic School" of poetry, he execrated Byron's *Don Juan* as "furniture for the brothel" that was designed to pollute the ingenuous reader with a poisonous mixture of "impiety [and] lewdness" and thereby to corrode and destroy "the religion, the institutions, and the domestic morals of the country." About Robert Herrick he noted: "Without being intentionally obscene, he is thoroughly filthy. . . . In an old writer . . . I never saw so large a proportion of . . . trash or ordure." Similarly, Southey dismissed Robert Malthus' theory of the primacy of the libido, "independent of the reason and the will," as "diarrhoea of the intellect," as an insult to womanhood, and "as false in philosophy as it is detestable in morals."[10] Perhaps this horror of sensuality, "the cursed enchantment of hell" (VI, 93), also accounts for Southey's general dislike of music.

No doubt Southey conceived this horror, the fear of letting go, in part in reaction to his aunt, the tempestuous and at the same time unresponsive Miss Tyler. Her hysteria about dirt, moreover, could not but produce certain fixations in her nephew as well. Coleridge notes that the only time he saw Southey get angry with his wife was "on occasion of her sportfully putting a little milk in his mash which (a drop or two) fell on his jacket & he feared would stain it." Conversely, Southey's letters and familiar writings contain not only frequent animadversions about cleanliness and its opposite but a good many scatological jokes. "All men of cold constitutions," Coleridge observed, "are naturally immodest. . . . So Southey —while he keeps clean of *one* outlet, he does not care what filth comes out of the other Orifices."[11]

III   *Religious Views*

The fatal bifurcation of Southey's nature is perhaps most glaringly evident in his ambivalence toward religious belief. On the one hand, though he professed to repudiate scoffers like Voltaire who "cut up the wheat with the tares," Southey was himself a rationalist in the formidable tradition of Pierre Bayle, John Toland, Thomas Middleton, and other dreadnoughts of the Enlightenment who boldly fought their century-old battles over again and who tirelessly collected instances of religious "folly and fraud," "superstition" and "priestcraft," miracle-mongering "hagiomania" and "mystical quackery," Christian and pagan alike, in order to hold them up for general scorn and disenchantment. While in Portugal, Southey had nothing but ridicule for Catholic "mummery" like the feast of Corpus Christi, which he called "the Body of God" so that one might "see the nakedness of the nonsensical blasphemy." On the night preceding the "raree-show" of the procession, he sneered, the streets are cleaned: "the only miracle I ever knew the wafer to perform is that of cleaning the streets of Lisbon." About the same time, the principal purpose of his major epic, *Madoc*, was to describe a "gentle tribe of savages delivered from priestcraft."[12]

Southey feared both Methodism, the "damned system of Calvinism," and the "accursed religion" of Popery as politically dangerous conspiratorial forces. But he feared even more the threat which the irrational appeal of religion and other "epidemics of the mind" posed to the rational judgment in the form of fanaticism and divisiveness. And when he contemplated visionaries from Richard Brothers, the "King of the Hebrews," and Joanna Southcott, the "Second Eve," to Saint Francis or William Blake, he had to conclude that "religious enthusiasm" was a highly infectious form of gratuitous lunacy that strongly testified to the "morbid anatomy of the human mind." Although Southey called himself "a believer in the truth of Christianity," his Christianity was the "reasonable" and "not mysterious" one of Deism. Belief for him meant rational assent to rational principles; faith in the fuller sense he disparaged as the mere satisfaction of an irrational "appetite." Even Joan of Arc was, after all, a "crazy Papist."[13]

Yet Southey betrays at the same time a powerful fascination for the objects of that "appetite," for the "pure charm and hidden moral of superstition and legendary lore" wherever these appear, whether in the fair humanities of Classical paganism, in remoter forms of heathenry, in the "fabulous Christianity" which he saw on the wane, or in the new sects and cults that made his own time seem an "age of credulity." Deep down, he could not but sense that to disparage "enthusiasm" and superstition was in the long run to sap the foundations of all religious conviction. "The Papists," he wrote in 1808, "are beyond all doubt Idolaters . . . but in flying from idolatry, what a fearful chasm have we left between man and God! What a void have we made in the Universe." And in the *Colloquies* of 1829 he was able to lament the decline of belief in this "age of reason" and to confess to his ghostly interlocutor that many would "think me superstitious, because I am not ashamed to avow my persuasion that there are more things in heaven and earth than are dreamt of in their philosophy."[14]

At times, Southey therefore exhibits a patent nostalgia for a lost Eden of emotional and imaginative freedom of belief, a longing to be delivered from the cold prudence of secular Protestant reason by the "blest illusion" of Catholic superstition. When stripped of its "tricks," he muses, Catholicism "is a fine religion for an enthusiast" who can "opiate his reason." It "seems made for human feelings, to supply all their cravings." "Never was goddess so calculated to win upon the human heart as the Virgin Mary." The fictitious Catholic narrator of the *Letters from England* (1807), Don Manuel Espriella, repeatedly waxes eloquent about the emotional richness of his religion, especially the worship of the "infinitely lovable and adorable" Virgin; and he laments the desolating spiritual and imaginative impoverishment of the Protestant heresy. Though Southey's principal intention is ironic, he betrays at times a wistful fondness for the mask he has assumed. Protected by this persona, he could even envy a visionary "madman" like Richard Brothers, a sort of Dr. Jones writ large, for being able to forget both past and present in the rapt contemplation of a glorious messianic future—"just as all other objects near or distant appear dark to him who has been looking at the sun."[15]

Southey had tried the Wordsworthian path of seeking in Nature a substitute for the exiled "Body of God." "Without becoming a pagan or a fool," he wrote," "we may allow imagination to people the air with intelligent spirits and animate every herb with sensation" and to make hill and grove "holier places than the temple of Solomon." But a deeper conviction told him that woods and rocks "are among the τα ουκ εφ' ζμιγ. It is within doors, and not without, that happiness dwells like a vestal watching the fire of the Penates."[16] Though often beautiful and "the passion of [his] youth," Nature was something alien that could not replace the Virgin.

Thus hemmed in by his rationalism, on the one hand, and by his humanism, on the other, Southey had to satisfy his spiritual needs surreptitiously by a pseudo-academic, antiquarian interest in the old mythologies—an interest that was prodigious and unappeasable and that issued in his fantastic plan to study and poetize every known religious system. Above all, his religious necrophilia focused on the "Catholic mythology" and its rank undergrowth of monkish stories, saints' and devils' legends, and apocryphal traditions. "I have ten thousand stories," he boasts, while rummaging for more. His Commonplace Books with their countless excerpts from his voluminous reading have, in places, the repellent fascination of an intellectual freak show and betray both a certain solicitude about, and a sneaking pleasure in, the things he ostensibly recorded for their sheer absurdity. The same is true of the published works into which he emptied much of this melange: the *Letters from England, Omniana, The Doctor,* and the notes to his long poems. *Omniana, or Horae Otiosiores,* for example, a book of shreds and patches collected from Southey's antiquarian column in the *Athenaeum* and published, with some additions by Coleridge, in 1812, is full of such samplings from the "Bibliotheca Fanatica," old wives tales, and other learned and curious matters. Endlessly fighting the hydra of superstitition, Southey seems determined to preserve every single head in amber.

In particular, he exhibits a peculiar and obsessive fascination with devils' lore and all forms of diablerie. "I am learned in Daemonology," he told Bedford; and his references to the Prince of Darkness are legion. Byron's *Vision of Judgment* is never more trenchant than when it has the Laureate propose to follow his *Life of Wesley* with a life of Satan. "Her dreams are usually of the Devil," Southey wrote of Joanna Southcott; but he might have said it about himself. Southey was a lively and often tormented dreamer. The dreams recorded in the unique "dreamlog" that he kept at various times are remarkable for their coherence and vividness of detail; but even more noteworthy is their preoccupation with death, naked and animated corpses, live burials, murderous skeletons, and the demonic and macabre in general. He was, in fact, prompted to begin this collection by just such a nocturnal horror:

I was haunted by evil spirits, of whose presence, though unseen, I was aware. There were also dead bodies near me, though I saw them not. Terrified as I was . . . still I reasoned and insisted to myself that all was delirium and weakness of mind. . . . At length an arm appeared through a half-opened door, or rather a long hand. Determined to convince myself that all was unsubstantial and visionary . . . I ran up and caught it. It was a hand, and a lifeless one. I pulled at it with desperate effort, dragged in a sort of shapeless body into the room, trampled upon it crying out the while for horror.[17]

A nightmare of the devil belonged to his earliest memories, and what had bedeviled him in childhood continued to haunt him still in his maturity.

He did not, of course, literally believe in the existence of demons; even in his dream, after all, he tried to reason them away. He joked about Saint Anthony and about Luther's bouts with Satan. He could not accept the doctrine of a hell of eternal torments; and, when an Anglican publication took him to task for disbelieving in the Devil because he had referred to him in his *Life of Wesley* as the "personified principle of evil," he merely replied, somewhat lamely, that one who believed in "anything spiritual" could not well deny the existence of "evil spirits" (*Correspondence*, 318). The grotesque diablerie of many of his ballads, however, suggests a continual need to exorcize by ridicule—by "making free with," as he boasts in the *Colloquies* (I, 244)—a specter his mind told him did not exist. At the same time, he was increasingly oppressed by the diabolic in human affairs, and he discovered the cloven foot and the stench of hell everywhere—in Bonaparte, in radicalism, in the Satanic School, in the steam locomotive, in the foundries of Birmingham, in the manufacturing system. If he tried to banish the myth, he fell under the drearier spell of the metaphor. When Byron read Southey's *Vision of Judgment*, he was not sure whether this was "Joanna Southcott or Bob Southey raving."

Southey thus illuminates in a peculiarly negative way a significant aspect of Romanticism: the crisis of the religious imagination produced by the Enlightenment and the Herculean endeavor of the Romantic poets to recreate a genuine mythic thinking for modern, historical man. Southey shared the need; but, unlike his greater contemporaries, he lacked the visionary energy and courage for a real quest of discovery. Almost the only Romantic to remain essentially untouched by Milton, he certainly could not follow either Blake or Wordsworth into their strange seas of thought. As to Wordsworth's Peter Bell, things to him "seemed [but] the things they were" (X, 373). And although Southey superficially shared Coleridge's dislike of Lockean empiricism, he had nothing but contempt for "metaphysics" and transcendental philosophy, and he lacked the imaginative sympathy necessary to "suspend his disbelief" or to contemplate superstitions as symbols or "facts of mind." A sketch for the rather trivial poem "Old Christobal's Advice" characteristically begins with the words "There is a lie in the life of St. Isidro which may perhaps make a ballad"; and, in a letter to Caroline Bowles (82), Southey remarked that, though saints legends were "very monkish and papistical," they were "well fitted for poetry." All of his mythological poems, while designed as "illustrations" of mythic beliefs are, in fact, exposures of clay-footed idols.

The only religious tenet Southey ultimately cared about was belief in an afterlife. The successive loss of five brothers and sisters, his parents, a beloved cousin, and a number of close friends, he said, had early "weaned" his heart from this world and "fixed its thought and desires upon a better state" in which there would be no separation. And when, in 1816, his brilliant ten-year-old son and playmate Herbert died—the "flower and crown of all my hopes and earthly happiness" whom he had loved with an almost frantic love "passing the love of women" (X, 384)—this belief became more necessary than ever: "If death were the termination of our existence . . . I should wish rather to have been born a beast, or never to have been born at all," for then "this world would be a mystery too dreadful to be borne—our best affections and our noblest desires a mere juggle and a curse" (*Life*, IV, 180; V, 12). The tenor of his dreams, moreover, bespeaks a deep-seated, primitive fear of death from which only a strenuous belief in an afterworld could shelter him.

Nor was he content with some kind of impersonal survival as part of a World Soul, or the like. In a letter to Caroline Bowles, he protested with comic abhorrence against any mystical posthumous merger into a single Great Humanity, in which he would be compounded bone and flesh "with Solomon and all his wives and concubines, and the whole court of Louis XIV and Charles II, and all the monks and nuns that ever lived, and all the radicals, and all the Turks, Jews, Infidels . . . deans and . . . dissenting ministers, and all bazaar ladies. No, no, no . . . We shall keep our identities there, and all our good feelings, and all our recollections . . . and we shall lose nothing but . . . sorrows, and frailties, and infirmities" (*Correspondence*, 223). Southey recoils as violently from contact with miscellaneous humanity as Elizabeth Tyler had shrunk from the contaminating presence of unwelcome visitors. Radical Pantisocracy and Aspheterism were as little attractive to him in Heaven as they had been in England or America. Heaven, to make life at all bearable, had to redress the evils endured on earth; and it had to do so individually. It had to respect domestic privacy and personal preference, to unite us with our loved ones down to the last pet, but not with our enemies or with general mankind. "Like the untaught

American," Southey once wrote, "I look / To find in heaven the things I loved on earth" (II, 233). It is the quintessence of his creed.

IV *Lyricism*

That an intense and powerful lyricism would spring from so dammed-up and divided a sensibility can hardly be expected. Indeed, Southey's lyrics are like runnels in a vast but shallow spillway, without music or deep current to move us, and not altogether undeserving of Southey's own disparaging motto: *Nos haec novimus esse nihil* (we know this is nothing). Yet his minor verse requires some notice, if only because, in its experimentation with new forms and themes, it reflects something of the spirit of the Romantic renascence. A handful of Southey's ballads, sonnets, and occasional lyrics can, moreover, stand on their own merit.[18]

Predictably, Southey's early poems are modeled on Thomas Gray, William Collins, and W. L. Bowles and to some extent on Mark Akenside, William Mason, and Thomas Warton. Like them, Southey reacted against the heroic couplet and returned to "Odes, Elegies, [and] Sonnets"; like them, he filled the old skins with the heady new vintage of Gothic sublimity, elegiac pastoralism, and sententious reflection; like them, he relied heavily on personified abstraction, solemn apostrophe, and swelling epithet. Few of these poems, however, match the best of their antecedents; their only interest lies in the novelty of their content.

This is especially true of Southey's attempts in the so-called major ode—all of them of the irregular, Cowleian type. Thematically, these range from the melancholy of the early "To Contemplation," through the anti-slavery agitation of "To the Genius of Africa," to encyclopedic poems like the mythological pieces "The Race of Odin" and "The Death of Odin" or like the "progress" poem on "Romance," a "Romantic" countermanifesto to Gray's "Progress of Poetry." At their best, these poems are not untalented. The opening stanzas of "To Contemplation" cleverly imitate both Gray and Collins. "To Horror" opposes the desolation of Nature's desert places to the ghastlier horrors of man's inhumanity to man. And "To the Genius of Africa" has moments of noble, if innocuous, rhetoric: "O Thou who from thy mountain's height / Rollest thy clouds, with all their weight / Of waters, to old Nile's majestic tide . . . By every drop of blood bespilt; / By Afric's wrong and

Europe's guilt,— / Awake! arise! avenge!" (II, 68 - 70). But too
often apostrophe degenerates into frigid rant, and panoramic vision
into a dull parade of learning. The two odes on Odin—both examples of a type of "Runic" poetry made popular by the
translations of Gray, Percy, and others—seek to utilize Gothic sublimity as a vehicle for libertarian sentiment but bog down in
mythological detail. "Romance," for all its enthusiasm about the
fairy way of writing, about Icelandic sagas and Arabian Nights,
about Spenser and Rousseau, does not succeed in making these
things interesting. The metrically ingenious "Triumph of Woman,"
a poem based on a story in Esdras and reminiscent of Dryden's
"Alexander's Feast," is a verbose, sentimental medley of
republicanism, romance, and religion.

Southey fares better with the monostrophic "minor," or Hora-
tian, ode. When writing irregular or free verse, Southey is generally
at the mercy of prosiness and verbosity. Even his highly personal
"The Dead Friend" about the death of Edmund Seward achieves
only intermittently any kind of emotional concentration: "Not to
the grave, not to the grave, my Soul, / Descend to contemplate / The form that once was dear. . . . It is but lifeless,
perishable flesh / That molders in the grave; / Earth, air, and
water's ministering particles / Now to the elements / resolved, their
uses done" (200 - 1). Equally unhappy are contrary experiments
with rigidly fixed forms like the Sapphic strophe, as in the notorious
"Widow": "Cold was the nightwind, drifting fast the snow
fell, / Wide were the downs, and shelterless and naked, / When a
poor Wanderer struggled on her journey, / Weary and waysore."
Besides being incorrectly scanned, the poem exhibits a total disjunc-
tion of form and content, as Canning's famous parody shows:
"Needy Knife-grinder! whither are you going? . . . Bleak blows the
blast;—your hat has got a hole in't, / So have your breeches."

Southey is at his best when he combines freedom and discipline,
tradition and innovation. His early attempts in Collins' rhymeless
"minor ode" stanza, like "To Hymen" and "Written on the First of
January," are still thoroughly mediocre. But when he varies the
stanza, a venture in which he took great pride, the result can be
something fresh and competent: "I looked abroad at noon, / The
shadow and the storm were on the hills; / The crags, which like a
fairy fabric shone, / Darkness had overcast" (164 - 5). In "The Ebb-
Tide," the same "envelope" is trimmed with rhyme and serves to

suggest the rise and fall of the tide in the river, which, in turn, is an emblem of the slow growth and rapid decay of all things—joys, kingdoms, and men: "Now o'er the rocks, that lay / So silent late, the shallow current roars; / Fast flow thy waters on their seaward way, / Through wider-spreading shores" (194). "The Destruction of Jerusalem," "The Death of Wallace," "The Spanish Armada," and "St. Bartholomew's Day" —all poems dating from the Westbury period and all dealing with critical moments in the history of man's struggle against tyranny—exhibit additional variants of the same stanza. So do several of the "Songs of the American Indians" of 1799: "The storm-cloud grows deeper above; / Araucans! the tempest is ripe in the sky; / Our forefathers come from the Islands of Bliss, / They come to the war of the winds" (208). Both syntax and diction effectively convey the sense of the "primitive" in this poem.

Mostly successful are also a handful of emblematic pieces that are reminiscent of Francis Quarles and George Wither, poets whom Southey greatly relished. The choice of the emblem itself is often the best part of the poem: an ivy-sapped oak as a symbol of British liberty ("What the travelers at distance green-flourishing see, / Are the leaves of the ivy that poisoned the tree"); or a holly to emblemize the poet's own life and personality—"harsh and austere" towards the outside world, but "gentle at home amid my friends"; comparatively sober of hue in youth, but still green and cheerful in the winter of age, and so on (191). The execution may be negligent, as in "The Oak of Our Fathers," and the thought is usually facile and pat. But a poem like "The Holly Tree" at least provides a simple image for what is mere unctuous preachment in the notorious "The Old Man's Comforts"; and "To a Spider," while rather diffuse in its random comparison of spiders to lawyers, statesmen, Satan ("Hell's huge black Spider"), and poets ("Thy bowels dost thou spin, / I spin my brains"), pleases by its informal yet controlled rhythm and by its kindly yet unsentimental ecological spirit.

Some of the most engaging and least hackneyed of Southey's lyrics are, in fact, addressed to animals; and we could wish that the author of "The Three Bears" had written more poems of this sort. Southey seems more at ease with brutes than with people. As the College Cat had typified freedom and independence for him, so the "Dancing Bear" stands for slavery and exploitation. "The Pig, A

Colloquial Poem" (evidently a pendant to Coleridge's "The
Nightingale, A Conversation Poem") is even more sansculottist:
"The Pig is a philosopher, who knows / No prejudice.
Dirt?—Jacob, what is dirt?" Let Miss Tyler answer that! The pig is
not only no uglier than "A Lady in her dishabille" but is perfect in
his ways—as man is not!

The best of Southey's sonnets—he wrote some four dozen—are
also emblematic. The early "Sonnets on the Slave-Trade," though
well-meant and of some notoriety in their time, do not rise above
sentimental rhetoric, despite their harrowing tale of the ordeal of a
typical slave from his abduction in the slave ship to his Promethean
punishment for attempted rebellion: "High in the air exposed, the
Slave is hung; / To all the birds of heaven, their living food" (68).
Similarly, the "Amatory Poems of Abel Shufflebottom" (written in
the wake of Coleridge's "Nehemiah Higginbottom" sonnets) ex-
haust themselves in fairly humdrum parody of the effete language,
precious conceits, and sentimental fetishism of the Della Cruscan
poetry: Southey disapproved of "amatory poems" generally, and his
comedy is purely negative. Other of his sonnets are as mawkish and
sentimental as those he ridiculed.

A few, however, benefitted from the concretizing example of W.
L. Bowles, whose influential volume of sonnets had appeared in
1789. Southey's sonnet "Corston," for example, echoes Bowles's
"To the River Itchin," as it unsentimentally recalls the cheerless
boredom and the loveless loneliness of life at boarding-school and
only tentatively invokes the redeeming power of memory:
"Dreamlike and indistinct those days appear, / As the faint sounds
of this low brooklet, borne / Upon the breeze, reach fitfully the
ear" (102). The murmur of the brook, with which the poem begins,
becomes in the end a metaphor of recollection that unifies the poem
and anchors the perplexed feeling of the poet in a concrete image.
The "mild arch of promise" in the sonnet "The Evening Rainbow"
finally only emblemizes the "smile that Piety bestows" on a good
man in death, but not before the day, "changeful and many-
weathered," has been finely described as "Flashing brief splendour
through the clouds while, / Which deepened dark anon, and fell in
rain."

Southey rarely avoids sententiousness altogether; but his best
sonnets, all written in his *annus felix* at Westbury (the last of them
is significantly a farewell to "Martin Hall"), show a marked degree
of pictorial concreteness and objectivity, as in "To Winter":

A wrinkled, crabbed man they picture thee,
Old Winter, with a rugged beard as gray
As the long moss upon the apple-tree;
Blue-lipped, an ice-drop at thy sharp blue nose,
Close muffled up, and on thy dreary way
Plodding alone through sleet and drifting snows.
They should have drawn thee by the high-heaped hearth,
Old Winter! seated in thy great armed chair,
Watching the children at their Christmas mirth;
Or circled by them, as thy lips declare
Some merry jest, or tale of murder dire,
Or troubled spirit that disturbs the night,
Pausing at times to rouse the mouldering fire,
Or taste the old October brown and bright.

This sonnet, perhaps the only entirely good poem Southey wrote, is at once precise in detail and universal in import; and it succeeds because it deals with matters close to the poet's heart. Declaredly a poem about winter, it is also, but more unobtrusively than the "Holly Tree," a portrait of Southey himself: cold and crabbed in the eyes of the world, but quick to thaw by his own fireside; with a hearty taste for ale and, like his own uncle, the "Squire," a wealth of stories for little ears. The structure is unconventional—Southey rarely adheres to the traditional sonnet forms but invents hybrids and mutants at will—but it accords admirably with the content.

Almost wholly undistinguished is Southey's blank verse lyricism. His personal blank verse meditations, particularly those about his favorite theme of domestic peace and happiness, can be eloquent in an old-fashioned way. Such is the noble "Hymn to the Penates," one of Southey's most fervent poetic manifestos, a kind of post-Revolutionary creed proclaiming the worship of the "Household Deities" as the true road to the millennium: "Then shall the city stand / A huge void sepulchre, and on the site / Where fortresses have stood, / The olive grow. . . . This is the state / Shall bless the race redeemed of Man, when Wealth / And Power, and all their hideous progeny, Shall sink annihilate, and all mankind / Live in the equal brotherhood of love" (272). At times, Southey even rivals Coleridge's Conversation Poems in his mastery of a poetic middle style, as in "The Pig" or in the poem to his cousin Margaret (231). But he lacked the emotional and intellectual resources to sustain him in the prolonged free flight of the Greater Romantic Lyric; and his poems, though sincere and competent, are without the imaginative power and the troubled fervor of their betters. His language is prosy; his subjectivity is casual (as in "On My Own Miniature Picture"); his sentiment is facilely complacent (as in "Autumn"). Notwithstanding his animus against the intellectuality and "regular Jew's harp *twing-twang* of what has been foolishly called heroic measure" (IV, 7), Southey succeeds better in the Goldsmithian couplets of *The Retrospect* than in his blank verse lyrics:

> . . . No more was heard at early morn
> The echoing clangor of the huntsman's horn;
>
> . . . .
>
> The squire no more obeyed the morning call,
> Nor favorite spaniels filled the sportsman's hall;
> For he, the last descendant of his race,
> Slept with his fathers, and forgot the chase.
> There now in petty empire o'er the school
> The mighty master held despotic rule;
> Trembling in silence all his deeds we saw,
> His look a mandate, and his word a law;
> Severe his voice, severe and stern his mien,
> And wondrous strict he was, and wondrous wise I ween.

Even the four dozen or so inscriptions that Southey wrote are no exception. Consisting of epitaphs, monumental verses, and a few nature inscriptions, they have some interest because, in their predominantly historical and political orientation, they provide a contrast to, as well as a context for, the inscriptional verse and place poems of Wordsworth.[19] Moreover, in their specific occasion and in their epitomizing or hortatory function, they succeed at times well enough: "O Reader! what a world were this, / How unendurable its weight, if they / Whom death has sundered did not meet again" (III, 134). But here, too, the sentiment is generally flat, and the language is undistinguished, even bald: "Love, duty, generous feelings, high desires, / Faith, hope, devotion" (134). The series about the Peninsular War consists of versified gazette notices rather than poems about the disasters of war, and their few moments of concrete vision are disfigured by vindictive, body-counting partisanship:

> The Carmelite who in his cell recluse
> Was wont to sit, and from a skull receive

Death's silent lesson, wheresoe'er he walk,
Henceforth may find his teachers. He shall find
The Frenchmen's bones in glen and grove, on rock
And height, where'er the wolves and carrion birds
Have strewn them, washed in torrents, bare and bleached
By sun and rain, and by the winds of heaven. (117f.)

V Monodramas and Eclogues

Southey's most nearly successful mode of blank verse poetry,
apart from the epics, appears in two species of poems he derived
from German literature.[20] Both are forms of narrative with a
"dramatic turn" to suggest crisis and to create thematic focus. The
monodrama is essentially a suicide speech whose ultimate
antecedents are the Classical *Prosopopoeia* and "Heroide." Unlike
the dramatic monologue proper, it is rhetorical rather than psychological in emphasis: character tends to be monolithic, utterance,
declamatory rather than seemingly spontaneous. Even so, Southey's
monodramas move in the direction of specificity of manners and
situation. Most of them—"Lucretia," "The Wife of Fergus,"
"Ximalpoca," and "La Caba"—deal with the somewhat tired
theme of classical republican propaganda, the pollution of feminine
honor by a lustful tyrant. But there are some interesting variants.
Caba denounces her father for avenging her dishonor by betraying
his country to the Moors. Ximalpoca, a gentle Mexican cacique,
whose wife has been ravished by a neighboring ruler but who does
not want to bring war and certain defeat upon his weak people,
offers himself as a victim to the god Mexitli so as to escape the
reproach of recreancy and proclaims that he will continue to benefit
his people by joining the choir of tutelar spirits whose song propels
the sun and causes the rain to fall.

Southey's eclogues are similarly innovative without being quite
so exotic. Nominally in the tradition of Virgil and Spenser, they are
thoroughly unconventional even by eighteenth-century standards.
Particularly the *Botany Bay Eclogues* (1794, published 1797) are
cases in point. Instead of melodizing the pains and pleasures of
nymphs and swains, or else ridiculing low life in the manner of the
Augustan mock pastoral, these poems depict the plight of sailor and
soldier, of felon and prostitute at Britain's latest penal colony, view-
ing them not as malefactors but as victims of social injustice and
the social neglect that fosters crime. Like Pope's *Pastorals*, they con-
sist of four parts—two monologues and two dialogues—each of

them related to a different time of day.[21] Only one eclogue, however, is written in heroic couplets; and, in contrast to Pope's dazzling rococo style, Southey's is severely republican—stripped of all ornament and virtually of all poetry whatever.

The dialogues recall the pastoral convention of the poetic contest; but, instead of praising Phyllis and Rosalind, the competitors debate the pros and cons of their life as convicts, weighing the loss of wife and home against the gains of freedom from press-gangs and game-laws, from war and disease, vice and poverty. The monologues, which bracket the series, are more sentimental and declamatory and suffer from the absence of an implied audience. In "Elinor," a transported streetwalker bemoans her "guilt and sorrow" and her lost days of innocence at her father's seaside parsonage but then welcomes her new life, "here, at the farthest limits of the world," among the naked savages and solemn kangaroos, where Nature gives enough to all and superfluity to none. By contrast, the speaker in "Frederic," a felon benighted in the bush and terrified of a sudden and graceless end, realizes that society "made me what I was"; dismisses his fear of death and divine retribution; and resigns himself to a peaceful future of Penitence and humble sufficiency. The mixture of pietism and Pantisocracy in these poems is less than explosive, and the characters seem made mainly of wood and unction. But the situations are more credible than those of the monodramas, and "Australis" scores some palpable Godwinian hits against a corrupt system.

In the *English Eclogues* of the Westbury period, Southey discarded the monologue almost completely in favor of dialogues that are sometimes genuine dramatic exchanges, though at other times they are more mechanical repartee between a somewhat fatuous "traveller" or "stranger" who acts as straight man and a local person who is the main speaker—a framework Southey seems to have derived from Goethe's "Der Wanderer." What is most striking about these poems is the extent to which they parallel or anticipate the style and subject matter of the *Lyrical Ballads*. Stoic and Republican that he then was, Southey insisted even more emphatically than Wordsworth that in poetry "simplicity is all" and that all ornament is mere "froth and flummery."[22] In the *Eclogues*, he repeatedly gave his speakers a diction more markedly vernacular than anything in contemporary poetry outside of Robert Burns and permitted a humbleness of subject and a laxity of versification that seemed to critics like Francis Jeffrey to imply an all-out repudiation of art. Unlike Wordsworth, however, Southey tends to make his dialogues not only as simple but also as tedious as rustic conversations are apt to be. This is true especially of "The Last of the Family" and "The Old Mansion House"—both of them ruminations by old retainers on a country estate who are facing new ownership. The sentiments of these speakers, as they worry about the old fashions and the old trees, are likely enough, and Southey's knack of capturing the rustic idiom would do honor to a novelist; but, in verse, such realism looks dull and prosy.

Several dialogues evoke the plight of the poor. "The Wedding" makes the grim point that, for the pauper, wedding bells are bells of doom and children no blessing but a curse. In "The Sailor's Mother," an old woman is begging her way to Portsmouth to see her son who has been blinded in battle and may be dying. These poems derive some force from the outrageous glibness of the "traveler"-interlocutor, who, for example, tells the old woman that "Old England's gratitude / Makes the maimed sailor happy" and that, if the boy should die, she was fortunate to live in "a country / Where the brave sailor never leaves a parent / To weep for him in want; and who, when told that the boy was pressed into service as a punishment for wiring hares, is satisfied that "for broken laws, / This was no heavy punishment." No clear alternative viewpoint emerges, however, and we must wonder whether the interlocutor's ineptitude may be the poet's own.

The two most successful dialogues are those that deal with the susceptibility of simple minds to sensation and superstition. "The Grandmother's Tale" tells a story that Southey remembered from his mother about Moll, the collier woman, who had her throat cut by a smuggler for informing on him, and how the murderer, though acquitted, was driven by his conscience to confess and take his punishment. The poem, originally planned to end as a ghost story, concludes in a rather homiletic vein; but it also has some lively moments in its evocation of the children's appetite for "dismal" things and in its portrayal of the rough-voiced, masculine Moll, who swears oaths "like any trooper" but is full of tenderness for her asses that share her harsh existence. In "The Witch," a farmer, convinced that he is being jinxed by a crone whom he had threatened for robbing his hedge, charms his threshold with a stolen horseshoe and calls it a shame "That in a Chrisian country they should let / Such creatures live" instead of hunting them down and hanging them as in the good old days. The village curate reproaches his selfish and superstitious fear of what is in fact a harmless pauper who is slowly dying of cold and neglect. But the farmer persists that, charity notwithstanding, it is irreligious to disbelieve in witches and goes on with the job of nailing down the horseshoe. Southey's point is not exactly a subtle one: the psychology of such fears is left unexplored. But the poem contains at least something like a perspective and a picture of a state of mind beyond mere didacticism.

Perspective is apparent also in the two narrative eclogues, "The Ruined Cottage" and "Hannah," poems about forsaken womanhood that anticipate Wordsworth's similar narratives in *The Excursion*, especially the story of Margaret. "Henry the Hermit," lastly, tells a local anecdote that builds to an impressive climax when the hermit is found sitting in darkness on a stone, "dead, cold, and stiff, / The bell-rope in his hand, and at his feet / The lamp, that streamed a long, unsteady light" (VI, 179): an image that makes his death poignantly symbolic of his life—and of ours.

VI   *Ballads*

Characteristically, "Henry the Hermit," though in blank verse, is not grouped among the eclogues by Southey but among the ballads. Southey's lyricism proper is, for the most part, hopelessly paralyzed by his inability to create metaphor. Even the well-known "My Days among the Dead Are Past" about his love of books scarcely gets past the first four lines before lapsing into prosiness, which the ironic turn in the last line cannot redeem. Nor is his eye often on the object, even though his notebooks record numerous fine images from nature for use in poetry, such as the effect of wind and light, dew and frost, the flight of birds, the cry of bats, and the many nuances of trees. Southey is more in his element in the ballads. Conventional in thought and feeling as he was, he *could* tell a story vividly and convincingly, particularly when the presence of supernatural machinery preempted all but rudimentary psychological motivation. His ballads, most of them written during the *annus felix* at Westbury, cannot match the best of the traditional ones for stark universality, nor the best of Wordsworth's and Coleridge's ballads for psychological realism and symbolic force. But they need fear few other comparisons.

Like his fellow Romantics, Southey caught the fancy for ballads both from Percy's epoch-making *Reliques of Ancient English Poetry* and from the *Kunstballaden* which Percy's book had called forth—particularly those imported from Germany by William Taylor and others, such as G. A. Buerger's famous ghost-ballad, *Lenore*. Like Wordsworth, again, Southey found in the ballad an ideal of "plain, perspicuous English" free of Latinisms and Gallicism (*Memoir*, I, 453). Unlike Wordsworth, however, who despised the new "craving for extraordinary incident" and who chose as his subject situations from common life, Southey reserved such subjects for his eclogues and—like Coleridge, Walter Scott, and the irrepressible Matthew Gregory Lewis—wrote ballads predominantly on the German model of "Gothick" terror and the supernatural, developed in alternately grotesque and humorous ways. The proper subject of the ballad, he thought, was superstition; and his notorious objection to the "Rime of the Ancient Mariner" was not at all, like Charles Lamb's, to its "miraculous part" but to an obscurantism and an overelaborateness that made it, in his eyes, only a "Dutch attempt" at the true "German sublimity."[23] Southey is the dean of the Romantic supernaturalists.

Some of Southey's ballads, in fact, are of the realistic kind. As elsewhere, however, the realism is apt to harden into rhetoric or to dissolve into sentimentality. Thus, while Southey dismissed the manner of Wordsworth's "Idiot Boy" as "Flemish," his own "Idiot Boy," published anonymously earlier the same year of 1798 in the *Morning Post*, merely dulls a difficult and threatening subject with defensive pity, as Wordsworth's does not.[24] In "The Complaints of the Poor," a "Rich Man" who wonders, with singular "let-them-eat-cake" obtuseness, why "the Poor complain" learns through a series of brief roadside interviews with sundry beggars and prostitutes, that the Poor complain because they are in fact poor, sick, hungry, and cold. The poem is well-meant, but its very bluntness and its jury-rigged situation prevent sympathetic response.

Matters improve when Southey has a real situation to depict or story to tell. In "The Battle of Blenheim," an anti-war poem, an old German cottager tells his grandchildren, who have just unearthed a human skull, how a great battle was fought here once, how the land was wasted with fire and sword, how many women and children died, and how many thousands of corpses "lay rotting in the sun" on the battlefield. But, when the children exclaim against the wickedness of the thing, old Kaspar, though he cannot tell either the reason for, or the result of, the battle, insists that, nevertheless, "twas a famous victory" and that "Things like that, you know, must be / At every famous victory." Nature, as in Wordsworth's "We Are Seven," runs afoul of Reason; and Kaspar, kindly but conditioned by received ideas, defends the indefensible.

In "The Cross-roads," Southey excoriates the inhumanity of pious folk by citing the case of a young servant girl who was evidently hanged by her brutal employer but was declared a suicide and buried at a crossroads. The narrator remembers how she was carried upon a board "in the clothes in which she died"; how the wind blew off her cap, revealing her wide-staring eyes; and how she was laid "here in this very place: / The earth upon her corpse was pressed, / This post was driven into her breast, / And a stone is on her face." By permitting the facts to speak for themselves and by subordinating theme to character, Southey achieves something of the haunting ambiguity of the traditional ballad; and his technique of creating multiple perspectives through the use of dialogue invites comparison with *Lyrical Ballads*.

Like Coleridge and Wordsworth, Southey repeatedly deals with insanity and the psychology of guilt. In his early "Mary, the Maid of the Inn," a village beauty runs mad when, on a dare, she visits an abbey ruin at night and accidentally discovers that her betrothed is a murderer. The poem enjoyed considerable vogue, but in its sentimentality it appeals merely to our pity. By contrast, "The Mad Woman," another ballad based on local fact and one somewhat reminiscent of Wordsworth's "Thorn," focuses on the terror of guilt: it tells of an unwed mother, Martha, who went mad after burning her newborn child to avoid infamy, and who would sit in the snow among the graves in a frantic effort to quench the "fire" burning in her mind.

Remorse is also the subject of "The Sailor Who Had Served in the Slave-Trade," an Abolitionist ballad about a sailor who had been forced to whip a slave girl to death and who is pursued by the memory of her shrieks and by his fear of the Wicked One: "From place to place, from rope to rope / . . . He follows, follows everywhere; / And every place is hell: / O God! and I must go with him / In endless fire to dwell." The poem suffers by a comparison with the rich, sinuous ambiguity of the "Ancient Mariner," which it resembles in its use of repetition; and it savors too much of the evangelical tract, especially in its concluding sermon by the "Christian minister" about the power of prayer and faith in Christ—an ending that undercuts the polemic and one that Southey himself deplored. But the poem also has the plain-spoken virtue of the broadside.

Most interesting, perhaps, is "Jaspar," a ballad whose theme recalls Wordsworth's early play *The Borderers*. A ruffian who had years before killed and robbed a man persuades a hard-pressed laborer to commit a like crime in order to gain a companion in guilt and damnation. The two men lay their ambush at the place of the old crime; but Jonathan, unlike the obdurate Jaspar years before, is softened by nocturnal Nature's peaceful sounds and begins to fear the all-seeing eye of God. Jaspar assures him that "Nor eye above nor eye below / Can pierce the darkness here"; but, as he speaks, a "sudden light, / Strong as the midday sun" falls on the spot. "It hung upon the willow-tree; / It hung upon the flood; / It gave to view the poplar isle, / And all the scene of blood." The light may have been lightning—the night was wan and starless—but Jaspar turns into a maniac who forever haunts—heedless of "the summer suns, the winter storms"—the scene of his crime. The ballad is told with economy and a sense of symmetry, and the ambiguity of the denouement saves it from mere melodrama.

In the long run, however, even such qualified naturalism could not quite satisfy Southey's surreptitious craving for simple providential certainties. As in his long poems, he was most in his element in the ballads when he could represent human character and conduct as overarched by manifestations of a supernatural order of things. Belief in such manifestations might be a monkish superstition, but it was also a "blest illusion," as he calls it in "St Gualberto" (VI, 194), that was highly congenial in its implicit moral absolutism. When sufficiently dwarfed by a transcendental perspective, human actions lost much of their fearfully ambiguous and relative character, and human beings could be divided more comfortably into the sheep and goats of conventional authoritarian morality: a man who sells his soul to the devil can be understood but need not be forgiven. Many of the ballads are thus more explicitly supernatural than a poem like "Jaspar." Conversely, since their tone is often one of burlesque, they seem purposed to objectify Southey's demons and to exorcise them by ridicule.

At times, the result is merely bizarre, as for instance in the early "Donica," a sentimental and macabre story about a young man whose betrothed dies and returns as a vampire. The once popular "Inchcape Rock"—about a pirate who sinks a bell-buoy out of sheer

deviltry and ends up shipwrecked himself on the same spot with all
his plunder while the devil rings his knell below with the sunken
bell—is spiritedly told, despite a somewhat obscure time scheme.
But the senselessness of the deed—the source gives no motive, and
Southey does not care to supply one other than pure malev-
olence—renders the ironic epiphany somewhat hollow and contrived.

Other ballads, however, succeed in combining machinery and
motivation. "Lord William," a straightforward ghost story, tells of a
usurper who, during a nocturnal flood, is drawn to his death by a
specter boatman and by the corpse of his young nephew, the rightful heir, whom he had long ago drowned in the Severn. Intent on
saving himself and ignoring repeated cries of distress, William at
length sees a child seemingly marooned on a crag in the flood. The
boatman admonishes William to "reach and save"; and William,
touching hands that are "cold and damp and dead," realizes with a
shriek that he is holding "young Edmund in his arms, / A heavier
weight than lead." The boat promptly sinks "Beneath the avenging
stream" and the murderer with it: "He rose; he shrieked; no human
ear / Heard William's drowning scream." The incessant shrieking
may be irritating, and the fact that Lord William's fate is sealed by
what appears to be an act of compassion is confusing. At the same
time, the evocation of an elemental poetic justice, underscored by
the closing echo of the poem's opening lines ("No human ear but
William's heard / Young Edmund's drowning scream"), is more
convincing than the contrived irony of "The Inchcape Rock."
Moreover, the suggestion that Lord William is destroyed as much
by remorse and persistent selfishness as by the supernatural agents
makes the latter esthetically acceptable.

"Rudiger" also unites pathos and mythos effectively. Here a
mysterious knight, a demonic version of the Lohengrin figure, takes
his first-born child to be sacrificed to an evil spirit as the stipulated
price for his success in the world, but is prevented by the mother
and perishes himself instead. The character of Rudiger is hardly
developed, and the concluding scene in which the demon's black
arms rise out of a cave is rather blatant. But the mother's mounting
anxiety as the swan-propelled boat takes them down the silent
moonlit river and her terrified resolution as she snatches the infant
from the demon's grasp give the poem a certain authenticity. Oddly
enough, the mother's name is Margaret; and, since the diabolizing
of the knight and the attempted child sacrifice were Southey's own

inventions, it may not be amiss to see in the story an unconscious manipulation of his own predicament as a child, an attempt to confront his idols of the cave.

In its denouement, "Rudiger" foreshadows *Thalaba.* Even closer in spirit is "St. Patrick's Purgatory" in which a typical Southeyan hero and forerunner of the Destroyer, Sir Owen, goes on an archetypal night journey in quest of a glimpse of Paradise. After having been shrouded and coffined for a precautionary Service of the Dead, the knight is conducted to a mystic cave, the entrance to fearful realms of ice and fire, a "frozen waste" of "ice-rocks in a sunless sky, / On ice-rocks piled," and a desert of fire where "the air he breathed was red." He almost perishes each time but is saved by prayer and by perfect faith in God. The ice divides, the fire is quenched, and the hero reaches the Paradisic garden beyond. The narrative is quarried from the same enchanted mountain from which came the profounder ordeal at pole and tropic of Coleridge's Mariner and the vision of Xanadu; and Southey's ballad, worked and reworked effectively as it was, is less than the great Romantic night journeys only because its hero, like all of Southey's questers, lacks the moving grace of human weakness.

"Bishop Bruno" likewise catches at least something of the simplicity and directness of the popular ballad: "The bony hand suspended his breath, / His marrow grew cold at the touch of Death; / On saints in vain he attempted to call, / Bishop Bruno fell dead in the palace-hall." But most of Southey's remaining supernatural ballads lack the unity of effect achieved in these poems. Instead, they exhibit an awkward mixture of somber didacticism and frivolous improvisation that ultimately springs from Southey's peculiar personality, though the immediate cause may have been the haste with which the poems, most of them written as pot-boilers for the *Morning Post,* were often composed. By posing as jolly improvising "Robert the Rhymer," Southey evades artistic responsibility along with moral commitment, Byron's sneer at the "balladmonger" is not entirely without justification.

"God's Judgment on a Wicked Bishop" is a case in point. A cautionary tale, it relates the Rhenish *Mauseturm* legend of the wicked prelate who burned a barnful of paupers as so many "rats that only consume the corn" and who was in turn devoured by an army of avenging rodents. There are some moments of authentic terror in the poem when the bishop finds his portrait eaten out of its frame and when he is awakened at night by the cat's screaming, "mad with fear" at the advancing nemesis. But Southey just missed the chance to create the genuine revolutionary fable he had perhaps intended. The villain is not made real; and the climax turns terror to comedy:

> Down on his knees the Bishop fell,
> And faster and faster his beads did tell,
> As, louder and louder drawing near,
> The gnawing of their teeth he could hear.
>
> And in at the window, and in at the door,
> And through the walls, helter-skelter they pour,
> And down from the ceiling, and up through the floor,
> From the right and the left, from behind and before,
> From within and without, from above and below,
> And all at once to the Bishop they go.

The cantering (and often limping) doggerel, used in many of these poems, seems more apt for a Visit from St. Nicholas than for a symbolic Storming of the Bastille. For a child, the humorous overtones may be a welcome relief from the horror of the "furious Alastors"—we remember Southey's early traumas from "dismal" ballads—but the adult reader is irked by the poet's evident uncertainty of purpose.

Artistic uncertainty also mars the famous "Old Woman of Berkley," Southey's principal attempt to equal the admired *Lenore*. When William Taylor, who had tried his hand on the same subject, called Southey's poem "unquestionably the best original English ballad extant," Southey complacently replied: "Mine is the ballad of a ballad-maker, believing the whole superstition, and thereby making even the grotesque terrible; yours that of a poet, decorating a known fable, laughing behind a masque of fear" (*Memoir*, II, 106, 112). The truth is however, that Southey does not quite achieve the "suspension of disbelief" either in himself or in the reader and that, far from rendering the grotesque terrible, he makes the terrible seem merely grotesque. He was annoyed when Payne Collier referred to the poem as a "mock-ballad"; but Collier was not far wrong.

The Old Woman, we are told, has led a fiendish life; she has anointed herself with "infants' fat" for her witchcraft, sucked the breath from "sleeping babes," and broken by charms the sleep of death." Now the Devil will fetch her; "and I who have troubled the dead man's grave / Shall never have rest in my own." To keep her "wretched corpse" from the clutches of the Fiend, her coffin is chained to the floor; and "the Monk her son, and her daughter the Nun," together with fifty priests and choristers, begin a three-day vigil behind barred church doors. For two nights they manage to ward off the hellish rout with bells and prayer; but, on the third night, the tapers are "extinguished quite"; and Satan, aglow with infernal light, carries the church. "He laid his hand on the iron chains, / And like flax they mouldered asunder; / And the coffin lid, which was barred so firm, / He burst with his voice of thunder." He bids the quaking corpse to rise and "come with her Master away"; and, like Lenore and her ghostly lover, though less peacefully, they take off through the night on a black charger. The Old Woman's cries are audible "for four miles round," and "children at rest at their mothers' breast / Started, and screamed with fear."

The story is told with speed and due attention to the incremental repetition of the folktale. Moreover, the recurrent motif of children—the Old Woman's infant victims, the nursing babes who start at her last scream, and her own children who cannot redeem her—gives the poem thematic weight and coherence. However, as in the ballad about Bishop Hatto, though less glaringly, the theme is undercut by stumbling doggerel and by untimely levity about beads and saints-worship. And, instead of creating an archetypal symbol of women that are the bane of childhood at the same time that, through children, they would be saved from themselves, the poem remains at the level of the quaint and macabre.[25]

Saints' and devils' legends attracted Southey again and again, but he rarely sought to understand them or to recover their symbolic potential. "Queen Orraca and the Five Martyrs" indeed, is a wholly admirable saint's legend that is told with economy and quiet conviction about a Portuguese queen's pardonable (and futile) endeavor to circumvent the fate prophesied to her by the martyrs: "Who sees us first, the King or you, / That one that night must die" (VI, 153). But most of the other pieces remain purely anecdotal, and their comedy is largely banal and tedious: St. Antidius, who rides the devil through the air in order to absolve a dying pope from mortal sin; St. Romuald, who fights the devil all night by "splashing holy water" but otherwise thinks it wrong "for Dust and Ashes to fall out with dirt" (94); the "Pious Painter," who spends his life portraying Lucifer and, rather like Southey himself, is haunted at night by "what he so earnestly wrought on by day"; and the rest. Similarly ponderous is the late "The Young Dragon" (1829), in which a virgin-devouring scion of the Old Dragon succumbs to the explosive force of John the Baptist's thumb which the resolute father of a prospective victim purloins from the reliquary and sends down the dragon's throat. The poem was written, Southey said, to eschew serious feelings by playing with the grotesque. He could have said the same about most of the other ballads as well.

Sometimes, Southey's diablerie can be unequivocal—as in "Cornelius Agrippa," the story of the sorcerer's apprentice who has his heart torn out by the devil for reading "unlawful books." But Southey usually tries to have it both ways. He loves to ponder, he says in "St. Gualberto," "The mingle-mangle mass of truth and lies, / Where waking fancies mixed with dreams appear, / And blind and honest zeal, and holy faith sincere." The ballad, after relating how the saint punished a company of worldly monks by invoking a sudden flood that destroys their palatial monastery, reflects at length about the pernicious effect such saintly fervor would have had on the glories of British architecture and then proceeds to tell about the "blest illusion" that first turned the saint from a path of blood and vengeance to the service of God (187, 194). Southey thought "St. Gualberto" the best of his metrical tales; and, if we still find it engaging despite its prolixity, we perhaps do so because Southey, in writing of this saint whose name he had borrowed years before in his luckless *Flagellant* adventure, openly faced a fundamental ambivalence that all too often merely undermines his poetic intentions.

CHAPTER 4

Mythopoesis: Thalaba *and* Kehama

I *Epic, Romance, and Mythography*

FROM early on, as we have seen, Southey's leading poetic ambition was to "illustrate" the major mythologies of the world. In part, this intention reflected the common notion that epic poetry required a mythological and allegorical superstructure and that new "systems" were needed to replace the overworked Classical pantheon. But Southey soon learned to dislike the notion of "machinery" conceived as a poet's didactic or simply fanciful embroidery of an otherwise realistic story. His real interest was in myth itself, in what he understood, however dimly, not as a mere literary convention but as the original symbolic expression of a people's peculiar way of apprehending and interpreting reality. In concert with eighteenth-century criticism, he held that the narrative poet was foremost an "historian of manners" who should exhibit "the manners and, what is more difficult, the habits of feeling and thought" of a given time and place (*Letters*, I, 173). The key to these "habits" was myth.

Southey's first impulse toward myth had come from Picart's *Religious Ceremonies*; but the decisive inspiration came from the *Dramatic Sketches of Northern Mythology* by the Norwich physician Frank Sayers, a disciple of Gray and Mason. Sayers, though a painstaking scholar, was not much of a poet and was less of a dramatist; but on Southey his set pieces on Norse and Celtic myth made a deep impression. Sayers' use of unrhymed verse—modelled partly on Greek drama, partly on *Ossian* and the verse of the German poet F. G. Klopstock—became a model for Southey's own irregular stanzas, in both romances and odes; and the mythological content impressed upon the younger man a conception of the poet as a cultural historian who, by depicting the "manners and mythologies" of different nations, would add greatly to man's un-

81

derstanding of man. Myths were not merely corruptions of Biblical history, as many thought, but avatars of truth or inspiration that were worthy of being depicted in their particularity, irrespective of any theoretical common denominator. Mythopoesis, then, was not mere indulgence in exotic flights of fancy but part of the Romantic exploration of human consciousness.

Some of Southey's mythical studies were lyrical in character and in scope. The two "Runic" odes on Odin, both modeled on Sayers' monodrama "Oswald" as well as on Gray's "Descent of Odin" and Percy's translation of the famous "Death Song of Ragnar Lodbrog," are of this kind, as are the "Songs of the American Indians," by-products of the researches for *Madoc;* and these were to have been followed by others on a global scale. For the most part, however, Southey thought in terms of full-length poems, including epics about the Deluge and Mohammedanism and three metrical romances about the "Hindoo, Persian, and Runic mythology" (*Memoir,* I, 371).

There is something quite Wagnerian in these projects; and, although most of them never materialized, they are intriguing and indicate that Southey's romances, frothy as they may be, emanated from ideological fissures that traverse the whole age. Thus the poem about the "most magnificent" Teutonic mythology was intended to contrast "the oriental picture in Thalaba" with a portrait of the "Northern" ethos of freedom and hardy independence—the revolutionary spirit that overthrew the "blood-cemented throne" of the Caesars (a theme that also intrigued Wordsworth);[1] Even more revealing is Southey's attempt at the subject of the Deluge, a myth peculiarly relevant to an age of cataclysm and one that a number of mythographers regarded as the myth of myths, the prototype of all later mythologies.[2] Inspired partly by the recent spate of Biblical epics by German authors like Klopstock, Bodmer, and Gesner, Southey planned to fuse Biblical and Talmudic lore, the lately rediscovered Book of Enoch, and Thomas Burnet's *Sacred Theory of the Earth,* with his own Pantisocratic ideas as the framework for a gigantic cosmodrama in hexameters about universal corruption (brought about by the infernal trinity of monarchy, priestcraft, and atheism), destruction, and renewal. An arrogant young revolutionary was to employ "evil means" for noble ends and thereby to succumb, like Robespierre, to the evil he had set out to eradicate. Meanwhile, Noah's son Japhet, "the European," was to emerge as the true Southeyan hero and as the founder of Pantiosocracy in the regenerated world (the awkward motif of the "general embarcation" was to be de-emphasized).[3] Southey was probably wise to relinquish this ambitious plan; but, in some ways, the "Noachid" was the myth of the age, and it remained constitutive for Southey's writings as his many scattered images of Flood and Ark attest.

Equally telling is Southey's interest in the *Zend Avesta*, which he intended to use as the basis for a poem about a Persian prince whom a series of persecutions by the powers of darkness would transform into a paragon of virtue. The sharp moral dualism of Zoroastrianism, and its obsession with death and uncleanness, could not but appeal strongly to Southey; and although this project was also abandoned, its idea that evil is formative and therefore conducive to good was central to Southey's thought and became the leading theme of the third of his planned romances, *The Curse of Kehama*.

That poem, in fact, finally incorporated most of the earlier schemes. Ironically enough, Southey found the Hindu pantheon unattractive—grotesque, unmanageable, and "fitter for the dotage dreams of [the Orientalist] Sir William Jones, than the vision of the poet." At the same time, however, he felt that "somebody should do for the Hindoo gods what Dr. Sayers has done for Odin." In its wealth of divine personages and stories, moreover, the Hindu mythology, like the Norse, offered a viable alternative to the traditional epic with machinery, namely a "theodrama" in which the gods were not merely the "wire-workers" but "the acting as well as aiding personages." Thus the Hindu romance became in the end the final upshot of Southey's long search for the mythological poem.[4]

The fatal flaw in all these ventures, as we have seen in the preceding chapter, is Southey's peculiar ambivalence about "superstition." The dilemma emerges most clearly from yet another abortive attempt at epic, the projected poem on Mohammed. Like Voltaire and Goethe, and later Carlyle, Southey was intrigued by the phenomenon of Mohammed and the disturbing implications it had for the question of religious inspiration, as well as by the historical parallels between the rise of Islam and the French Revolution. The poem, projected in eight hexameter books in collaboration with Coleridge, was to trace the career of Mohammed from the Hegira to the conquest of Mecca.[5] Among its episodes the famous miracle of the cave and the spider—the only portion that materialized (X, 374 - 82)—would stamp the Prophet's mission with providential Nature's approval, and the parable of Mohammed and the Mountain would show him as not a miracle-monger but an enlightened religionist and stoic teacher of *islam* or "submission" to the nature of things and the will of God. But the project, like the others, was bound to fail, not only because Southey became quickly disenchanted with hexameter as a suitable medium for a long poem, but because he could not suspend his disbelief sufficiently to create Mohammed as the hero of a serious work. After initial endeavors to judge him, like Joan, as a sincere "enthusiast" who really thought himself inspired, Southey rapidly fell back on the old view of the Prophet as an "imposter" or as, at best, a victim of delusion and fanaticism. Consequently, even if he kept "the mob of wives . . . out of sight" (*Memoir*, I, 325), as he had intended to do with the "general embarcation" in the Noah story, and made Mohammed's nephew Ali the real hero, he could not get on with a "Mecca Delivered" whose Godfredo was either a fool or a knave, and at all events a polygamist, though its Rinaldo were perfection itself.

In all of his mythological projects Southey thus appears caught between the Enlightenment's latitudinarian interests and its residual ethnocentrism or new positivist arrogance. His compromise was to turn from epic to romance. Myth and history, uniquely if precariously fused in the great epics of the past, would henceforth be strictly segregated. In the epics, the supernatural would appear, if at all, as the product of credulity and priestly imposture, as a political or pathological factor rather than a metaphysical dimension, and thus merely as a culture's weakness rather than also as its strength. The poet could thereby retain the effect of "machinery" without having to countenance its "absurdity." But all the mythic lore that was too good to be trounced or forgotten would be mounted into "romances"—poems of magic and fancy void of historical content in which the supernatural could be exploited for symbolic and didactic purposes, as well as for sheer effect, but would otherwise be morally neutral.

II   Thalaba the Destroyer

Thalaba the Destroyer (1801), the first of the romances,[6] is probably the most influential and historically the most important of Southey's long poems. Few readers have been as enthusiastic about it as Cardinal Newman who considered it the most "morally sub-

lime" of English poems. But the young Shelley reckoned it his
favorite poem, and both he and Keats followed its lead in some of
their verse narratives. Moreover, its outrageous modernity provoked Francis Jeffrey's notorious first attack on the "Lake School of
Poetry," the brilliant if unfair and indiscriminate *tour de force* that
launched the *Edinburgh Review*, and thus earned the "Lake" poets
at least the dignity of formidable criticism.

What made *Thalaba* distinctive as well as provocative was above
all its flamboyant exoticism. Southey himself regarded the poem,
with some justice, as the most original romance since *Orlando
Furioso* and the *Faerie Queene* and as being to poetry what William
Beckford's *Vathek* was in prose. Oriental and pseudo-Oriental tales
had been popular in England since the first Englishing of Gallard's
Arabian Nights—not to mention heroic drama and baroque opera.[7]
But most of these works, *Vathek* excepted, were Oriental in name
rather than in spirit; and their exoticism was either purely sen-
sational or a makeshift vehicle for satire and commonsense didacticism. Southey brought a more objective attitude to bear, an interest perhaps more scholarly than poetic but no longer merely
rhetorical. Above all, he was really the first to dignify the type by
casting it in verse.

Much of the originality of *Thalaba* consists also in its use of the
rhymeless, irregular stanzas which Southey inherited from Dr.
Sayers. Sayers had used them to conjure up "gothic" sublimity. His
disciple regarded them as equally suited for combining "Oriental"
abandon with the austere stoicism of "Mahometry," and as a happy
medium between the ornate formalism of the *arabesque*, with its
"childish love of rhyme," and the sublime "monotone" of blank
verse.

Southey's basic formula is one of extreme naturalism. "Follow
your ear," his recipe read, "taking mere convenience for your
guide, except where the subject brings with it . . . its own
measure." Unfortunately, the overall effect is often one of
formlessness; and, although Southey chafed under the demands of
the Spenserian stanza when he wrote the *Tale of Paraguay* and felt
that having to "zig-zag" after rhymes kept him from "following the
natural course of thought and feeling, which always leads one the
best way, and generally the shortest" (*Correspondence*, 51, 78), the
Tale progresses more smoothly and rapidly for all its supposed tack-
ing and veering than *Thalaba* which sails rudderless before currents
of "convenience" and squalls of "thought and feeling." At times

Southey employs parallelism, the "thought rhyme" then newly discovered as the dominant formal principle of Biblical and Near
Eastern poetry[8] and, as such, appropriate to an *arabesque:* "Or
comes the Father of the Rain / From his caves in the uttermost
West? / Comes he in darkness and in storms? / When the blast is
loud; / When the waters fill / The traveller's tread in the
sands. . . ." (IV, 80). Over large stretches, however, the verse is in-
distinguishable from rhythmical prose; and the reader is apt to
stumble over pure prosaisms like "I know the rest. The accused
Spirits were called" (113). The regular coincidence of verse and syn-
tactic units frequently produces monotony despite the constant
variation of line length; and the heavy use of anaphora, repetition,
and apostrophe can become irritating. Even so, Southey's quasi-
futurist experimentation with a "musical" style that would capture
"the accent of feeling" (IV, 7) is noteworthy for its novel endeavor to
adapt form to content.

The poem is set in the time of Harun-al-Rashid. It depicts the
struggle of a race of powerful sorcerers who dwell in the "Domdaniel" under the roots of the sea to escape their prophesied
overthrow at the hands of a champion of God and traces the eventual fulfillment of the prophecy through the young Moslem
Thalaba. As the story unfolds, the magicians are on the verge of
success, having just massacred the family of the noble Hodeirah
from whom the "Destroyer" was to come. But one of Hodeirah's
sons, Thalaba, has escaped by God's grace, together with his mother
Zeinab. As they stagger through the desert, they come upon the
remains of the earthly paradise of Irem, whose lone survivor tells
them a harrowing tale of hybris, doom, and penance. Here Zeinab
dies. Thalaba, now fully orphaned, is eventually found and adopted
by the patriarch Moath and grows up in pastoral simplicity.

Meanwhile, the gruesome Domdanielites have been watching the
"life-flames" of Hodeirah's family expire one after another, only to
discover that one of the feared race is still alive. One of their crew,
the magician Abdaldar, is dispatched to reconnoitre. He eventually
finds the boy in his new home; but he is blasted by a simoom before
he can do any harm, leaving Thalaba in the possession of a magic ring
whose stone, enclosing a spark of the "Eternal Fire" of hell, bestows
uncontestable power upon the wearer. A demon who tries to recover
the ring is challenged by the young hero and is forced to reveal the
murderers of Hodeirah and the reason for the murder. At Thalaba's
command, the demon also restores Hodeirah's arms—except for the

"fatal sword," which lies wrapt in impenetrable flames in hell.

Thalaba, now a young man and deeply in love with Moath's beautiful daughter Oneiza, realizes that he must sacrifice his personal happiness to the duty of avenging his father and of destroying the Domdaniel. A mysterious message in "Nature's own language" confirms his decision and directs him to depart "when the sun shall be darkened at noon." The eclipse eventually occurs: "The day grows dark; the birds retire to rest; / Forth from her shadowy haunt / Flies the large-headed screamer of the night." And, while "Far off the affrighted African / Deeming his God deceased, / Falls on his knees in prayer," Thalaba, reposing his trust in the Invisible, plunges resolutely into the "dreadful noon": "They heard his parting steps, / The quiver rattling as he passed away" (88 - 91).

He is promptly led astray in the desert by the magician Lobaba, who, disguised as a sage, attempts to deprive him of the protection of Abdaldar's ring. Unable to do so by stealth or sleight, Lobaba tries to seduce the young man into invoking the ring's magic and thereby to subject him to the powers of darkness: "Nothing in itself is good or evil, / But only in its use" (119). But Thalaba renounces all use of magic as impious. Divining the true nature of the tempter, he tries to despatch him with his father's bow. The arrow recoils; but a sandstorm rises, "driven by the breath of God"; and Lobaba perishes. Thalaba, parched and bewildered, is saved by a pool of water that a pelican had collected for her young.

Past Harun-al-Rashid's Baghdad with its pomp and pleasure, the "delegated youth" hastens to fallen Babylon, now a lair of wolves and scorpions and the habitation of devils, to search for the exiled angels Haruth and Maruth, traditionally the guardians of all magic lore. From them Thalaba must learn what special "talisman" his task requires, or so his mother's wraith has told him. Uncertain where to turn among the moon-lit ruins, he encounters a sinister young warrior, Mohareb; and he is guided by him to an infernal, bituminous cave where Zohak, the descendant of Shedad, is punished for his sins by two serpents that grow from his shoulders and feed on his brain. Zohak blocks their way, but Mohareb throws a sop to the Promethean Cerberus, and the questers enter the central vault. When Thalaba challenges Haruth and Maruth to disclose the nature of the needed talisman, the arrogant Mohareb realizes that his companion is not, like himself, a prier into forbidden secrets but a pious "prayermonger" and tries to kill him. He is foiled by Abdaldar's ring; but, when he sneers that Thalaba would have been helpless without its magic, Thalaba throws it into the abyss. They wrestle, and Mohareb is cast down. Thalaba invokes the angels again and learns that the needed talisman is "Faith."

Emerged from the macabre gloom, Thalaba is carried by a reinless courser to a "wild and wondrous scene" and comes to the famous earthly paradise of Aloadin, the Old Man of the Mountain, of whom Southey had read in the works of Samuel Purchas and John Mandeville. Through a narrow gorge and iron gates, Thalaba enters a garden of "odorous groves," "gorgeous palaces," and "rich pavilions, bright with woven gold"; and he revels in the "streams of liquid light," the brilliant flowers expanding their "paradise of leaves," the sound of falling water and murmuring trees, the song of nightingales, and the scent of jasmine and orange (177 - 9)—"a proof," Southey wrote, "that I can employ magnificence and luxury of language when I think them in place" (*Life*, II, 95). In a sumptuous banquet hall, Thalaba feasts with the gay company there assembled. But he refuses to drink any wine, in obedience to the Prophet's commandment; and, when a "troop of females," whose "transparent garments to the greedy eye / Exposed their harlot limbs," begins a lascivious dance, he resists temptation by thinking of his beloved Oneiza. At length, he rushes from the hall to the river, past unveiled and beckoning women, and into the silence of a grove—just in time to rescue a maiden from a pursuing ravisher. The maiden turns out to be Oneiza herself, kidnapped hither to serve as a "Houri" in this "Paradise of Sin," where young men are seduced into becoming assassins for the diabolic Aloadin. Thalaba and Oneiza confront the sorcerer, kill him, and thereby destroy his devilish Bower of Bliss and all its denizens. The paths open, and the victorious couple take their solitary way "awestruck and silent down the stony glen" (205).

They are found and honored by the Sultan who would have been Aloadin's next victim. Thalaba wants to rest on his laurels and insists on immediate marriage to Oneiza. But Allah disposes otherwise. As they enter the bridal chamber, Oneiza, like Zeinab before her, is taken by Azrael, the Angel of Death. Thalaba remains to pine at her grave—a raving madman who is shunned by all and who is tormented nightly by a ghostly Oneiza with the disclosure that God has abandoned him. Eventually, his foster-father Moath, in search of his lost daughter, finds Thalaba, recognizes the nightly visitant as a vampire, and kills it. The real spirit of Oneiza thereupon appears to whet Thalaba's blunted purpose.

This is the main turning point of the story, and its lesson is plain: suffering is the necessary pruning without which no vine can bear fruit (226). Thus taught, Thalaba sets out again to search for the Simorg, the mystical "Bird of Ages" who dwells in the mountain of Kaf. On his way to this new oracle, he comes to a land of eternal snow. A comely old woman whom he finds spinning and singing (in rhyme!) in a cave turns out to be the sorceress, Maimuna. Thalaba duly entangles himself in the magic thread of this Northern Circe and is transported in a magic chariot to the island sultanate of Mohareb, "Whom erst his arm had thrust / Down the bitumen pit" (235) and who has meanwhile risen in the ranks of the dark forces.

Fortunately for our hero, the camp of his adversaries is somewhat divided. During a gruesome séance, Maimuna's sister Khawla, "fiercest of the sorcerer brood" (232), has learned that the death of Thalaba is fatally linked to that of Mohareb. The sultan, sensing that Khawla would not scruple to sacrifice him, thereupon seeks an alliance with Thalaba. He returns Abdaldar's ring to him, instructs him in a diabolic version of Manicheism, and tries to persuade him to abandon the harsh and unprofitable service of Allah and to join those who offer more tangible rewards. Talaba, of course, stalwartly resists this second temptation in the wilderness and affirms his faith in the goodness and supremacy of God and the certainty of moral progress: "in the Manhood of the world, whate'er / Of folly marked its Infancy, of vice / Sullied its Youth, ripe Wisdom shall cast off, / Stablished in good, and, knowing evil, safe" (248).

Meanwhile, Khawla labors to destroy Thalaba by dreadful voodoo magic, but Abdaldar's ring once again protects the hero. Maimuna tries to aid her sister by fetching a horrible "grave-wax." But as she views "the secrets of the grave," she learns that it is the day of the Universal Sabbath, when "all created things adore / The Power that made them" and no evil may betide (258). Under its healing influence, she repents, frees Thalaba from her spell, and returns him in a whirlwind to the snow country, where she conveniently expires.

Thalaba travels on and almost perishes in the numbing cold, until, in the midst of the wilderness and the "dizzy floating of the feathery sky" (274), he comes upon a garden with a cottage, an island of summer created by a mysterious "Font of Fire." In it, he finds a sleeping damsel, Laila, who has been secreted there by her father to protect her from impending doom. She has never heard of Allah or the Prophet, we learn, and her only companions are ephemeral men and women made of snow by her father's magic to serve her and then to melt again.

Of the various encounters in the poem, this is the most human and moving: the embattled avenger, haunted, grown suspicious, yet weary of his burden and longing for unencumbered companionship, and the lonely, innocent girl who first mistakes the frozen traveler for another of her snow attendants and then is enraptured to discover that he is a warm and breathing human being like herself. Of course, their joy does not last long. The father of this young Miranda, whom she worships as the greatest and best of men, is no Prospero but the evil magician Okba, the murderer of Hodeirah and his children. When Okba, now a much-suffering man, punished by years of foreknowing that he would lose his daughter through Thalaba, discovers the dreaded avenger, he resignedly begs him to speed the inevitable. But Thalaba refuses—even when Azrael appears once again to confirm Laila's kismet and a somber voice from above warns him that either she or he must die. Noting the young man's recalcitrance, Okba thinks him forsaken of God and tries to stab him. But Laila rushes in between and receives the fatal blow. Once again Azrael has taken a woman from Thalaba's side. But, while Okba curses God's justice for slaughtering the innocent, Thalaba is now filled with pity for the old man's anguish and self-destructiveness.

Guided by a mysterious Green Bird, the hero journeys to the Vale of the long-sought Bird of Ages. The Simorg, however, merely exhorts him and directs him to a dogsled already appointed for him. A long, fearful ride returns Thalaba at last to the green world. There the Green Bird takes leave of him, begging him to forgive and save Okba "from endless death." Thalaba realizes that the gentle creature is in fact the penitent spirit of Laila, and he vows to "put off revenge, / The last rebellious feeling" (310).

The story now approaches its climax. Thalaba comes to a mysterious fountain and boards a small boat piloted by a damsel who, he later learns, is doing penance for having detained a previous champion of God in "the arms of love." To the rhythms of a rhymeless ballad measure somewhat reminiscent of *Lenore* and the *Ancient Mariner*, the boat begins to move down the stream and into a river and eventually carries its two inmates "without an oar, without a sail" across a moonlit ocean. At day-break, they arrive at a wild, rocky coast. Thalaba casts Abdaldar's ring into the sea to signalize his final and complete submission to the will of God; per-

forms his last ablutions; and, re-entering the boat, is swept by the
rising tide into a cavern and to the adamantine gates that lead to
the Domdaniel.

Past an ancient warder, whose run-out hourglass shows "the hour
appointed," Thalaba enters a "dead atmosphere" of sulphurous in-
candescence and descends in silence and solitude—"all earthly
thoughts, all human hopes / And passions now put off" (329)—to
an abyss of total darkness. There he finds Othatha, the champion
whom love had lured from the path of duty, bound to the rock with
fiery chains. He frees the Promethean penitent and sends him back
to the "lovely Mariner" beyond the gates. Then he plunges down
the abyss on a winged chariot and proceeds towards an intense
green light in the distance—the burning eye, as it turns out, of a
fierce Afreet who guards the inner gate of the Domdaniel. Thalaba
looses an arrow into the Afreet's eye and forces his way through the
gate. Khawla and Mohareb spring upon him; but he shakes them
off and, rushing toward his "life-flame," triumphantly tears from it
his father's lost sword.

As the flame surrounds and irradiates the hero, the "Living
Image" of Eblis in the inner cave strikes upon a Round Altar made
in the image of the World, thereby causing a tremor that convokes
the wizards from everywhere, "by Hell compelled [to] Oppose the
common danger; forced by Heaven / To share the common doom"
(337). But their arms are powerless against Hodeirah's sword; and,
when Thalaba shatters the shield and scimitar of their champion
Mohareb, they flee to the protection of the Living Idol. Okba alone
still opposes the hero, asking to be killed in expiation of the evil
done by him. But Thalaba spares him for Laila's sake and exhorts
him to seek forgiveness while he can. The voice of the Prophet is
heard commending Thalaba and bidding him to name his reward.
Thalaba prays for Okba and resigns himself to the Prophet's will:
" 'I am alone on earth; / Thou knowst the secret wishes of my
heart! / Do with me as thou wilt! Thy will is best.' " As he plunges
the sacred sword into the Idol's heart, the ocean vault falls in and
crushes all. "In the same moment, at the gate / Of Paradise,
Oneiza's Houri form / Welcomed her husband to eternal bliss"
(342).

Even a plot summary like the foregoing reveals the poem's faults
all too clearly. Intent mainly on exhibiting a congeries of myths and
manners, settings and superstitions, Southey pays little heed to
structure and economy. Instead of using plot and character to

develop, deepen, and resolve genuine moral or psychological problems, he merely rationalizes his extravaganza with a fairly pat moral formula regarding the rewards of duty and perseverance. The result is a dizzying array of gaudy "arabesques" and wasted, or imperfectly realized, poetic opportunities.

The chief weakness is the diffuse and tortuous plot which eddies and meanders without any firm principle of progression as the hero posts from stage to mysterious stage. Preliminary sketches for the poem in the notebooks show that Southey was more concerned about accommodating a maximum of legend and lore than about constructing a plot; and the eighty-odd pages of notes that accompany the text, crammed with excerpts from and references to the leading eighteenth-century Arabists and travelers, point to the same antiquarian impulse.[9] A multiple plot in the manner of Ariosto or Spenser could have absorbed the wealth of detail; but *Thalaba* is as severely unilinear as *Joan of Arc*. As a result; too many different things happen to the hero, and we tire of his quest before it is over.

In the very first book the action is nearly smothered by the colorful and moving but frankly irrelevant tale of Irem.[10] The legends of Haruth and Maruth, of Zohak, Aloadin, and the Simorg are similarly tacked on. There are, indeed, some indications of incremental or otherwise purposeful repetition. Thalaba passes through three false paradises, and in or near each of them a woman—mother, wife, filial friend—is taken from his side by the Angel of Death to be restored to him at last in the true Paradise. But since the recurrence does not appear to modulate or clarify the original idea significantly, it seems in the final analysis repetitive and even obsessive. Again, the visit to the Bird of Ages not only duplicates the descent to Haruth and Maruth but is, in its meager results, absurdly disproportionate to the bulky Maimuna and Laila episodes that lead to it. Conversely, the Khawla-Maimuna episode appears largely gratuitous in its necromantic gruesomeness. That it involves in fact the second of Thalaba's major temptations—the lure of power after that of sensuality in Aloadin's paradise—is lost in the hocus-pocus. There is, to be sure, some thematic development: the hero achieves his final triumph not merely through physical prowess (as in the Aloadin episode) but through a series of renunciations—of home, love, power, revenge, and finally of life itself. But, on the whole, the ways of God appear not so much mysterious as merely circuitous and redundant; and the hero's itinerary is at once too obviously and too arbitrarily determined to emerge as a genuine Islamic "path of purification."

The poem exhibits some potentially effective symbolic motifs. Thus Thalaba's "life-flame"—a pale-blue will-o'-the-wisp at first, "upon whose shrinking edge / The darkness seemed to press," but then a mighty blaze, "bright as the summer lightning when it spreads / Its glory o'er the midnight heavens"—early portends the eventual victory of light over darkness (50). But Southey does not sufficiently isolate and develop such motifs. The recovery of the father's sword from the life-flame is a splendid archetypal moment; but it comes too late in the story and without due preparation and is buried in the rush of events. Conversely, much is made of Abdaldar's ring, evidently a symbol of unlawful power and, like the sword, a fine, quasi-Wagnerian motif. But why Thalaba should accept it *twice* and, without using it, still enjoy its protection is given no better explanation than the facile one that "Blindly the wicked work / The righteous will of Heaven" (155, 253).

Again, the poem is rich in vivid imagery that is often concerned with light, as in the fine Shelleyan image of snow-flakes falling "like fire" through the red glow of a sunset (274). But the images often have the stark insular discontinuity to which Wordsworth objected in *Ossian*, and their esthetic is rhetorically asserted rather than immediately felt: "How beautiful is night! . . . In full-orbed glory yonder Moon divine / Rolls through the dark-blue depth. . . . The desert-circle spreads, / Like the round ocean, girdled with the sky. / How beautiful is night!" (9). Like all of Southey's writings, moreover, the poem lacks fresh and fitting metaphor. Such a deficiency is particularly painful in a supposedly "Oriental" poem. But Southey, with characteristic insularity, despised the "metaphorical rubbish" of Arabian Tales as heartily as he disliked the Song of Songs (IV, 37). His fancy may conceive the "deathy," "bluey," and "flamey" horrors of his story as somehow significant, but his heart is evidently not in them. When he suddenly compares the sulphurous glow in the Domdaniel to "A yellow light, as when the autumnal Sun, / Through travelling rain and mist, / Shines on the evening hills" (329), his figure is not only quite un-infernal but poignantly English and un-Oriental.

It is thus perhaps a fitting irony that, despite all the ethnic trappings, the poem's main source, the "History of Maugraby" with its legend of the Dom Daniel of Tunis, is not genuinely Oriental but is part of a spurious sequel to the *Arabian Nights* that was published in France by two literary hacks, Dom Chavis and M. Cazotte, and translated in 1792 as *Arabian Tales or a Continuation of the Arabian Nights Entertainment.* The sinister Manicheism of a seminary of powerful necromancers who make it their business to abduct and corrupt the sons of Princes could not but appeal strongly to the ex-Flagellant; but it is not much more Arabian than *Ossian* is Celtic.

Accordingly, Southey's hero, while intended to exemplify *Islam*—or more correctly that fatalism which Southey regarded as the cornerstone of "Mahometry"—is in fact of a rather Zoroastrian hue; and his prim, impregnable virtuousness appears as out of place in the sanguine world of Harun-al-Rashid as Moses would in Camelot. There are glimpses of an all-determining Divine Will that appoints both the locusts and the birds that devour them and that thus preserves the moral ecology of the universe (87). But Southey had no love for mysticism. That appears not only from his perfunctory treatment of the *Simorgh*, the great mystic symbol of the oneness of life in Moslem legend, but also from the description of the Living Image of Eblis, whose left hand sustains the "naked waters" of the ocean vault, while its sceptered right decrees earthquakes and tidal waves on its globe-shaped altar: the being that is at once Preserver and Destroyer is not divine but diabolic. The poem is thus essentially dualistic: Allah against Eblis, light against dark.

Even then its Manicheism is that of an adolescent's daydream. The problem of evil which the poem raises is neither defined nor resolved but is merely sensationalized. Thalaba, the "delegated youth," is a dream hero whose grotesque and unreal campaign against Evil *per se* is an index of the dreamer's own innocence, superficiality, or paranoia and, at any rate, of his vainglory. At once merely personal and vaguely metaphysical, daemonic and domestic, Thalaba's quest wholly lacks a political middle ground: his victory, while purporting to be an act of universal redemption, produces no visible practical good other than his own promotion to beatitude. "Perhaps the Anti-Jacobin criticasters may spare Thalaba," Southey wrote; "it is so utterly innocent of all good drift." Though he later called his hero "a male Joan of Arc" and once thought of making the Domdaniel into an allegory of "the evils of established systems," the poem represents, in fact, a complete political disengagement.[11]

Altogether, Southey lacked the nerve to make evil truly seductive or virtue genuinely hazardous. As a result, his hero is never in any

real danger of being corrupted by lust, ambition, fear, or hate, or of
being sapped by conflicting obligations. Except for an early out-
burst of Job-like impatience and a spell of outright madness, he per-
sonifies the ideal of Submission which it is his *raison d'être* to exemplify; and his sole weakness is a modest desire for domestic happiness. Essentially a Stoic and Puritan in exotic trappings, Thalaba
is at once a late descendant of Spenser's Sir Guyon and a shadowy,
very old-fashioned forbear of Shelley's heroes. But, unlike those
figures, Southey's "idealisms of moral excellence" have neither the
intellectual substance of real allegory nor the imaginative depth of
true myth. Unlike Mephistopheles, who is part of Faust, or Jupiter,
who is Prometheus's own remorseless superego, Lobaba is merely
the converse of Thalaba. Domdaniel may be the popular hell, or it
may be Dr. Vincent's Westminster or some other region of
Southey's private nightmares; but it is seen as purely external, not
as also a symbol of the hell within. Thus, despite its many impressive moments, the poem as a whole is machinery rather than
metaphysics.

III   *From Cintra to Greta Hall*

Myth becomes more nearly symbolic in *The Curse of Kehama.*
When Southey completed that poem he was thirty-five and a much-
altered man. He had planned it as early as 1800 and had rapidly
progressed with his "Hindoo romance of original extravagance"
during 1801 and 1802. But then the work ceased for years—partly
because other labors interfered but also because Southey was discouraged by the poor sale of *Thalaba* and *Madoc.* At length,
however, in the spring of 1808, he met Walter Savage Landor, who
not only urged him to continue his mythological series but
generously offered to pay the publishing costs if necessary. Southey
thereupon resumed work on *Kehama,* largely recast it, and not only
finished it by the end of 1809 but immediately embarked upon yet
another epic, *Roderick.* Southey was always grateful for Landor's
enthusiasm and generous faith which, he said, "awakened in me old
dreams and hopes [that] had been laid aside" and without which he
"should never have written verse again."[12]
   Much had changed by then in Southey's life. Between 1800 and
1801, he and Edith had been back in Portugal to improve his health
and to gather material for a history of that country. As before, he
was appalled by the filth and squalor of Lisbon, by the grinding

poverty and ignorance, disease and brutality rife among the populace, and by the lawlessness and corruption, laziness, fraudulence,
and superstitious fanaticism of Portuguese society, conditions that
seemed to him to cry for a revolution. But he passionately loved the
voluptuous, sun-drenched land, particularly the famous region of
Cintra, "the most blessed spot in the habitable globe," where a man
could "eat grapes, and ride donkeys, and be very happy." He spent
much time in Mr. Hill's large library and in the monastic and public
libraries in and around Lisbon. But what left the deepest imprint
upon his memory was the far-flung donkey rides he took with Edith
through the mountainous countryside adazzle with oranges and
olives, twisted cork-trees and sparkling chestnuts, gay lizards and
brilliant fireflies—a land at once rich and mellow, soft yet strongly
contoured under the blazing sun. His descriptions of moonlit
"waters that shine like midnight snow" or of ocean fogs marching
upland like an army of darkness have a lyrical intensity rarely found
elsewhere in his writings. For years afterward, he dreamed of his
"paradise," and yearned for the "life and joy-giving power" of its
air: "even to breathe was a pleasure there."[13]

Returned to England, Southey finally abandoned the thought of
studying law and resolved to live by authorship alone. For six
months he tried his hand as private secretary to Isaac Corry, the
Irish Chancellor of the Exchequer. But the post, though lucrative,
was essentially a sinecure; and its specious glory repelled Southey
enough to make him resign. For some time, he played with the idea
of entering the diplomatic service, as a means of returning to Portugal. In general, however, he was determined to live by his pen,
even if that meant the drudgery of writing poems for the *Morning
Post*, reviewing dull books for the periodicals, translating from the
Spanish and Portuguese, or turning out scholarly editions and other
ephemera. Years of unremitting "task-work," of having to "spin out
the very guts of one's brain" for daily subsistence, later led Southey
to admonish aspiring poets to choose anything rather than literature
as a livelihood; but there was never an alternative for himself.

At the same time, a series of personal tragedies severed the
remaining links with his own youthful past and gave a fateful turn
to his life. In 1801, his beloved cousin Margaret Hill had died; early
in 1802, he lost his mother. The birth of a first daughter, Margaret,
consoled him over the loss of the two other Margarets; but when the
child, on whom he doted, died of hydrocephalus the following year,

it all but broke his heart; and he never wished to see Bristol, the scene of these tragedies, again. Urged by Coleridge, the bereaved parents traveled north to Keswick—on a "visit" that lasted to the end of their lives.

At first, Southey still planned to make Portugal his permanent abode. But that dream gradually faded, particularly once the increasing incapacity and final defection of Coleridge had imposed upon Southey the burden of providing for two families instead of one. Meanwhile, the beauty of the English Lake Country began to grow upon him and to inspire in him, he felt, a surge of poetic power. Greta Hall, situated with its gardens and orchards on a low hill inside a sharp bend of the noisy Greta River on the outskirts of Keswick and commanding a spectacular view across Derwent Water and its mountains into Borrowdale, increasingly replaced Cintra in his affections. "Nothing in England," he wrote with little exaggeration, "can be more beautiful than the site of this house. Had this country but the sky of Portugal, it would leave me nothing to wish for" (*Letters*, I, 232).

Lastly, the Peace of Amiens in 1802, which freed Britain from the reproach of reactionary war-mongering and placed responsibility for future hostilities on the shoulders of the French, restored to Southey the love of his country from which, like most Republicans, he had been alienated during almost ten years of war with revolutionary France. Moreover, the increasing arrogance of Napoleon gave Southey's "holy hatred of tyranny" a new and more comfortable direction. The sun of liberty might once have risen in the East; but it had now clearly traveled to the West; and even those who had always sought it there were less wrong-headed than those who were still looking for it in the East. Henceforth, Southey would study how to ready the world for a *pax Britannica* and for "the eventual triumph of the English language over all others" by colonization or even by force of arms (*Life*, II, 215, 329).

The principal poetic expression of these news ideas was *Madoc*, completed in 1805, the year of Trafalgar. But of necessity *The Curse of Kehama*, too, besides carrying on the interrupted mythological series, reflected the new orientation. On the one hand, the otherwordliness of Hinduism could not but appeal strongly to Southey, especially after his recent losses. On the other hand, his growing interest in English colonial expansion in India and elsewhere gave a new importance to his old subject. "Take the Hin-

doo superstitions for your machinery," William Taylor had written
as early as 1801, "[and] its celebrity [will] grow with the empire"
(*Memoir*, I, 375).

Here again, Southey also reflected contemporary changes of
taste, for Brahmin India had begun to replace rationalist China in
the exotic fancies of the West. The opulent creations of India's
religious imagination, hitherto largely dismissed as absurd,
effeminate, and obscene forms of superstition, were now beginning
to be described, translated, and interpreted dispassionately, largely
owing to the pioneering efforts of Sir William Jones, the discoverer
of Sanskrit and founder of the Royal Asiatic Society. Speculation
was rife about the relationship between Hinduism and the myths of
ancient Egypt, Greece, and Israel, and in particular between the
Hindu *trimourti* and the Christian Trinity; and Hindu myth had
been repeatedly recommended as suitable machinery for epic.

Here, too, of course, Southey's puritanical rationalism was too
strong for a ready suspension of disbelief. He knew *Sakuntala* and
the *Bhagavad Gita* in translation, and he had read the most recent
authorities on India—Thomas Maurice, Pierre Sonnerat, Jones,
and the writers of the *Asiatic Researches* (which he reviewed). Yet
Hinduism was to him "of all religions . . . the most monstrous in its
fables and the most fatal in its effects," and his main worry was how
to keep its "deformities" "out of sight"—like Mohammed's "mob
of wives" and Noah's "general embarcation"—and how to
"compensate for the extravagance of the fictions" by "moral sublimity" (VIII, 7). As elsewhere, Southey could not refrain from
tilting solemnly against the windmills of "superstition" even while
using their torque to drive his poetry.

Even so, *The Curse of Kehama* is a striking poem. Centrally, it
embodies a vision of evil which, though still grotesque, is not
without terror and symbolic force. Instead of the preposterous
sorcerers of the Domdaniel, there is now a human ruler in whom
evil takes the intelligible form of lust for power and universal domi-
nion. The subject, which Southey had already intended to treat in
his Noachid, had a new urgency for him. For he had by now come
to see in the rise of Napoleon not only a betrayal of the Revolution
but a total calamity for mankind, and in Bonaparte himself an in-
carnation of evil, a kind of Antichrist, whose titanic endeavor to
unite all mankind under his sway was nothing less than a diabolic inversion of the millennium. Ever disposed to view political realities
in terms of moral absolutes, Southey could find the figure of

Kehama, like that of Coleridge's Kubla, a lesson to the age as well as a timeless archetype.

IV   The Curse of Kehama

Taking hold of a tenet of a degenerate form of Brahmanism, that prayers and sacrifices are "drafts upon heaven" which compel the deity to grant the worshipper's demands, Southey depicts in Kehama an Oriental potentate and chief Brahmin who, by means of terrific austerities and countless sacrifices to the god Siva, has reached nearly absolute power and who only needs the lordship over the kingdom of death and the Amreeta, the Water of Immortality, to complete his design of self-deification. Kehama thus appears as a Satanic counterpart of Prometheus, the Romantic superman challenging the Divine Establishment—a conception so disquieting even in its Satanic guise to a bourgeois mind like that of Southey's friend Wynn that he pronounced it revolting and unintelligible. But, while seemingly on the verge of absolute freedom, Kehama is of course in reality totally enslaved by the passions of pride, ambition, and hatred that drive him inexorably toward a terrible fate.

Kehama's involuntary antagonist is the peasant-pariah Ladurlad, the Southeyan hero, by now middle-aged, who, through patience under unmerited enmity and suffering, not only wins ripeness for himself but helps to bring about the downfall of tyranny. Ladurlad has just saved his daughter Kailyal from the lust of Kehama's son Arvalan by killing the dissolute prince, whose spirit now haunts the world as a ghoulish demon of revenge. The grief-stricken Kehama vows that he will make war on the death-god Yamen himself and meanwhile seeks to satisfy his dead son's thirst for vengeance by condemning the killer to a fate worse than death. While the obsequies of Arvalan, with which the poem opens, are still in progress, the rajah pronounces a terrible curse on the pariah that exiles him not only from society but from nature: from the elements, from food and drink, from time, sickness, and death, and—worst of all for Southey—from sleep.

The terror of such a plight is the peculiarly Romantic one of exile from Nature and from every source of self-oblivion, of perpetual imprisonment in the solitary cell of consciousness; and Ladurlad thus joins the number of those sleepless cosmic sufferers that haunt the Romantic mythology: Cain, the Wandering Jew, the Ancient Mariner, Manfred, and above all Prometheus. Ironically, however, as in the case of Cain and the Wandering Jew, the curse also protects the sufferer and enables him to pass fakir-like through fire and water and to perform heroic deeds beyond the might of ordinary mortals. When Kailyal seeks asylum from Kehama by clinging to a statue of Marriataly, the patroness of the poor, and is pushed, in the ensuing struggle, into the river with the idol, Ladurlad can rescue her without being touched by the element. Later, when Kehama is about to perform the hundredth of his Vedic horse sacrifices which will make him lord of the first sphere of the world, his archers are powerless to prevent Ladurlad from spoiling the rite by mounting, riding, and thus desecrating the victim. Hence the poem's (rather homely) motto—Grecized by Coleridge from one of the proverbs of Southey's "half-saved" uncle Tyler—that "curses are like young chickens, they always come home to roost."

The poem, better constructed than the preceding ones, divides into two equal parts, each comprising twelve books or cantos. The first half, largely episodic and replete with details of Hindu cosmology, exhibits the growth of Kehama's power while foreshadowing the happiness that awaits the virtuous at the end of their trials. The remainder, less sprawling and more dramatic, conducts the narrative through a series of crises to its climax and unexpected reversal. Here, too, mythological detail bulks large, so that the story appears at times expressly constructed to accommodate it; but the overall effect is that of an integrated whole, without gratuitous excursions of the sort found in *Thalaba*.

Part One turns primarily around Kailyal, the beautiful and innocent maiden of sentimental convention, who is persecuted by the lustful Arvalan, now a powerful *asura* or evil demon. After her rescue from drowning, she is left forsaken by the wretched Ladurlad, who, "selfish in misery," flees into the night to bear his torments alone (VIII, 45). Promptly pursued by the nightmarish Arvalan, she finds sanctuary in the temple of Pollear, the elephant-headed god of travelers. Eventually, she faints at the foot of a deadly manchineel tree (transplanted for the nonce from the West to the East Indies). But she is found and rescued from its poisonous dews by Ereenia, one of the winged "Glendoveers" (*gandharvas*), the "most beautiful" of the *suras*, or good spirits; and she is then taken by him to Casyapa, the Sire of the Gods, who sits in the sacred grove on Hemakoot, the Holy Mountain, "Where, underneath the Tree of Life, / The Fountain of the Sacred River sprung" (50).

Under the healing influence of the Tree of Life, Kailyal recovers from the effects of the poison tree. But Casyapa denies her asylum because he is afraid of the Almighty Man, whose growing power has begun to threaten heaven itself. The Glendoveer thereupon conveys her in an ethereal "ship of heaven" to the Swerga, the Paradise of Indra, the god of the elements. Indra, too, refuses Kailyal asylum, lest mortality "unparadise the Swerga"; but he relents when she begs only to be reunited with her father. Ereenia is dispatched to fetch the torment-driven Ladurlad; and father and daughter, reunited with the blessed spirit of Ladurlad's wife Jedillian, find temporary refuge from Kehama's curse in a lower paradise on Mount Meru, the cradle of the heaven-sprung Ganges.

They are attended by the affable Ereenia, who tells them of ancient times when Vishnu, the Preserver, would assume human form to deliver mankind from calamity and who imbues them with faith and hope that tyranny would pass away at last and "Evil yield to Good": "For there are Gods who look below: / Siva, the Avenger, is not blind, / Nor Vishnu careless for mankind" (91). A pure, spiritual love develops between Kailyal and Ereenia which even the arrows of the mischievous god of love, Camdeo (*Kamadeva*), are powerless to infect with carnal passion. Kailyal grows ever more lovely and ethereal; and the sun, the moon, and all the *suras* and *devetas* (gods) linger overhead to "bless that blessed Company" (93).

Meanwhile, Arvalan, smarting from his recent defeats, obtains help from Lorrinite, an unspeakably venomous witch who works in the employ of the bloodthirsty "Calis," or female demons. Lorrinite locates the whereabouts of Ladurlad and Kailyal in her horrid crystal made of a thousand gouged-out eyes, equips Arvalan with magic arms, and sends him to Mount Meru in her dragon car. But the magnetic ore of the mountain acts on the yoke of the dragon team so that the car is dashed against the rocks and Arvalan is helplessly wedged into an ice rift. Unfortunately, Kehama has at the same time succeeded in completing the hundredth *aswamedha* and invades the first heavenly sphere. While the *devetas* flee to the second sphere, Kehama seizes the Swerga, and Ladurlad and Kailyal have to relinquish their "Bower of Bliss."

For a while, they live in peace in an idyllic glade. Ladurlad develops into an accomplished Stoic with "a heart subdued, / A resolute, unconquer'd fortitude, / An agony represt, a will resigned" (118). Kailyal, on the other hand, like another Sakuntala, charms the wild beasts with her beauty and is adored by fish and fowl. Action resumes when a band of yogis, in search of a bride for their god Jaga-Naut (Juggernaut), carry Kailyal off to their holy city where she is drawn in procession on the notorious car of the seven-headed idol while frenzied worshippers immolate themselves under its iron wheels. Having been conveyed onto the sacred bridal bed by temple harlots, the girl is beset by a lecherous Brahmin who pretends to impersonate the deity and who in the process becomes possessed by the "accursed soul of Arvalan." Ereenia appears to defend Kailyal but is overpowered by the witch Lorrinite and her crew and is carried to the vaults beneath the ocean. Left once more to face the horrid Arvalan, Kailyal frustrates his renewed attack by suicidally setting fire to the bridal bed and the temple. Luckily, Ladurlad arrives and, shielded by the curse, carries her to safety.

Together, they search for the kidnapped Ereenia. After much wandering, they reach the seashore at the sunken city of Mahabalipur, the ancient seat of the demon king Baly, who, like Kehama, had tried to rival the gods and was overthrown by an avatar of Vishnu. While Kailyal remains on shore, Ladurlad descends "like a god" into the parting waters. Through silent streets and once paradisic gardens now grown with coral and marine vegetation, he comes to the glowing "Chambers of the Kings of old" beneath Baly's palace, where the embalmed and naked bodies of the ancient kings sit in ghostly, frozen majesty. Here Ereenia lies, chained and guarded by a monstrous *naga*. After six days of wrestling with the serpentine horror, Ladurlad's sleeplessness prevails, and he frees Ereenia.

Rescuer and rescued return to the despairing Kailyal. Once again they are set upon by the forces of Arvalan. Fortunately, however, it is the day when Baly, who after his overthrow became the judge of the dead, makes his annual visit to the earth. Appearing suddenly like Shelley's Demogorgon, he seizes the evil host with his hundred arms and plunges them "To punishment deserved and endless woe" (161).

Kehama himself now falls in love with Kailyal, woos her to become the consort of his eternal reign, and lifts the curse from Ladurlad as an incentive. But his offer is spurned, and he thereupon not only re-inflicts the curse on the father but strikes the girl with leprosy. Kailyal, having fought down the carnal fear that she might lose Ereenia's love, rejoices at being at least secure from further sexual molestation: once again Kehama's curse becomes a blessing.

Ereenia has meanwhile set out on a perilous quest to awaken the god Siva who thrones, alone and inaccessible, on Mount Calasay, beyond the seven worlds and the outer darkness. We learn of the god's sanctuary enclosing the Fountain of Light, the mystic Rose, and the unspeakable *lingam*, the sacred phallic symbol of the Destroyer. Having at last reached the place, the faithful Glendoveer calls upon the god to awaken and put on his terrors "For mercy's sake." As he strikes the self-poised Silver Bell, the mountain dissolves in a blaze of light, "Even as a morning dream before the day," and Ereenia plummets down with a small voice in his heart that bids him to carry his appeal to Yamen, the god of the dead: "He hath the remedy for every woe; / He setteth right whate'er is wrong below" (175f.).

With this lofty variant of the redemptive quest, the poem approaches its crisis—once again a night journey, as in *Thalaba*, but exceeding, Southey wrote, "in grandeur anything that I have ever yet produced or conceived," (*Memoir*, II, 228). Over the roaring darkness of the outer ocean, Ereenia, Kailyal, and Ladurlad embark for hell in a crazy boat. They pass the quiet ocean, where Kehama's curse once again ceases to operate; and, after traversing an icebound shore where spirits await their summons to judgment, they plunge down a vast abyss to the adamantine stronghold of Padalon, the Hindu hell and purgatory. A one-wheel chariot, which protects mortals from the fires of hell and immortals from fruitless pity, carries them through one of the gates of Padalon and across a razor-thin bridge over the fiery gulf, where the rebellious spirits of the damned exult over their imminent deliverance, to the city of Yamenpur which shines in unearthly brilliance and is ringed by gigantic subterraneous thunderstoms. Here Yamen, his aspect at once terrible and benign, sits on a throne supported by three fiery arch-sinners, the inventors of what Southey once called the "Trinity of Evil": Wealth, Power, and Priestcraft. Ereenia announces his message from Siva and is told to await "in patience and in faith" the approaching hour of fate.

A dead silence suddenly falls over the infernal kingdom, for the "Man-God" at last approaches, self-multiplied and in the fullness of his power, to harrow hell. He deposes Yamen and renews his suit for Kailyal; but her "virtuous will" remains unshaken even when he threatens to make her father the fourth of the burning throne-bearers. Now the rajah demands the Amreeta, the nectar of immortality, and a huge, ghastly skeleton rises from a marble sepulchre as from one of Southey's nightmares to proffer the cup to him and

Kailyal. Boasting of his triumph "over Death and Fate" and of his having risen to be Siva's equal, Kehama drinks, ignorant in his pride that the Amreeta assumes the character of its partaker. In his veins the divine mead promptly turns to poison, giving him eternity indeed, but an eternity of torment, the fate he had pronounced upon Ladurlad. Thus the curse comes "home to roost," the eye of the awakened Siva falls full upon the rajah, and he has to take his appointed place as the fourth of the fiery atlantes. Yamen resumes his throne; Kailyal is commanded to drink next; and, as she does so, she becomes an immortal spirit and is told to ascend with Ereenia to the Swerga. Ladurlad, granted death by Yamen, falls serenely asleep to awaken in the blessed Yedillian's bower, where, as the poem typically concludes, "All whom he loved he met, to part no more."

The fearful career of the Universal Tyrant thus comes to a sudden, inglorious end; and evil, after so much fear and trembling among gods and men alike, easily succumbs to a trick of fate that is only less arbitrary than the earlier intervention of Baly. The poem is, therefore, at once too crass in its situation and too facile in its resolution to succeed fully even as a moral allegory. The crude idea that God can be coerced through austerities and sacrifices need not be so if rendered symbolical. But Southey, in his largely patronizing concern with "manners," does not attempt any such transmutation. Evil in the poem accordingly remains almost as abstract as it is in *Thalaba*. Arvalan, while the spawn of one of Southey's nightmares, is mere Gothic machinery; and the more he overacts, the less terrifying he becomes. Kehama himself commands some awe through his stern remoteness and some belief through his pathetic affection for his son and his passion for Kailyal. But the mainspring of his actions, his bizarre cosmic megalomania, is as unconvincing as the crass malignity of his fiendish offspring. As elsewhere, Southey's obsession with evil is matched, perhaps inevitably, by his inability to comprehend it.

Only Lorrinite, though as grotesquely Gothic a witch as her Dom-danielite sisters, bears features that reveal something about the etiology of evil. She had been unlovely in her youth, we are told, and therefore had remained unloved. Finding no outlet, her passions rankled and turned to poison: she "hated men because they loved not her / And hated women because they were loved." Thus, in despair, she "tempted Hell to tempt her, and resigned / Her body to the Demons of the air," becoming "at once their mistress and their slave," so as to be able to "wreak her vengeance on mankind" (98). It may be that Elizabeth Tyler sat for part of this portrait of malignant frustration. At any rate, evil here for once stirs not just complacency but compassion and accordingly appears authentic.

Similar weaknesses appear on the side of good. Except for some initial stumblings, Ladurlad, like most of Southey's heroes, is as severely virtuous and Kailyal is as fatally sweet and sexless as their enemies are wicked and lewd. What should have been a harrowing portrait of the hero's trying to overcome the dreadful desolation imposed upon him by the curse becomes, therefore, another piece of sentimental melodrama. At the same time, however, though both Ereenia and Ladurlad occasionally perform heroic feats, the action is now primarily assigned to the villain. More clearly than Thalaba's, Ladurlad's virtues are the passive ones of Stoic endurance and pious faith in providence; and his deeds, though spectacular, accomplish nothing decisive. The reversal does not come about because of anything the hero does or suffers or, as in *Prometheus Unbound*, through the hero's regenerative conquest over himself; it occurs solely because the villain at last gratuitously overreaches himself.

The ironic parallel between Kehama's self-deification by sacrifice and Ladurlad's becoming "god-like" through his ordeal is potentially profound and would seem to point to Ladurlad as a Promethean revolutionary in whom oppression itself becomes a source of revolutionary power. As it is, Casyapa's promise of the redemptive role of suffering is wholly ambiguous—"And, when the Wicked have their day assigned, / Then they who suffer bravely save mankind" (110)—and his subjoined exhortation to "leave the event, in holy hope, to Heaven" makes plain that the hero can be no Prometheus, neither rebel nor redeemer, no champion of either men or gods, but only a much-suffering bystander who meekly trusts in the justice of some nebulous Providence while endeavoring to "exist in pain / As in [his] own allotted element" (118). That is of course a viable conception of heroism; but in the cosmic framework of the theodrama which Southey adopts, we expect a more decisive causal relationship between the actions of the hero and the events of the story. Perhaps one reason for Ladurlad's curious inconsequence is that, much as Southey hated and feared a godless and self-serving humanism such as Kehama represents, he yet could not bring himself to make his hero an active champion for what is after all the *ancien*

régime of the *devetas*. As always in Southey, the real denouement is
not liberation but death.

The reader who wants to enjoy the poem must not look for any
subtle or unified vision of nature, history, or the human psyche but
must be content with an array of lively if not always fully authentic
descriptions of luminous and somber exotic settings and
mythologems and with a rudimentary symbolism. From the lurid
pomp of the funeral of Arvalan with its chanting and wailing, its
torchlight reflected on the bald heads of the Brahmins, the
propped-up corpse nodding to the tread of the bearers, and the
blaze and violence of the *suttee*; through the powerful thanatopsis
at Mahabalipur; to the climactic vision of the Oriental Inferno of
Padalon and its fury and pain, the poem abounds with the sublime
and picturesque, rendered in often merely abundant but sometimes
evocative detail. Southey's imagination always seems most fully
aroused by the theme of death. Moreover, as in *Thalaba*, Southey
delights in depicting various paradises, earthly and heavenly, in
terms which, though never sensuous, are colorful and at times
genuinely lyrical.

At the top of the list is the Swerga, the garden of Indra, where a
gigantic raintree drinks the dews of heaven with its thousand
branches and sends them down through romantic glens and gleaming cataracts into a lake from which in turn a thousand rivers branch
out to water paradise:

> On that ethereal lake, whose waters lie
> Blue and transpicuous, like another sky,
> The Elements had reared their King's abode.
> A strong, controlling power their strife suspended,
> And there their hostile essences they blended,
> To form a Palace worthy of the God.
> Built on the Lake, the waters were its floor;
> And here its walls were water arched with fire,
> And here were fire with water vaulted o'er;
> And spires and pinnacles of fire
> Round watery cupolas aspire,
> And domes of rainbow rest on fiery towers,
> And roofs of flame are turreted around
> With cloud, and shafts of cloud with flames are bound.
> Here, too, the Elements forever veer,
> Ranging around with endless interchanging;
> Pursued in love, and so in love pursuing,

In endless revolutions here they roll;
For ever their mysterious work renewing;
The parts all shifting, still unchanged the whole.
Even we on earth at intervals descry
Gleams of the glory, streaks of flowing light,
Openings of heaven, and streams that flash at night,
In fitful splendor, through the northern sky. (63)

Here we have the Romantic vision of Nature as motion and harmony amid strife, with echoes of "Kubla Khan" and anticipations
of Shelley. On a lower plane, Ladurlad and Kailyal find refuge in a
paradise less sublime than picturesque and pastoral—a "green and
sunny glade" overarched by "an aged Banian tree" as by a temple,
with a murmuring brook and a pellucid, lotus-bearing lagoon that
glows "like burnished steel,"—where Kailyal's presence returns
nature to Edenic peace and innocence. Finally, there is the
necropolis of Baly, a Xanadu sunk beneath the tumult of the sea. Its
golden summits still peer above "the dark green deep that rolled
between"; its ancient temples, "Once resonant with instrument and
song, / And solemn dance of festive multitude," now hear "no
voice save of the ocean flood / Which roars forever on the restless
shores" and the "lonely sound of winds" in "solitary caves"; its
thousand palaces stand silent and beautiful in the "everlasting
stillness of the Deep," steeped in sunlight and seagreen and surrounded by gardens that flash with coral and marine life.

> The golden fountains had not ceased to flow;
> And where they mingled with the briny sea,
> There was a sight of wonder and delight
> To see the fish, like birds in air,
>   Above Ladurlad flying.
> Round those strange waters they repair,
> Their scarlet fins outspread and plying;
> They float with gentle hovering there;
> And now upon those little wings,
> As if to dare forbidden things,
>   With wilful purpose bent,
> Swift as an arrow from a bow,
> They shoot across, and to and fro,
> In rapid glance, like lightning go
> Through that unwonted element. (146f.)

This poetry is of a fairly high order and of considerable metrical dexterity. In adopting for *Kehama* a rhymed form of the irregular verse of *Thalaba*, Southey remarked cynically that he was probably "corrupting," with "French cookery," the already "diseased and pampered" taste of the English public (*Letters*, I, 156). But he also knew that blank verse, "the noblest measure [in] our language," would not suit *Kehama*. "There must be quicker, wilder movements; there must be a gorgeousness of ornament also—eastern gemwork, and sometimes rhyme must be rattled upon rhyme" (*Life*, III, 145). The result is a poetry more nearly "Oriental" than anything in *Thalaba*. The language of *Kehama* is still all too often drearily prosaic, crusted over with abstractions like faith, hope, love, will, fortitude, patience, piety, resignation. Even at its best, Southey's art is uneven, and vivid images and sonorous phrases mingle with banality and flabby rhymes. Yet in passages like those quoted above we catch a glimpse of the great Romantic dream of Paradise and hear, though in somewhat reedy tones, a version of its elusive melody.

CHAPTER 5

The Course of Empire: Madoc

I *Genesis*

OF all of Southey's epic projects, *Madoc* was his most ambitious and elaborate and the one about which he thought most and longest. Modeled on nothing less than "the Bible, Homer, and Ossian" (*Life*, I, 238), it was to "outdo" all epics but the *Iliad* and *Paradise Lost* and to assure Southey's immortality as the most original poet since Homer. Coleridge, too, prophesied that *Madoc* would excel the *Aeneid* and urged its completion with typically intense vicarious involvement.

The genesis of the poem spans Southey's entire formative period. The subject of the legendary twelfth-century Welsh prince and colonizer of America was first suggested at Westminster by Southey's school friend Wynn, who claimed lineal descent from Madoc's brother Rhodri.[1] Projected and begun in prose as early as 1789, the work had grown to a book and a half of verse by 1794, when it had to yield to *Joan of Arc*; it was recommenced early in 1797 and completed in its original version during the productive year at Westbury. Almost immediately, however, Southey decided upon major alterations. The fancied association—typical of eighteenth-century speculative mythography—of Madoc with the mythical Inca founder Mango Capac now seemed forced and artificial. The scene of the American action would therefore have to be shifted from Peru to some other, less hackneyed location; and incidents based upon the "customs and superstitutions" of that region would have to be "woven into the work . . . so neatly as not to betray the junction." Altogether, what Southey had written so far was no more than a "first sketch" that would have to be fleshed out with "manners" before it could become his "Jerusalem Delivered."

After a two-year dormancy, the poem accordingly underwent complete remodeling, the bulk of this work being done at Keswick.

Its original fifteen books were expanded by more than a third, revised, and divided into two parts to correspond to the *Odyssey* and the
Iliad respectively. The text of what is now Part One, the "Odyssey
part," was virtually rewritten and made to accommodate an
"Odyssey-like" wealth of "scenery, manners, and traditions" which
Southey had gone to Wales to collect during the autumn of 1801.[2]
Toward the end, Southey grew doubtful of the wisdom of reworking
a juvenile plan for so many years and felt that the poem was lacking
in vitality. But, with Coleridge's encouragement, he persisted. Early
in 1805, the poem was published, essentially in its present form, and
was dedicated to Wynn, its spiritual father.

Like all of Southey's narratives, *Madoc* today alienates by its
remoteness. Yet its story of the discovery and settlement of America
by a band of disaffected, freedom-loving Welshmen was anything
but esoteric to the young poet. Linking contemporary interest in Indians and in Welsh antiquities with the old dream of Pantisocracy,
the poem bade fair to unite private vision and communal myth, present and past, in true epic fashion.

Despite Southey's penchant for the exotic, he always longed to
write an "English epic" on a "Welsh or English story" that could
make him "feel like a cock on his own dunghill." Over the years, he
pondered a variety of national subjects, ranging from the legendary
founding of Britain by the Trojan Brutus to the struggle of the
barons against King John and the merry outlawry of Robin
Hood—not to mention the matter of King Arthur, which had
engrossed him even in the days of his most fervent anti-British
Republicanism.[3] He found fault with all of these subjects, however,
and none of them materialized. But if he never wrote an "English
epic" proper, it is perhaps because *Madoc* came so close to being
one. The poem owes its remodeling into its present double-barreled
form precisely to Southey's search for a British theme.

In choosing a Welsh setting, Southey paid tribute to the "Celtic
revival" which, though past its yeasty Ossianic phase, was still in
full swing, nourished by Romantic nationalism and primitivism, and
which naturally centered on Wales as the last stronghold of the ancient Britons. After the Franco-philia of *Joan of Arc*, Southey now
looked to Wales for vestiges of "native" British manners and morals
undefiled by Saxon and Norman ways. The speculations of
Celtomaniacs like William Stukely, Edward Williams, and Edward
Davies had convinced him, moreover, that the religious "system" of
the Medieval Welsh "bards" was the "patriarchal faith" as derived,

via the Druids, from the "real and true faith" of the Celtic descendants of Japhet. Wales was the true Britain, the once and future England of Gray's *Bard*.[4]

Initially, of course, *Madoc* was not so much a patriotic poem as a large-scale projection into the past of the old scheme of Pantisocracy, or rather of that more general Utopian dream of exodus to a brave new world which Pantisocracy had sought to embody. In time, however, the two impulses merged. The celestial gleam of Pantisocracy, after first retreating from America to Wales, not only faded into the light of common domesticity and the bourgeois symbiosis of Greta Hall but gradually turned into the glare of an unabashed colonialism. Bishop Berkeley's famous line, "Westward the course of empire takes its way," comes at the end of a poem that envisions a new golden age of harmony with nature in the New World. Southey's thought took a similar turn. What began as a Utopian gesture of revolt eventually became a nationalistic and imperialistic millennialism that identified missionary ideals with colonial interests and preached a *pax Britannica* of "making the world English."[5]

Madoc reflects this metamorphosis. Far from being "too much associated with the . . . pantisocratic philosophy," as William Taylor feared, it is, in fact, Southey's epic of foundation—his answer to the *Aeneid* and particularly to the *Lusiad*, then recently translated by Julius Mickle and recommended by him to English readers as "the Epic Poem of the Birth of Commerce" and colonialism. Southey regarded Camoens' hero, Vasco da Gama, as in reality "more atrocious than Pizarro" and the Portuguese conquest which he spear-headed as "the chief cause that barbarised the Mohammedans" and prevented the development of an enlightened commercial civilization among them. Southey would tell the full cautionary story of the rise and fall of the Portuguese empire in the "History of Portugal." Meanwhile, *Madoc* would sing how colonizing should be done the British way.[6]

II Madoc *in Wales*

The action of the poem is set in the latter part of the twelfth century during the reign of Henry II. Owen Gwynned had become king of North Wales (Gwynned) after dispossessing his nephew Cynetha and blinding and emasculating him. After Owen's death, David, the third of his six sons, had in turn usurped the throne, kill-

ing his older brothers Yorwerth (Edward) and Hoel and imprisoning
or exiling the rest. Madoc, the youngest, had thereupon joined
forces with Cadwallon, the natural son of the wronged Cynetha,
and, with a band of hardy adventurers, had put to sea in search of a
newer world. Returning now to Wales in order to recruit additional
settlers for the colony he has succeeded in founding overseas,
Madoc arrives at ancient Mona (Anglesey) in time to witness the
marriage of his surly brother to a "Saxon" princess, Emma Plan-
tagenet, the sister of Henry II. During the wedding banquet, he
relates his adventures—much like Odysseus at Phaeacia, though
without the circumspection of the wily Greek.

After the fratricidal battle between David and Hoel, Madoc
begins rather undiplomatically, he had realized that his life was in
danger from the usurper. He had therefore resolved to leave the
strife-torn old world and to stake his fortunes on the noble
Cadwallon's Faustian theory "That yonder waters are not
spread / A boundless waste, a bourne impassable," but that "manly
courage, manly wisdom" would find "Some happy isle, some undiscovered shore, / Some resting-place for peace" beyond the
sunset (V, 36). Accompanied by old Cynetha, Madoc, Cadwallon,
and their followers had sailed West. After weeks of uncertainty,
storms, and threats of mutiny, they had come to an exotic shore
riotous with color and the flash of dolphins and fireflies and peo-
pled by noble, loin-clothed redskins. They had coasted along the
shore and were received hospitably by the children of the
wilderness. A captive of one of the tribes they visited, Lincoya,
became Madoc's man Friday and guided the Welsh adventurers up
the Mississippi—"By shores now covered with impervious
woods, / Now stretching wide and low, a reedy waste," and
through rich valleys, "League after league, one green and fertile
mead, / That fed a thousand herds"—to the dwellings of his own
people, the pastoral Hoamen.

This peaceful tribe, Madoc soon discovered, was tributary to the
noble but aggressive and priest-ridden nation of the Aztecas and
was forced to furnish victims for the sacrificial rites of the Aztec
idolatry (the action antedates the Aztec migration to Central
America). Arriving in time to save two children from the clutches of
an Aztec priest, Madoc persuaded the timid Hoamen and their
sorrowful dowager queen, Erillyab, to resist the oppressor; and he
resolved to go in person to Aztlan, the Aztec capital, to negotiate
with the Aztec king, Coanocotzin. Coanocotzin responded to

Madoc's ultimatum by taking him to the top of a huge temple to impress upon him the folly of provoking war: " 'They tell me that two floating palaces / Brought thee and all thy people: when I sound / The Tambour of the God, ten Cities hear / Its voice, and answer to the call in arms' " (58). Madoc viewed the imperial city—"her far-circling walls, / Her garden groves and stately palaces, / Her temple's mountain-side, her thousand roofs" and "battlements all burnished white, which shone / Like silver in the sunshine" (56)—and his mind misgave him. But the sight of heaps of human skulls and of the mummified corpse of Erillyab's husband made to serve as a lamp turned his doubt to indignation; there could be no peace until the practice of human sacrifice was abolished.

A vast army, arrayed in the pomp and pageantry of war, promptly advanced from Aztlan. But their numbers were no match for the strategically deployed forces of Madoc and his allies; their arrows and stone maces recoiled from the iron-clad ranks of the Welsh; and their own armor of wooden helmets and woven habergeons resplendent with gold and gorgeous plumery proved ineffectual against the Welsh swords and battle-axes, spears and longbow shafts. When, moreover, their king suddenly fell ill of a mysterious disease, their morale collapsed. Many were captured, including their gallant general, Yuhidthiton, and his brother Malinal; the rest were routed or killed. The prisoners expected to be sacrificed; but Madoc set them free with an offer of peace and further mollified the enemy by sending his leech, a man skilled in the lore of the "Sages and Bards of old," to heal the ailing Coanocotzin (69).

In the negotiations that followed, a rational compromise was struck. The Aztecs were to retain possession of the land, which they, in contrast to the shiftless nomadic Hoamen, had reclaimed and cultivated. But the Hoamen were to be free from bondage and tribute, and the infernal custom of human sacrifice was to be abolished. The priests at first demurred, afraid of the wrath of their baffled gods. But the venerable Cynetha exhorted them to renounce their bloodthirsty idols and to return to the Universal God of Natural Religion, once known to all nations, a God of love and kindness, rather than of fear and thraldom: " 'Him who laid / The deep foundations of the earth and built / The arch of heaven, and kindled yonder sun, / And breathed into the woods and waves and sky / The power of life' "—the Great Spirit " 'who in clouds / And storms, in mountain caves, and by the fall / Of waters, in the woodland solitude / And in the night and silence of the sky / Doth make his being felt' '' (74). Madoc's will and Cynetha's eloquence prevailed, and the hatchet was solemnly buried. "What followed was the work / Of peace, no theme for story" (79).

So ends Madoc's narration. The remainder of *Madoc in Wales* concerns the prince's endeavor to gain support for his colony among the disaffected nobles of Gwynned. The action not only provides pegs for Welsh scenery and "antiquities" but defines Madoc's enterprise, in three main scenes, in terms of both continuity with an older order and revolt against the present one. The first scene takes place at "ancient Mathraval." Madoc meets the famous Poet-Prince Owen Cyveilioc[7] and is advised to appeal to the *gorsedd*, or Congress of Bards, which is about to convene on a solitary hill nearby. Soon the "Bards of Britain," in their sky-blue robes, assemble solemnly at the "Druid circle," as of old, to initiate new aspirants to the "high degree and sacred privilege / Of Bardic science and of Cimbric lore" (93). As Madoc listens to the green-robed candidates' probation songs he is overcome with nostalgia for the old ways. But then Caradoc, the youngest but most gifted of the candidates, advances and turns the tide. Inspired by the "flow of waters" and the "motions of the moonlight sky," he sings of Madoc's Merlinian quest for a new world of Liberty, Peace, and Plenty, and rallies support for Madoc by declaring himself Madoc's follower in the task of renewing the glory of Arthur's people beyond the seas (94).

The second scene, added in revision, shifts the perspective. After an excursion to Deheubarth (South Wales), where he gains an unexpected ally in his exiled brother Ririd, Madoc crosses over to the Holy Isle of Bardsey, the burial ground of the Welsh chieftains and saints, to take leave of his "great progenitors." His "natural piety" prompts him to endow an annual requiem mass, whose "pomp and solemn circumstance," however, contrasts sharply with the simple dignity of the *gorsedd* and is described with typically Southeyan mixture of fidelity and condescension. Here Madoc also meets Llewelyn, the son of Yorwerth and rightful Prince of Wales, who is biding his time to regain the throne. Madoc urges him to join his exodus, but Llewelyn pleads his duty to Wales and to vengeance.

Revolt becomes explicit in the third scene at Bangor. Returning to Mona, Madoc first makes a sentimental stop at the mountain refuge where he had first met Cynetha and Cadwallon and finds the place occupied by a young woman and a boy. The lovely refugee turns out to be the great Hoel's mistress Llaian and his son, young

Hoel. Madoc joyfully takes them along. They pass through Bangor, just as Baldwin, the "Saxon Prelate" of Canterbury, is in the act of excommunicating Owen Cyveilioc with bell, book, and candle for his contumacious refusal to join the Crusades. When Madoc protests, the prelate sneers at his "barbarism" and orders him to abandon his impious New World enterprise and to take the cross instead. But Madoc is as good a British nationalist and crypto-Protestant as Joan of Arc had been a French one—a representative of the "pure faith" (108) which, Southey believed, derived from the "patriarchal" religion of Druidism and had made the Welsh Bards early champions against the "yoke / Of Rome."[8]

> 'Barbarians as we are,
> Lord Prelate, we received the law of Christ
> Many a long age before your pirate sires
> Had left their forest dens: nor are we now
> To learn [it] from . . . your mongrel race! . . . Tell
> Your Pope, that, when I sail upon the seas,
> I shall not strike a topsail for the breath
> Of all his maledictions!' (126f.)

Baldwin retaliates by removing from holy ground the remains of Owen Gwynned, on the pretext that Owen had been excommunicated for an "unlawful marriage." But Madoc learns of the plan and surprises the primate at the nocturnal disinterral. Threatening a general uprising, he cows him into surrendering the royal remains for secret transfer to the New World, where they are in due course deposited "by Cynetha's side . . . / All wrongs forgotten now . . . / From foul indignity of Romish pride / And bigot priesthood, from a falling land / Thus timely snatched" (225).

The Bangor episode, a favorite with Southey, completes both the hero's emancipation and the thematic development of the poem. At Mathraval, Madoc had been impaled on the horns of the Romantic dilemma, nostalgia for a glamorous past and longing for a Utopian future, until Caradoc showed him the way out by redefining the future *in terms* of the past. At Bardsey, "natural piety" performed an act of sunderance from both past and present. At Bangor, Heroic past and Republican future are fully reconciled, as Southey opposes his poem's theme of exodus to the crusader myth of Tasso.

Madoc now settles down for the winter at Mona. Both he and Emma, the queen, vainly try to get David to release Rodri, the remaining son of Owen. With spring come and the ships ready, Madoc once more pleads with the suspicious king and begs him to rule with justice and the love of his subjects rather than by force and fear and foreign allies. David's heart is softened to the extent that he orders Rodri released for deportation with Madoc. But his decision comes too late: Rodri has already escaped from prison.

There follows the embarkation of the colonists, a scene which Southey hoped would outdo Camoens' model in the fourth *Lusiad*. While the ships are readied—"Their sails all loose, their streamers rolling out / With sinuous flow and swell, like watersnakes / Curling aloft"—a mass is celebrated on shore, and then the adventurers embark: "Youth beauty, valour, virtue, reverend age,— / Some led by love of noble enterprise; / Others, who, desperate of their country's weal, / Fly from the impending yoke; all warm alike / With confidence and high heroic hope, / And all in one fraternal bond conjoined / By reverence to their Chief" (141). Among the voyagers are not only Madoc, Ririd, and their sister Goervyl; Llaian and young Hoel; and Caradoc, the young Bard; but also, unknown to him, Caradoc's childhood sweetheart, Senena, who has fled from a hateful impending marriage, disguised as a page, to follow her despairing lover.

As the ships glide out into the night, they are hailed by a boat. Rodri appears with Llewelyn, his gallant liberator, to bid Madoc farewell, since he is resolved to help his nephew depose the usurper and restore Wales to its rightful ruler. Madoc bewails the prospect of civil war; but Llewelyn (one day to be called the Great) assures him that he need not fear for Britain: "Though her Sun / Slope from her eminence, the voice of man / May yet arrest him on his downward way. / . . . The Bard of years to come, / Who harps of Arthur's and of Owen's deeds, / Shall with the worthies of his country rank / Llewelyn's name. Dear uncle, fare thee well" (147).

The speech makes for a rather ironic conclusion to Part One. Evidently intended to exempt the hero from any charge of deserting his country in an hour of need, it in effect fairly undercuts the earlier apotheosis of Madoc's cause as a Mosaic, or Noachic, exodus from a doomed world by juxtaposing it to the advent of a Messianic, Arthur-like king come to restore his people by restoring the legitimate succession, a Bardic Joshua able to make the sun stand still in heaven. The precariousness of Llewelyn's image may hint at the futility of his optimism; and, indeed, we know from history—and from Gray's *Bard*—that the hoped-for renascence did not last and that the sun arrested by one Llewelyn went down with another less than a century later. Nevertheless, Southey's Republican fable here unexpectedly reverts to the royalist ideal of traditional epic, with the effect that Madoc himself dwindles from a true Utopian into an adventurer and colonialist.

Without this shift of emphasis, Southey would perhaps have done well to have ended the poem here. In its larger framework of Welsh history, the American adventure and its clash of cultures is interesting and is comparable in purpose and proportion, if not in power and dramatic nuance, to Odysseus' exotic flashback narrative at the court of Phaeacia. The Welsh narrative itself is shaped more by scenic and antiquarian than by epic impulses and as a result is somewhat desultory for a hero's story, as well as of doubtful historicity; but it appeals to a variety of Romantic interests—patriotic and picturesque, sentimental and libertarian. And though, as always, thought tends to be commonplace and pathos shortwinded, the quality of the writing is almost uniformly high, and there are memorable and moving passages of description and rhetoric, as well as suggestive images, such as those of the setting and rising sun, or that of the lone beaver trying to repair his dams (99). A concentrated effort to tighten the structure, to add dimension to character, and to transform curious data imaginatively into expressive symbols might have resulted in a poem of enduring interest. The uncertainty of Madoc's success or failure, moreover, would not only have accorded with what history knows of him but would have left the reader elated with a sense of promise and fearful chance beyond the moonlit waves.

Quite apart from the fact, however, that the poem was from the start meant to be primarily about America, it was not in Southey's expansive nature to forego a more detailed description of Aztec religion and manners than the flashback could accommodate or to pass up the chance to depict a ponderous campaign against priestcraft and superstition in the name of a sentimental Christian rationalism. Thus the reader may not stay behind to watch the hero fade, like Tennyson's Ulysses, into the vastness of an uncertain destiny, but is forcibly carried along to the undiscovered country to witness the profusion of events and circumstances that make up the "Iliad part" of the poem: *Madoc in Aztlan.*

III   Madoc *in Aztlan*

Southey's epic thereby becomes, in fact, the crowning effort of eighteenth-century English literature to deal poetically with the

American Indian; coinciding, as it did, with the Lewis and Clark Expedition, it was also the last.[9] Indians had figured in English literature since the middle of the seventeenth century as part of the stock-in-trade of heroic-exotic drama and romance. In the eighteenth century, the Red Man appeared not only in plays and operas but in narrative and lyrical poetry, in prose fiction, and in Utopian and satirical literature. The most popular Indian nation was that of the Peruvians: their sufferings under Spanish greed and fanaticism exercized sentimentalists from William Davenant to Richard Brinsley Sheridan and Helen Maria Williams, and their sun worship and Inca government enchanted an age obsessed with reason, natural religion, and the *rêve exotique*. Few works, of course, did justice to the Indian: blood-thirsty, devil-worshipping Hobbist brutes take turns with the Noble Savage of sentimental primitivism. *Madoc*, too, is not above reproach in this respect. Though an expert on both Spanish and English sources, Southey does not really transcend the stereotypes but often merely intermingles "savagism" and primitivism. However, his shift of scene from Peru represents a break with cliché, and his characters afford at least glimpses of cultural and psychic forces beyond simple abstractions.

To be specific: Madoc, upon returning to the New World, discovers that the "Violence and bloody Zeal" he sought to escape from (113) are in fact inescapable. His settlement, Caermadoc, is prospering; but relations with the natives have become strained. The Aztecas, predictably, have returned to their old superstitions, swayed by the hocus-pocus of their wily, dispossessed priests. The restoration of the bloody rites proceeds at first in secret and under a show of continued cordiality; but presently Yuhidthiton, the noble but misguided Aztec general, declares openly his people's return to the worship of the gods of their fathers and revokes the peace, despite Madoc's attempts to dissuade him. Yuhidthiton's young brother Malinal alone remains loyal to the Britons.

To make matters worse, trouble is also brewing among the Hoamen. Neolin, a self-proclaimed shaman of the "Snake God," insists that the god has possessed him during his mystic vigils to demand his ancient tribute:

> 'It came to me
> In darkness, after midnight, when the moon
> Was gone, and all the stars were blotted out;

> It gathered round me with a noise of storms,
> And entered into me, and I could feel
> It was the Snake-God rolled and writhed within;
> And I, too, with the inward agony,
> Rolled like a snake, and writhed. "Give, give!" he cried:
> "I thirst." His voice was in me, and it burnt
> Like fire, and all my flesh and bones were shaken.
>
> . . . .
>
> Sons of the Ocean! why should we forsake
> The worship of our fathers? Ye obey
> The White Man's Maker; but to us was given
> A different skin and speech and land and law.
> The Snake-God understands the Red Man's prayer,
> And knows his wants, and loves him. Shame to us,
> That . . . we have let his lips be dry!' (215 - 8)

Abetted by the degenerate son of Queen Erillyab, Amalahta, who at once hates the strangers and lusts for Madoc's sister Goervyl, Neolin easily imposes on the credulous Hoamen, who, having learned from their late "Beloved Teacher" Cynetha to look on their old gods as Evil Ones, begin to fear that even devils must have their due.

During the annual "Feast of Souls," when the Indians assemble the shriveled corpses of the year's dead for interment at their ancient burial ground—"a deep and shady dell, / Fronting a cavern in the rock,—the scene / Of many bloody rites ere Madoc came,— / A temple, as they deemed, by Nature made, / Where the Snake-Idol stood" (235)—Neolin, with a mad shriek, proclaims the presence of the God and with a "long, shrill, piercing, modulated cry," causes a huge serpent to emerge from the cave and coil around him. The priest demands "Blood for the God," snatches up a little boy, and in a whirling ritual dance throws him to the sacred monster. Madoc confronts the frenzied worshippers, denounces Neolin as a traitor, and vows to feed him in turn to his fetish. The priest welcomes such a fate as a "consummation" and reward of his faith—"to rest in him, / Body with body be incorporate, / Soul into soul absorbed, and I and He / One Life, inseparable, for evermore" (241). But he promptly uses the awe that his show of "fortitude" has evoked even in Madoc to lure the serpent forth again and to demand Madoc's blood. Madoc thereupon kills both Neolin and the monster—the latter in a manner reminiscent of Hercules' fight with Cacus in the eighth *Aeneid*—and consigns them to a pyre, together with the

Snake God idol he found in the cave. The Hoamen, overawed by the "mighty Deicide," are duly converted and baptized.

At Aztlan, meanwhile, altars have been wreathed and human victims readied for the annual visit of the Aztec gods: of Tezcatlipoca, "Maker he / And Master of created things," who "sits upon a throne of trophied skulls, / Hideous and huge" (206); of the wind god Quetzalcoatl; of Tlaloc, the god of waters; and, above all, of Mexitli, "woman-born, who from the womb, / Child of no mortal sire, leaped terrible" (257).[10] But though twilight begins to fall on the worshippers as they wait nervously amid the uproar of song, pipe, and drumbeat and the glare of sacrificial fires, no sign of theophany occurs. At length, Tezozomoc, the High Priest, appears, ghastly from ten months of vicarious penance for the iniquities of his people. The gods will not come, he proclaims, until they have been propitiated by the strangers' blood. So Coatlantona (Coatlicue), "the gentle mother of [the] guardian God" Mexitli, has revealed to him in a trance (263). A truculent young warhawk, Tlalala, thereupon offers to capture a "stranger's child" for the gods and is seconded by his friend Ocellopan. The pair ascend the great *teocalli* to "devote [themselves] to Heaven" before the grisly image of Mexitli. The chiefs mingle their blood in a golden bowl, which the High Priest consecrates and then gives to the two young warriors to drink. Suddenly, the eternal flame leaps up, signaling the presence of the god. The victims are cast into the fire, and the plumed and panoplied chieftains perform the sacred dance of the "mystic wheel."

From theopathy and theomachy the narrative now shifts to military action. The two young Aztecs succeed in capturing not only young Hoel but Madoc himself. While a procession of hymning temple virgins carries the child to be immured alive as a victim to Tlaloc, Madoc is chained to the great altar stone and is forced to undergo a series of sacrificial single combats, which Southey describes with Homeric gusto. Fortunately, the ritual is interrupted by the arrival of the Welsh fighting force under Cadwallon; and Madoc is freed by the gentle daughter of a priest, Coatel, a one-time ritual spouse of Lincoya and now his secret bride. Coatel also enables Madoc to free the terrified Hoel. At the same time, the treacherous Amalahta attacks the now defenseless Caermadoc in order to carry off the Welshmen's wine and women; but he is routed by the Welsh under the spirited leadership of the loyal Malinal, Madoc's sister Goervyl, and the devoted Senena, still disguised as a page. Madoc eventually reaches the battlefield of Aztlan, where Cadwallon's Welsh and Lincoya's Hoamen have been fighting all night by moonlight and the distant glare of the sacrificial flames. Fired on by their fanatical priests, the Aztecs are still holding out, despite heavy losses; but their resistance collapses when Madoc kills their king Coanocotzin in single combat and, having hacked his way into the city and the temple precinct, succeeds in smashing the idol of Mexitli.

While the Britons cleanse the battlefield of its corpses and raze the temples of Aztlan, and Aztecs gather in the nearby city of Patamba to cremate their slain chieftains and to sacrifice the chieftains' wives and slaves. The rite completed, Yuhidthiton is acclaimed as the new king, annointed and crowned by the priests, and sworn "to protect thy subjects, to maintain / The worship of thy fathers, to observe / Their laws, to make the Sun pursue his course, / The clouds descend in rain, the rivers hold / Their wonted channels, and the fruits of earth / To ripen in their season" (338). Morale is fully restored when, during the ensuing games, acrobatics, and maze dances, the temple of Mexitli suddenly seems to be shrouded in flames and the smashed idol of the god mysteriously reappears undamaged.

The Aztecs thereupon set out to regain the capital. An embassy sent to Aztlan to demand the withdrawal of the Welsh from Aztec soil draws a firm reply from Madoc: "To this goodly land / Your fathers came for an abiding-place, / Strangers, like us, but not, like us, in peace. / . . . Bloody and faithless, to the hills they drove / The unoffending children of the vale, / And, day by day, in cruel sacrifice / Consumed them." Now "God hath sent the Avengers here." There will be no peace with the "tyrant race" until "they bow the knee, or leave the land to us, / Its worthier Lords" (360). In answer, the Aztecs launch a massive attack from the lake.

> Their thousand boats, and the ten thousand oars
> From whose broad bowls the waters fall and flash,
> And twice ten thousand feathered helms, and shields,
> Glittering with gold and scarlet plumery.
> Onward they come with song and swelling horn;
> While, louder than all voice and instrument,
> The dash of their ten thousand oars, from shore
> To shore, and hill to hill, re-echoing rolls,
> In indistinguishable peals of sound
> And endless echo. (363f.)

But unknown to the Indians, the Welsh have in the meantime dismantled their ships, transported the parts overland, and reassembled them on the lake of Aztlan—a small-scale imitation of Cortez' celebrated logistical feat. Like Cortez, Madoc is thus able to rout the enemy by simply ramming their boats and sending thousands to Tlaloc and the fishes.

Even now the Aztecs' will to resist is unbroken, at least among the leaders, though they are divided about the proper course of action. While the high priest Tezozomoc counsels dissimulation and treachery, Yuhidthiton insists that the will of the gods and the nation's destiny are to be ascertained honorably in open battle. The decision is taken out of their hands by the turn of events. According to the Aztec calendar, an age is about to end in a cataclysm that may extinguish the sun and destroy mankind. To insure the sun's renewal, the priests, gashed and smeared with witch's brew, prepare to burn a live victim at the summit of a sacred mountain, while the townspeople veil their women's faces and extinguish all fires in the city. Southey, who had already alluded to this custom in *Joan of Arc* (I, 120), describes it vividly and suspensefully, contrasting man's superstitious fears with the serenity of unconscious nature. "Westward the Sun proceeds; the tall tree casts / A longer shade; the night-eyed insect tribes / Wake to their portion of the circling hours; / The waterfowl, retiring to the shore, / Sweep in long files the surface of the lake." Fearfully the Aztecs watch "the spreading glories" of the sunset.

> And, when at length the hastening orb hath sunk
> Below the plain . . . still on the light,
> The last green light that lingers in the West,
> Their looks are fastened, till the clouds of night
> Roll on, and close in darkness the whole heaven.
> Then ceased their song; then o'er the crowded vale
> No voice of man was heard. Silent and still
> They stood, all turned toward the East, in hope
> There on the holy mountain to behold
> The sacred fire, and know that once again
> The Sun begins his stately round of years. (373, 375f.)

Instead of the sacrificial flame, however, a flood of lava suddenly erupts from the mountain and engulfs the wretched Tezozomoc and his crew, while, below, Patamba is buried beneath the waters of the flooding lake.

Convinced at last of heaven's disfavor, Yuhidthiton resolves to yield and to depart with the remnant of his people. Tlalala urges continued resistance; but the king, pointing to Madoc's galleys as they busily search the lake for survivors, repudiates further war against the "noble enemies." Sending out messengers to all the tribes, he gathers the bold and hardy about Mexitli's image for the historic southward migration and consigns the rest to Madoc's care and "easy yoke." As the march gets underway, Tlalala announces that he will neither leave nor outlive his country and strides off to kill himself. Even the sight of his boy and his wife Ilanquel, both rescued by Madoc's ships, cannot shake his resolution. He commends them to Madoc's protection and falls upon his javelin, after having first, in a fine poetic gesture, veiled Ilanquel's face with his mantle: " 'Woman, thou mayst not look upon the Sun, / Who sets to rise no more' " (392).

Ironically, thus, *Madoc in Aztlan* ends with an exodus and a setting sun, just as *Madoc in Wales* did. But the poles are now reversed. If the exodus from Wales had been dwarfed by the prospect of a messianic restoration in Wales itself, it is now the founding of the new kingdom that is undercut by the exile of the Noble Savage—the victory of Aeneas by the defeat of Turnus. More properly, the moral issue, already ambivalent in *Madoc in Wales*, between Kingdom and Exile—between Pharaoh and Moses, as it were—is now decided largely in favor of the former. Moses-Madoc establishes himself as an enlightened Pharaoh and prospers. At the same time, Aztec Pharaoh turns into a Moses of idolatrous fanaticism and priest-rule—who is to be put down in time by the "heroic Spaniard's unrelenting sword" when Heaven, as Southey rather appallingly concludes, will make "blind Zeal and bloody Avarice / Its ministers of vengeance" (392). Such, it seems, are the exigencies of progress.

The effect of these reverses on the reader, however, is less one of conscious irony than one of ambivalence and conflicting intentions. Primitivism alternates with savagism, and what began as a myth of Utopian revolt winds up as a saga of the White Man's burden. Vacillating between the two conceptions, Southey lacks the skeptical integrity that enabled a Byron or Keats to see and engage both sides of a question dialectically.

In striking contrast to Byron's ironic claim that his *Don Juan* was an "epic" composed "with strict regard to Aristotle's rules," Southey asserts solemnly that *Madoc* "assumes not the degraded title of Epic" and is therefore not subject to "the rules of Aristotle"

(9).[11] Despite such anti-Classical bluster, however, Southey does not fully free himself from the conventions and stereotypes that always tend to survive an exploded ideal. Though the hero's struggle is initially against Empire, his story is still essentially one of conquest and establishment. Likewise, much of the action is still military, though the poem's avowed values are agrarian and missionary: the "work of peace" is "no theme for story." As in mock-epic, intention clashes with convention; but unlike the mock-epic, there is no firm ironic resolution of the discrepancy.

Madoc himself, like Joan before him, is ostensibly a pacifist and republican whose aim is to be good rather than to be great. Yet much of his action is that of a charismatic military leader, and at the crucial moment he decides the issue by single combat like any traditional hero, and does so without apparent scruple. Interestingly enough, Southey's *Commonplace Book* outline of the poem did not provide for the slaying of Coanocotzin but had Madoc appear at the battle solely to placate the Welsh hawks and persuade them to withdraw (IV, 204). Clearly, however, Southey found himself unequal to the task of rendering "goodness" without the glamor of "greatness," and Madoc thus became both a regicide and even a "Deicide." Southey tried to confront this dilemma belatedly in his "Anglo-American Iliad" (*Letters*, II, 213), *Oliver Newman* (1811 - 29), a poem set in New England during King Philip's War, whose titular hero, an ex-Cromwellian and son of the regicide Goffe, rises from the ruins of the Commonwealth to become the New Man and "a new character in heroic poetry": the hero of non-violence (X, 351). The poem tellingly remained a fragment.

As elsewhere, moreover, both art and scholarship in *Madoc* are impaired by a rationalistic absolutism and ethnocentrism only less exclusive than the religious absolutism that Southey so abhorred. Out to mind the manners of other nations, Southey finds them interesting only for their quaint or lurid barbarism and consequently renders them an object, at times of horrified fascination, but more often of mere smug curiosity and, in the footnotes, of pedantic garrulousness. Despite his claim to historical accuracy, he does not scruple to mix genuine Indian "manners" with customs reported of the Arabs or the Chinese, customs that are comparable only in their common remoteness from European habits and from an abstract philosophical ideal. Moreover, though fairly faithful and often picturesque in describing the external forms of religious rituals and the like, Southey does little to probe into their inner spirit, whether to comprehend the appalling mystery of human sacrifices or to ponder the sources of religious phenomena in general.

A case in point is the Snake God incident, which was Southey's favorite episode in the poem, together with the disinterment of Owen. Both the poet and the anthropologist in Southey endeavor to do justice to Neolin and to depict him as a sincere and in some way impressive, if brutally misguided, fanatic—as when Neolin asserts the Red Man's right to his own gods, voices his eagerness to be reunited with his totem, or solemnly derives his sacerdotal authority from an original oneness with it: " 'Before this generation, and before / These ancient forests,—yea, before yon lake / Was hollowed out, or one snowfeather fell / On yonder mountain-top, now never bare,— / Before these things I was. . . . / And I beheld the Spirit, and in him / Saw all things, even as they were to be' " (216). The upshot, however, is not any sustained insight into a people's collective unconscious—their Idols of the Tribe—but merely a crasser version of the Bangor episode: the hero's defying and overcoming of a priest, that archbogy and scapegoat of Enlightenment criticism. For all his professed interest in Indian beliefs, Southey is only too quick to diabolize them into the blasphemous lies of fiendish "miscreants." Like Arvalan or the demon of "Rudiger," Neolin's Snake-God remains a melodramatic projection of the poet's own puerile obsessions—an Idol of the Cave, indeed.

What specifically hamstrings Southey's anthropology and keeps him a prisoner of simple dualisms is the absence of any evolutionary philosophy. While pioneers like David Hume or J. G. Herder had long since begun to understand religious thought as something evolved from more primitive intimidations, Southey still clings to the conventional notion of "superstition" as the corruption of a pristine universal truth (natural religion or primitive monotheism). He would have been as much appalled at the thought of any kinship between the beliefs of a Neolin or Tezozomoc and the Apostles' Creed as a generation later Bishop Wilberforce was at the imputation of his descent from an ape. In consequence, the "pure faith" that Madoc preaches to the Hoamen is not only radically opposed to the "pomp of hellish piety" of the Indians (207) but—besides being strongly authoritarian for all its emphasis on love and charity—bears only a nominal resemblance to twelfth-century Catholicism. It is, instead, essentially Southey's own ideal of rational religion, dressed out with a few Catholic trappings and rationalized as the "patriarchal" faith. Catholicism was, as Southey repeatedly observed, too much like the "Mexican idolatry" to be anything but compromising to a Southeyan hero.

The capital charge against Southey is thus not that he is too remote but that, instead of exploring the remote sympathetically in order to discover its humanity, he merely surveys it by present standards of the parish in order to annex and convert it or else to declare it a desert for scapegoats. Southey not only lost his way in Utopia to find it in Old Sarum, he left the strait path to Cosmopolis for the beaten track of Empire and Mission.

The same narrow rationalism governs Southey's conception of character. "A common magician can make snow-people, but flesh and blood must be the work of a Demiurgos," Southey wrote of the difference between *Thalaba* and *Madoc* (*Memoir*, II, 110f.). Yet the main characters of his epic are almost as underdeveloped and overdetermined as are those of his romances—either paragons of virtue without passion and self-interest except for the most innocuous of sentimental affections, or, like Amalahta, the direct contrary. We may note in particular that early plot-sketches had provided for several interracial marriages: Madoc was to marry Erillyab, and his sister and Cadwallon were to have native spouses as well. But, in the poem, all this happy miscegenation is omitted, except for a conditional betrothal between Goervyl and Malinal. Lincoya and Coatel, moreover, end tragically—Coatel is sacrificed for her part in Madoc's escape, and her lover, upon hearing the news, leaps over a convenient precipice to join his bride in the Land of Souls. Only the insipid and confessedly tangential Caradoc-Senena episode was allowed to supply a vague carnal interest. Sex is the mark of a beast like Amalahta.

Accordingly, Southey firmly rejected William Taylor's remark that Platonic affection was not in the nature of savages and that therefore Erillyab's feelings for Madoc should have been purely "Didonic"; and, where Taylor thought that the queen should side with her son, Southey at one time planned to have her "put Amalahta to death with her own hands." Evidently he preferred "savage heroism" in behalf of abstract moral principles to the unprincipled kindness of the blood. He eventually compromised by postponing Erillyab's arrival on the combat scene and dispatching Amalahta instead by the joint knock-down, drag-out action of Goervyl, Senena, and the wounded Malinal. But he always disliked the substitution, whereas it now seems, in its unheroic messiness, one of the most credible episodes in the poem.[12] Southey never outgrew the crippling habit of evading moral ambiguity by means of simple stances and simple, mutually exclusive alternatives of impulse and principle. Personality for him implies almost invariably a deviation from some abstract norm that is morally reprehensible in direct proportion as it is colorful and vital. There may be conversion, but there is no growth and little inner conflict. Even Yuhidthiton is not so much a complex character as he is a centaur of nobility and superstition. Only Tlalala, the "savage Regulus," wooden as he, too, is, approaches an integrity beyond facile dichotomies.

Maloc must thus be said to fail not only as a great poem but also as an endeavor to transcend the age's simplifications about the Indian. "The savage and civilised state," Southey wrote, "are alike unnatural, alike unworthy of the origin and end of man" (*Life*, I, 317). Such a view leaves the poet of "manners" to talk about what he cannot value and to oppose it to some vague "natural" ideal he cannot imagine concretely and credibly. *Madoc* is a colorful work, rich in contrasts and superficial excitement whenever, as in depicting the barbaric splendor of war or the mystic fervor of a Neolin or Tlalala, the poet gets the better of the moralist. In some ways, the poem even adumbrates the tragic vision of progress of, say, Keats's *Hyperion*. But Southey was no "camelion Poet" able to empathize with both foul and fair, and he had no clear evolutionary philosophy to supply the want of imagination.[13]

CHAPTER 6

Lucifer in Spain: Roderick and the Laureate Verse

I Southey and the Peninsula

O F the places associated with Southey's life and writings, none is so uniquely his own as the Iberian Peninsula. There he had fled from the ruins of Pantisocracy and had found his paradise, Cintra. There, at the same time, he had observed at close range the evils bred, or at least condoned, by Catholicism, an experience which so confirmed his Protestant and Enlightenment anti-clericalism that he remained an enemy of Catholic Emancipation even after it had become a liberal cause. There, also, he became steeped in the Spanish and Portuguese authors of his uncle's extensive library and developed both his interest in empire and his passion for books. So immersed, he at last resolved to become "a Portuguese student among the mountains" (Life, II, 281), to tend and enlarge his uncle's already unique collection (now become his), and to utilize its resources—and his own proficiency in Spanish and Portuguese—to describe and interpret Iberian culture and history to his countrymen.[1]

The most substantial early results of this undertaking, not counting purely journalistic publications, were Southey's prose renditions of Anadis of Gaul (1803), Palmerin of England (1807), and The Cid (1808)—the three romances of chivalry which even the anti-romantic Cervantes had thought worth preserving.[2] Of these, Southey's Cid is the most faithful to the original (the other two are somewhat bowdlerized) and the one most likely to interest the modern reader. It is mainly a translation of the sixteenth-century Chronica del Cid, to Southey "one of the finest things in the world" (Life, III, 171); but it also draws on a variety of other sources, including the earlier Poema del Cid, popular ballads and romances,

128

and several chronicles, all collated with a scholar's patience, and copiously annotated. The result is a comprehensive account of the Spanish hero—indeed, "a complete view of the heroic age of Spain" (*Memoir*, II, 193).

The prose style Southey developed for these works is modeled on Malory, the sixteenth-century English chroniclers, and the great Bible translations. It is vigorous, paratactic, matter-of-fact, and just quaint enough to suggest the era of the *Chronica* without impeding ready comprehension:

And the Cid having it at heart to take the town [of Valencia] . . . let make three engines, and placed them at the three gates of the town, and they did marvelous great hurt. And food waxed dearer every day, till at last dear nor cheap it was not to be had, and there was great mortality for famine; and they ate dogs and cats and mice. And they opened the vaults and privies and sewers of the town, and took out the stones of the grapes which they had eaten, and washed them, and ate them. And they who had horses fed on them. And many men, and many women, and many children watched when the gates were open, and went out and gave themselves into the hands of the Christians, who slew some, and took others, and sold them to the Moors of Alcudia; and the price of a Moor was a loaf and a pitcher of wine: and when they gave them food and they took their fill, they died.[3]

The romances were well received, and *The Cid* in particular was universally praised as a masterpiece of translation and is still serviceable today.

Publications like *The Cid*, with all their apparatus, were, however, mere "preliminaries" to Southey's projected *opus maximum*, the "History of Portugal," the "Pyramid labor" that he hoped would be the supreme vindication of his life of letters. Conceived, like Gibbon's great work, in essentially epic terms, the "History" was to supersede Camoens' *Lusiad* as well as Gibbon's *Decline*. It would replace Gibbon's centripetal and classical model of Roman civilization by Camoens' expansive Renaissance ideals of knight and navigator, chivalry and commerce, but would temper these with Gibbonian critiques of the evils of barbarism and fanaticism. Relatively isolated from the rest of Europe, Portugal promised epic "wholeness and unity" in her history. At the same time, she could be viewed as a kind of microcosm of Europe at large. Her epic rise to power and the "gradual destruction of [her] noble national character" by the "cancer of Romish superstition"

made her an important object lesson, and the "detestable barbarity" of her colonial exploits would serve as a warning to Britain,
her imperial successor in the India of Tippoo Sahib. Besides, she
was virgin ground for an English historian. By adding the
strangeness of novelty to the beauty of ancient truth, Southey could
hope to produce a work such "as the world has never yet seen."[4]

Ironically, the world never did see it. Southey left it unfinished at
death, and only a small part of what must have been a voluminous
manuscript is extant.[5] In the meantime, however, events were bearing out Southey's historical perspective; for the Spanish Peninsula
was about to become the scene of Napoleon's peripety and a prime
cause of his downfall. By occupying allied Spain in March, 1808, ostensibly to marshall forces against Portugal, and by then using internal dissension to place his brother Joseph on the Spanish throne,
Napoleon precipitated the popular uprising of the *dos de mayo*
which not only escalated into a costly and ultimately fatal war—the
first guerilla war in history—but awakened a subjected Europe to
the realization that the giant was not invincible and that a national,
popular effort might accomplish what imperial armies had failed to
do. Moreover, the attack on Portugal provoked Portugal's old ally,
England, hitherto satisfied with its maritime sovereignty, to enter
into a landwar that ended only at Waterloo. Between August, 1808,
when the British first landed in Portugal and defeated the French at
Vimeiro, and the summer of 1813, when they won the decisive battle of Vittoria and prepared to invade France—at least until
Napoleon's Russian disaster roused the Continental powers—the
Peninsula was the spot where Europe's political destiny hung chiefly in the balance.

Southey early foresaw the fateful issue of what he came to regard
as the "most glorious war recorded in the British annals" (*Letters,*
III, 318), and he eagerly engaged his pen in its behalf. From the
middle of 1809 until the end of 1812, he chronicled the events of
the war in John Ballantyne's *Edinburgh Annual Register*—an enterprise that established him as a columnist and prose-writer of rank
and that eventually resulted in the three-volume *History of the
Peninsular War* (1823 - 32). At the same time, he commemorated
the victories and defeats of that bloody struggle—Coruna, Talavera,
Torres Vedras, Ciudad Rodrigo—in a series of inscriptions and
epitaphs, as well as in his first laureate poem, the *Carmen
Triumphale.* Only an epic, however, could do full justice to the
momentous events of the time and, by evoking the great heroic

past, put them into proper perspective and thereby rouse the nation to a sense of its duty and destiny.

Southey, to be sure, had begun to feel forsaken by the muse. The time was past when he all but lived on the "nitrous oxide" of poetry and immortal fame. The careless happiness of the grasshopper—"singing merrily among the canes, God bless him!"—had had to yield to the drudgery of the ant; and *Madoc* and *Thalaba*, were moldering on the shelves, bringing neither fortune nor fame. But now there was a "glorious revolution in Spain," a "holy War" of "virtue against vice, light against darkness, the good principle against the evil one"—a fire that would consume Bonaparte and, at the same time, clear the ground for a Republican form of government! "The truth of the present history," Southey wrote in July, 1808, "is, that a great military despotism in its youth and full vigor—like that of France—will and must beat down corrupt establishments and worn-out governments, but that it cannot beat down a true love of liberty, and a true spirit of patriotism." Spain and Portugal, cleansed by the fire of war, would unite in a commonwealth or federal republic! "Since the stirring days of the French Revolution I have never felt half so much excitements in political events." "Nitrous oxide" was still to be had![6]

What plainer duty, then, could the poet have—especially at the moment when England seemed to have "betrayed the cause of Spain and Portugal" at the Convention of Cintra—than to rally support for that cause by recalling the betrayal of Spain to the Enemy of Christendom, the Moors, in the days of yore and by extolling her heroic struggle against that deadly foe? The retelling of the deeds of Spain's national hero, the Cid, had been a timely first step: "Ruy Diez, dead as he is, will do more against Bonaparte than all the kings of Europe have done." But something more was needed. Southey would therefore once more write an epic of foundation—a "poem upon Pelayo, the restorer of Spain," a song about the passing of the old, feudal, order and about the birth of a new one out of the holocaust of foreign domination.[7]

II Roderick

Plans for such a poem had in fact been ripening for some time. Southey had first explored the subject in 1802 in the "monodrama" on the legendary Cava, "Spain's Helen" (as Cervantes calls her), whose rape by the Gothic king Rodrigo had supposedly led to the

Moorish invasion. By 1805, he had resolved to crown his epic series with a poem on the same subject to be called "Pelayo," in which he would not only set forth the "Catholic mythology" but would exhibit those "strong feelings and passions" which he admitted had been wanting in his previous epics. The events following upon the *dos de mayo* finally provided the necessary spark, but also a new emphasis. Now entitled "Pelayo" or "Spain Restored," the poem, as begun in the summer of 1808, was primarily revolutionary in outlook. Its titular hero, the leader of the *reconquista* and founder of the Spanish monarchy (718 - 37), would be closely akin to the Joan of Arc of fifteen years earlier, a noble youth sent by heaven to liberate the country from foreign yoke and to initiate a new, indigenous order. Roderick, the royal ravisher, would be the villainous embodiment of the *ancien régime*.

Between that conception, however, and its execution fell the shadow of events that speedily converted Southey from the impenitent "heretic" and "Jacobin" he had still called himself until then (*New Letters*, I, 511) into the monarchist and authoritarian of his laureate years. In 1810 he had still been able to welcome the young Shelley in Keswick as the "ghost" of his own past (*Life*, III, 325). That ghost now faded before the terrifying specter of mob rule and "bellum servile" raised by the Burdett and Luddite riots and by the assassination of the prime minister Spencer Perceval.[8] As a result, Southey's poem assumed a different, essentially royalist complexion. The restoration of the monarchy, an embarrassed concession to history in *Joan of Arc* and a side issue in *Madoc*, now became a central theme. The hero, Pelayo, is not only king-maker to his son-in-law, Alphonso I of Leon, but is himself a king by dynastic prerogative as much as by popular acclamation. Moreover, the young hero is in turn outshone by a new interest in his predecessor on the throne, Roderick, the last of the Visigothic kings, the original villain. By showing Roderick as "more sinned against than sinning" (IX, 173) and by improving upon the penitential posthumous existence ascribed to him by monkish chroniclers, Southey exonerates both him and monarchy as such. "Pelayo or Spain Restored" thus became *Roderick, the Last of the Goths, a Tragic Poem* (1814).

The resultant double plot grows out of two sets of events. The immediate point of departure is the collapse of the Visigothic monarchy under the Moorish invasion which, according to tradition, had been instigated by the powerful renegade Count Julian in retaliation for the rape of his daughter Florinda by Roderick.

Behind that picturesque foreground, a dimmer but equally important backdrop reveals itself gradually by means of flashback, allusion, and inset story—a tale of internal dissension, dynastic conflict, and "Treason, like an old and eating sore" having sapped the country's strength from within (17). After a prolonged dynastic rivalry, we learn, Witiza had succeeded Chindasuintho as king of Spain and had disposed of Chindasuintho's sons by blinding one, Theodofred, and by murdering the other, Favila—the latter at the instigation of Favila's wife, who had become his mistress. Pelayo, the young son of Favila, had fled into exile. But Roderick, his older cousin, had recovered the throne and avenged his father's blindness on Witiza. Unhappily, Roderick spared Witiza's brother Orpas, the Archbishop of Seville, as well as Ebba and Sisibert, the offspring of Witiza's adulterous union with Pelayo's mother. All three in time turned renegades and abetted Julian's betrayal of Spain to the Moors.

The poem opens with the Gothic overthrow at the eight-day battle on the Guadalete (711 A.D.). Following the tradition of the monkish *Chronica del Rey Don Rodrigo* that Roderick had not died in that battle but had escaped to become a hermit, Southey depicts the unhappy king as abandoning his battle-steed and war-gear at the moment of evident defeat and fleeing in peasant garb through the ravaged country. From the beginning, Roderick is characterized as conscious-stricken and remorseful. His days are filled with anguish at the suffering and desolation he feels he has caused. His nights are haunted by visions of bleeding Saviors and ravenous fiends—remnants of the "Catholic mythology" once contemplated—and above all by the damning image of the violated Florinda.

He is eventually comforted by an aged, saintly monk, Romano, whom he finds in a deserted monastery awaiting martyrdom from the Moors and who resolves to forego that luxury in order to minister to the king. The two men escape to a hermitage on the west coast, where Romano eventually dies. Roderick, now alone and burdened with himself and nature's indifference to his "human form divine," wavers between self-vindication and despair and struggles to ward off temptation by mortifying his flesh and praying to the blessed "father" Romano. One night, however, his mother Rusilla appears to him in a dream. She is mournful and in shackles. But when she calls on Pelayo for deliverance, her chains break and her widow's weeds change to radiant armor: "A bloody Cross / Gleamed on her breastplate . . . her helmed head / Rose

like the Berecynthian Goddess crowned / With towers; and in her
dreadful hand the sword / Red as a firebrand blazed" (33).
Southey's monkish source represented similar visions as diabolic
delusions designed to tempt Rodrigo from his path of penitence.
Southey's Roderick, however, regards the dream as a sign from
heaven to quit his life of solitude and inhuman discipline, as
Romano had once given up his martydom, in order to aid his
mother and his country. Salvation is to be earned by service to man
rather than by the barren self-torment of the anchorite.

From here on, Roderick's movements are freely invented. Aged
and emaciated beyond recognition, the king begs his way north
through the occupied country to mountainous and unsubdued Can-
tabria. In the ruins of recently sacked Auria, he comes upon a young
woman named Adosinda, who is in the midst of burying her husband, child, and parents. The scene is notable for its vindictive
spirit. The sole survivor of the city, Adosinda relates how the
Moorish captain had spared her to be his concubine but had
respected her request for time to mourn her dead, and how she had
thereupon beheaded the "loathsome villain" in his sleep. The fury
of this Judith rekindles the "pride and power of former majesty" in
Roderick sanctified now by "duty and high heroic purposes." He
joins her in dedication to bloody revenge, a duty, as she puts it, inspired alike by "Love, hatred, joy, and anguish and despair / And
hope and natural piety and faith" (48f.). Since Roderick refuses to
reveal his name, Adosinda baptizes him "Maccabee" and sends him
forth on his mission of vengeance, while she herself proceeds to
organize resistance in the mountains.

Roderick's first stop is the monastery of St. Felix. There he learns
that the Gothic barons are either helpless or apostate and that
Spain's only hope, his cousin Pelayo, is kept hostage at the Moorish
court at Cordoba. "Maccabee" undertakes to contact Pelayo and is
ordained as a priest. Resuming his journey, he overhears travelers at
an inn who mourn their losses and curse King Roderick's soul. He
protests and is seconded by an old man whom he, almost betraying
himself, recognizes as his old tutor Siverian. In the first of a series of
vindications of the king that punctuate the narrative, Siverian
asserts that the Moors would have come even without Count
Julian's invitation, and that the atrocities of Witiza and the treason
of Witiza's kin did more to deliver Spain into the hands of the
enemy than Roderick's one "deed of shame." Since Siverian is
likewise on a mission to Pelayo, the two men proceed together.

Arrived at Cordoba, they decide to spend the night at Roderick's paternal mansion, the scene of his childhood and later of his triumph over Witiza. As they kneel at the tomb of Theodofred, a majestic figure in sackcloth and ashes emerges from the gloom to challenge them. It is Pelayo, who has been given leave to pray at the grave of his wretched mother. "Maccabee" tells him of the "living spark" which "From Asturia's ashes, by a woman's hand / Preserved and quickened, kindles far and wide / The beacon-flames o'er all the Asturian hills" and adjures him to lead Adosinda's recruits in the "work of holy hatred" (86). Pelayo accepts the "crown of thorns," and Roderick kneels as the first Spaniard to swear allegiance to the new king. His homage seals his own forfeiture of the throne but gives him that "heavenly peace" which, we are told, "follows painful duty well performed" (89).

Pelayo returns to Cordoba to plot escape in concert with young Alphonso, his fellow hostage and his future son-in-law and heir. They are presently joined by the hapless Florinda, who seeks refuge from having to marry the miscreant Orpas. Disguised as peasants, the three slip out of Cordoba at sunset and, by hidden paths, make their way through the moonlit night to a rendezvous with "Maccabee" and Siverian.

The scene that follows in one of the most moving and successful of the poem and, indeed, was Southey's own favorite. The setting is romantic: a "lonely grove" before dawn, "when the stars were setting, at what hour / The breath of Heaven is coldest," the cork-trees illumined by the campfire, which "cast upon the leaves / A floating, gray, unrealizing gleam." While the other travelers enjoy the sleep of the just, Florinda confesses herself to Roderick, not recognizing him in his priestly appearance and, indeed, at first unrecognized by him. In the course of their interview, we learn that Florinda had loved Roderick "Tenderly, passionately, madly," and, seeing him unhappy in his marriage, had presumptuously dreamed herself his queen. Roderick's marriage had been political and had remained both loveless and barren. His queen, Egilona, as we have already learned earlier, was a captious and vain woman who has since adulterously married the Moorish governor Abdalaziz. Meeting the king alone one evening, Florinda had discovered that he harbored feelings similar to her own and, suddenly terrified, had vowed to become a nun. When Roderick had met her again to tell her that Rome would annul his childless marriage to Egilona, she had perversely insisted on her vow, with the result that the king, overcome with desire, had seduced her so as to force her to renounce her vow, "Here then, O Father! at thy feet I own / Myself the guiltier; for vengeance mastered me, / And in my agony I cursed the man / Whom I loved best" (114).

Florinda's confession thus corroborates and supplements Roderick's own earlier endeavor, when he was still a recluse, to extenuate his crime. At that time, he had recoiled from such thoughts that seemed to reveal an unregenerate spirit; but he now accepts Florinda's insistence that he "Sinned not from vicious will or heart corrupt, / But fell by fatal circumstance betrayed." Florinda's pent-up emotions find relief in tears; and, together with the deeply shaken "Father," she kneels to pray "For Roderick, for Count Julian, and myself,— / Three wretchedest of all the human race, / Who have destroyed each other and ourselves, / Mutually wronged and wronging" (115f.).

The scene is far from perfect. While the perversity of Florinda's past behavior represents an advance from the flatness of Southey's usual character portraits, it still lacks substance to be fully convincing. The brittle illogic of her action seems less an outgrowth of her psychology than a convenience for the poet, enabling him to exculpate the king without simply abandoning the rape motif of the legend. Even so—and in spite of the inevitable declamatoriness of Southey's dialogue—the scene is a touching one, and the predicament it recalls surprises by its humanity. For once Southey seems to have confronted reality without barricading himself behind moral absolutes. There are clear autobiographical overtones. Roderick's reluctant and ill-advised "wedlock to an ill-assorted mate"; his suffering from "hope deceived, [a] soul dissatisfied, / Home without love, and privacy from which / Delight was banished first, and peace too soon / Departed"; and his finally encountering "a heart attuned, a spirit like his own, / Of lofty pitch, yet in affection mild, / And tender as a youthful mother's joy," whose sympathy made his chilled and shrunken feelings "open forth like flowers / After cold winds of night, when gentle gales / Restore the genial sun" (28f.)— is that not the story of Coleridge, the heartbreak of whose hapless marriage, hopeless love for Sara Hutchinson, and homeless wandering could not but oppress Southey's spirit, and for which, despite his noisy self-righteousness, he must have felt in some measure responsible? And does not, conversely, Florinda's ironic admission to "Maccabee," "I thought / Thou wert a rigid and unpitying judge; / One whose stern virtue, feeling in itself / No flaw of frailty, heard impatiently / Of weakness and of guilt. I wronged thee, Father!" (116), sound like an echo of Coleridge's standard reproach of Southey—who, in fact, liked to regard himself as a sort of Maccabeus—and a plea of not guilty? I do not insist on a conscious personal allegory; but if emotional currents run deeper here than elsewhere in Southey, it is perhaps because—instead of merely constructing models of morals, manners, and mythology—he for once used poetry to face, if at a bias and only for a moment, a truth of his own life.

The scene between Roderick and Florinda is a turning-point in the poem: it completes the interpretation of the past and thereby clears the ground for future action. After days of devious travel, the fugitives reach the seat of Count Pedro, Alphonso's father, among the Asturian hills. They find the castle thronged with armed men who have flocked to Adosinda's crusading call and are waiting for the reluctant Don Pedro to lead them. The unexpected recovery of the royal hostages removes all uncertainty. Pedro and Pelayo resolve to bury their families' ancient feud and seal their friendship by arranging a betrothal between their children, Alphonso and Herme-sind. The future king of Leon is knighted by Pelayo, and Roderick makes him swear ceaseless war "Through every generation," until "this insulted land hath drunk / . . . the last invader's blood" (129).

The ceremony is interrupted by a Moorish commando sent to capture Don Pedro in reprisal for Alphonso's escape; the Moors are quickly routed by the Asturians. When Pelayo learns from a captive that a similar task force is advancing against his own castle, he tries to intercept it by a forced march but arrives to find the place deserted. Fortunately, his fears are quickly allayed. As Siverian had already told him in Cordoba, his sister Guisla, taking after her dis-solute mother, has consorted in "loose and shameless love" (145) with the renegade lord Numacian. Pelayo's wife, Gaudiosa, had thereupon put herself and her children in hiding—just in time, as it turned out, to escape capture. Moreover, Adosinda, appearing shortly after the raid, had pursued and massacred the Moors and retrieved Pelayo's household, including Roderick's mother Rusilla and the renitent Guisla herself. Apprised of Gaudiosa's whereabouts, Pelayo early the next morning ascends to the mountain-fastness of Covadonga, where the Deva wells from a sacred cave—a place someday to be hallowed by the graves of Alphonso, Hermesind, and Pelayo himself. His bugle call tells the stunned cave-dwellers of their unlooked-for happiness; and Pelayo, like Robert Southey returning to Keswick from abroad, soon embraces his restored family.

At the same time, Roderick feverishly tries to fortify his soul for an encounter with his mother. He finds Rusilla with Florinda who, in obedience to "Maccabee's" counsel, has done her utmost to exonerate the king to the queen. Rusilla, too, fails to recognize her son in the gaunt priest before her; but Roderick's dog Theron knows his master and rises to lick his hand. Roderick hastily withdraws into a grove. There Siverian finds him, weeping at the dog's neck; and, half-suspecting "Maccabee's" true identity, he expresses his conviction that Roderick is alive and may return some day to restore his reign. Roderick resists temptation, however, and humbly goes to promote Pelayo's acclamation among the gathering chieftains. At the coronation ceremony, Roderick himself carries the buckler on which the king-elect is elevated. The mountains echo to the cry of *Real*; and, amid rather fulsome rhetoric about vengeance and the centuries of carnage to come, "Spain is born again" (189). Soon afterwards, Roderick finds himself in the arms of his mother. She, too, dreams of restoration to the throne, but Roderick begs her not to tempt him: his heart has died to the world, and his hopes are for the world to come.

The scene now shifts to the camp of the Moors, who are advancing from all sides to crush the incipient revolt. With them are the renegades: the traitor Count Julian; Sisibert and Ebba, thirsting for their half-brother Pelayo's blood, "As if that sacrifice might . . . efface the shame / Of their adulterous birth, and . . . emancipate / Thenceforth their spirits from all earthly fear" (198); and Orpas, the ex-Metropolitan and arch-villain of the piece. Already disappointed in his aspirations to royalty, Orpas now hopes to gain possession of Count Julian's domains and, having failed to achieve his goal through marriage to Florinda, tries to sow suspicion against the count among the Moorish leaders by citing Florinda's recalcitrance and refusal to embrace the Moslem faith as proof of Julian's unsoundness. Julian defends himself against the charge of apostasy. He has used every means to convert his daughter, short of compulsion, which the law of the Prophet forbids; and as for heresy, he retorts that such a charge is itelf heretical under the "wiser law" of Islam, "which, with the iniquities / Of thine old craft, hath abrogated this, / Its foulest practice!" (204). Julian then dispatches a message to Florinda that entreats her to return, promising her both "liberty of faith" and safety from Orpas.

Florinda responds by slipping into the Moorish camp after sunset, accompanied by Roderick. The ensuing scene between the three instigators of Spain's plight corresponds to the earlier interview between Roderick and Florinda. The setting is again picturesque. Camp fires gleam among the trees of the wooded slope where the Moors have pitched their tents, smoke curls from among the tree-tops to the evening sky, and the muezzin's sonorous voice proclaims the hour of prayer to the hushed multitude and with "melodious modulation" invokes "the highest name" (207): Southey seems momentarily to have forgotten his animus against the Moors. Julian's tent is pitched "an arrow's flight" above the camp in an idyllic glade. A fountain wells out of a rock under an oak, like Horace's Bandusian spring or the "fountain of the fairies" of *Joan of Arc*. The Count is performing his ablutions "Moor-like" when Florinda and Roderick come upon him.

A tense debate about religion ensues. Julian, having registered acid surprise to find "honesty / And sense of natural duty in a Priest," advances the Deist argument against religious absolutism: "from every faith, / As every clime, there is a way to Heaven," since all men are children of the "All-Father." Roderick grants the premise but denies the conclusion. There is but one "gospel-truth"; and, although natural religion suffices where positive revelation is not given, the latter becomes binding once it is known. Those who, "born amid the light, to darkness turn, / Wilful in error," forfeit their salvation. Besides, creeds are known by their fruits. Christ's law, "Forgive as ye would be forgiven," is the law of peace; by turning from it, Julian has only brought misery to Spain and remorse to himself (212 - 6).

Julian at first retorts hotly that there can be no forgiveness for "Roderick's crime"; but when Florinda thereupon implores the "Redeemer" to heal Julian's heart of "the grief / Which festers there," the old man, abashed, concedes that he might have been wrong but that "Things are as they will be; and we, poor slaves, / Fret in the harness as we may, must drag / The Car of Destiny where'er she drives, / Inexorable and blind" (219). Roderick naturally denounces such fatalism as "sophistry," palpably false since man has Will and Conscience. When Julian counters—rather illogically—with Nihilist and Manichean sentiments, Roderick admits that "The happiest child of earth" would "from the gloom and horror of his heart / Confirm thy fatal thought, were this world all." For "who could bear the haunting mystery, / If death and retribution did not solve / The riddle, and to heavenliest harmony / Reduce the seeming chaos" (220f.). Fortunately, however, as Southey writes elsewhere, "Free-will, God, and final retribution solve all difficulties" (*Life*, III, 17). Just as the pure spring at their feet becomes polluted and loathsome when it "reaches the resorts of men" but is cleansed at last in the sea, its "appointed end," so the "great stream of things" flows from good through transitory evil to greater good. And as the moon is clothed "with richer beauties than her own" by a passing cloud, so adversity serves to enhance the soul's beauty. "Ages pass away, / Thrones fall, and nations disappear, and worlds / Grow old and go to wreck: the soul alone / Endures, and what she chooseth for herself, / The arbiter of her own destiny, /That only shall be permanent" (222).

The debate, while central, is neither very dramatic nor truly dialectical. Julian is a mere multi-purpose straw man who is easily reduced to silence. Conversely, Roderick's theology is only nominally Catholic—the more nearly orthodox sentiments are put in Florinda's mouth—but consists of an eclectic mix of Deism, Stoicism, and Christian ethics. As a result, the concluding emblems of polluted stream and cloudy moon do not really mesh, the stream emblem, in particular, being imported somewhat incongruously from one of Southey's early Nature inscriptions. Even so, the scene is well placed and handsomely trimmed—a moment of quiet before the storm and, for the three sufferers, of respite under the "healing power / Of Nature."

> Alone in heaven the glorious Moon pursues
> Her course appointed, with indifferent beams
> Shining upon the silent hills around,
> And the dark tents of that unholy host,
> Who, all unconscious of impending fate,
> Take their last slumber there. The camp is still;
> The fires have mouldered, and the breeze which stirs
> The soft and snowy embers just lays bare
> At times a red and evancescent light,
> Or for a moment wakes a feeble flame.

As a nightingale begins to pour "To the cold moon . . . her deep and thrilling song," the "splendor of the night" and its sounds of water and bird song come to them "like a copious evening dew / Falling on vernal herbs which thirst for rain" (223f.).

In the remaining books, which depict the reversal of fortune and the beginning of the *Reconquista*, we see not only the Christians victorious but their foes self-defeated by intrigues and internal rivalry. News arrives from Cordoba that Abdalaziz has been assassinated. Incited by the pomp-loving Egilona, he had begun to rule like a king in the Gothic manner and had thereby furnished "artful spirits of ambitious mould" with a pretext for revolt. Julian counsels instant return to Cordoba to restore order there. The Asturian guerrillas in their fastnessness, he argues, will not be easily or quickly put down; force will not crush but merely feed their mountaineers' independence; time may weaken and divide, but force can only unite them, as Romans and Goths have had to learn in the past. However, Florinda's visit to her father's tent has deepened the suspicion of the Moorish commander, Abulcacem; and Orpas's insinuations convince him that Julian is about to change sides again and that his advice is intended to play into the hands of the insurgents. In order to avert this danger without provoking retaliation from Julian's loyal Myrmidons, Abulcacem, with Orpas's help, plots to have Julian assassinated in battle. For the present, he decides to attack the Asturians. Guisla has deserted to the Moorish camp in a gamble for her brother's possessions and has betrayed the rebels' hideout at Covadonga. Abulcacem intends to take them by surprise and smoke them out.

As it happens, Guisla's betrayal plays directly into Pelayo's hand. Anticipating the enemies' intentions and informed about their movements by his scouts, he withdraws into the narrow Deva valley and stations his forces along the valley's rims, while Pedro lies concealed near the entrance to close the trap. The Moors arrive at Congas and find Pelayo's castle deserted. Abulcacem remains behind with part of his troops, including Julian; the rest, under the command of Alcahman, the sacker of Auria, set out toward Covadonga. Rain and low mists conceal the deadly trap from the overconfident Moors. But as they approach Covadonga, the lifting fog reveals Adosinda high on a rock, in flowing garment, breastplate, and helmet, "one hand upon the Cross, the other raised in menacing act." In the best fashion of Gray's *Bard*, she denounces Alcahman, "Moor, Miscreant, Murderer, Child of Hell," and summons him to answer for the massacre at Auria: "In the Name of God, for Spain and Vengeance." At this password, a devastating torrent of logs and boulders descends from the mountains. The crash of the falling mass and the "shrieks of horror and despair and death" from the doomed host presently yield to silence, "through which the sound of Deva's stream was heard, / A lonely voice of waters, wild and sweet." Now Pelayo, a "dreadful joy" in his eyes, sets his Asturians upon the broken enemy, and "along the vale of blood / The avenging sword did mercy's work that hour" (242).

Meanwhile, a skirmish develops at Congas between Spaniards and Moors, and Julian is treacherously stabbed as planned. The stricken count orders his followers to avenge him by joining Pelayo's standards and calls for his daughter and her companion. He asks to be carried into a nearby mountain chapel named after St. Peter—"he who denied his Lord, and was forgiven"—and there renounces "the Impostor's faith." Roderick absolves him of his sins and, having administered Holy Communion to both father and daughter, reveals himself and begs Julian's forgiveness. The count urges Roderick to restore his kingship but then acquiesces in the "will and work of Heaven" and dies peacefully. Florinda, overcome by the turn of events, cries "My Roderick! mine in Heaven!" and expires in his arms.

With that the poem draws to its climax. As Julian's myrmidons desert to Count Pedro's lines, Orpas is dispatched by Abulcacem to "allay the storm his villainy / Had stirred" and appears for a parley, mounted (rather improbably) on Roderick's old battle-steed Orelio. Roderick advances toward him; calls the horse, who, like the dog earlier, recognizes his master; and, "with just and unrelenting hand," makes him throw the priest and trample him to death. Caressing Orelio, he mounts and draws Orpas's scimetar but is repelled by its "unholy shape" and calls for a "Spanish sword." He is given Julian's blade and, without waiting for armor, rides off against the advancing Moors. With his priestly "garb of peace" like "death's black banner shaking from its folds / Dismay and ruin," he seems like an angel of destruction or a saint come to champion God's chosen people. Presently Pelayo arrives with his troops from Covadonga and Roderick hastens to tell him that Julian's troops have joined the Spanish cause. When Pelayo and Siverian see him approach on Orelio, the truth dawns on them. Roderick, surmising from Pelayo's wistful look and gesture of obeisance that he is known, takes the weeping Siverian aside to ask for the old man's armor; and, having obtained his promise to look after his mother and to bury him beside Florinda should he fall in battle, he takes leave and returns to the field.

The Moors, already dismayed by the news of the disaster of Covadonga, now find themselves attacked on two fronts. Roderick, forgetting himself in the joy of battle, raises his old war-cry, "Roderick the Goth." Pelayo takes it up, and the battlefield resounds with "Roderick and Vengeance!" Experiencing his finest hour, the "dreadful Goth" mows down everything in his way, including the treacherous pair, Sisibert and Ebba. By nightfall, the Asturians have won complete victory. Roderick had hoped to die at last in battle; but, seeing "that the shield of Heaven / Had been extended over him once more," he bows "before its will." Once again he disappears; once again his horse and battle-gear are found abandoned by the side of a river, drenched in "Moorish gore." Centuries would pass "before, far off / Within a hermitage near Viseu's walls, / A humble tomb was found, which bore inscribed / In ancient characters King Roderick's name" (274).

III   *Structure and Style; Character, Setting, and Theme*

Southey said *Roderick* was "the best which I have done and probably the best that I shall do," (*Life*, IV, 90), and his contemporaries agreed with him. Not only friends, like Coleridge, Lamb, Landor, and William Taylor, praised it, James Hogg called it "the noblest epic poem of the age"; Byron, who had elsewhere sneered that Southey's "epic mountains never fail in mice," deemed it "the first poem of the time" and "as near perfection as poetry can be"; and even Jeffrey could not bring himself to damn it. Reviews were generally favorable, and, as a result, the poem sold well. While not a best-seller like the romances of Scott and Byron, it went through several successively larger editions that netted its author some seven hundred pounds in three years; and it was eventually translated into French and Dutch. Its success was no doubt largely due to the timeliness of its subject; even so, it is a superior poem.

For one thing, *Roderick* is more carefully constructed than its predecessors: its plot has the firm circular or helical form of the epic, and its episodes are fairly subordinated to the main design. We start with an end—the disaster of Xeres de la Frontida—and end with a new beginning—the legendary battle of Covadonga seven years later, the inception and mythical embodiment of the

Reconquista. Between battle and battle, defeat and victory, the action spirals from death to resurrection, from fall to regeneration, from division to reunion, from the old order to the new. Both battles end with the mysterious disappearance of the king. The parallel enables Southey to graft the actions he ascribes to his hero neatly into history, as though he were simply unfolding what time had erroneously conflated. At the same time, we are made aware of the distance we have come: Roderick does not merely expiate his past through monkish penances but seeks to rectify it and is therefore able to reenact and redeem it. His spiritual rebirth is complemented by political renewal. The plot thus emphasizes Southey's humanization of the old story.[9]

There are other instances of design. As Romano confesses and absolves Roderick at the beginning, so Roderick ministers to Julian toward the end. And as the first phase of the revolt is preceded by the nocturne between Roderick and Florinda, so is the second phase by the similar encounter between Roderick and Julian. The battle of Covadonga itself, moreover, is prefaced by Pelayo's reunion with his family at the same spot, a scene that, in its emphasis on scenic beauty and domestic sentiment, contrasts strikingly with the blood and thunder of the mist-shrouded ambush.

But the poem also has a good many structural and stylistic flaws. It suffers from the usual Southeyan combination of short-windedness and overelaboration. Its diction, which is generally ample and flexible, is often abstract and prosy and is marred by recurrent stock phrases; by trite redundancies like "needful food," "blooming bride," "grateful rest," and the like; and by needless Latinisms like "ornature," "foliature," and "argentry." Moreover, there is a frequent disproportion between character and action. Adosinda is too sketchily developed for the importance that the poet ascribes to her as "Sufferer, patriot, saint and heroine, / The servant and the chosen of the Lord" (50); and, as a result, her appearances do not rise far above melodrama.[10] Similarly, Guisla's villainy is mere machinery. Her passion for the renegade Numacian, rather than being the tragic cause of her disloyalty, appears simply as part and parcel of a gratuitous malignity which Southey utilizes for his plot but does not bother to explain otherwise than as an inherited trait. Sisibert and Ebba do not appear in person at all until Roderick encounters and kills them in battle. Alphonso, after a prominent start, virtually drops from sight, being barely mentioned in the battle as one who "Rejoicing like a bridegroom in the strife / . . . Bore on his bloody lance dismay and death" (259). The fence-straddling Count Eudon, on the other hand, serves merely as a warning example of the self-defeating nature of cowardice and neutrality but is altogether superfluous to the plot.

In general, the poem suffers from Southey's inability to render psychic processes, from his unwillingness to see beyond moral categories into the real confusion of conflicting interests, of obscure impulse and tenuous principle, that makes up human personality. Character is interpreted rather than depicted, and no figure ever says or does more than he knows or than his creator can readily label. Such two-dimensionality is tolerable in an ornate genre like opera or heroic play; but, in a realistic medium like Southey's, it easily becomes shallow and tedious. Roderick and Florinda, indeed, represent advances over previous Southeyan protagonists; but even here conflict is mainly between the characters' past and their present. Passion and virtue remain polar opposites. And although Southey goes so far as to ascribe rape to his hero, that act is quickly extenuated to a mere shadow of itself, and Southey liberates us from his excessively pious heroes only to saddle us with an overly remorseful one.

Even landscape at times exists only to be facilely and gratuitously moralized. A mountain stream, "with its shadows and its glancing lights, / Dimples and thread-like motions infinite," becomes a pat emblem of time running toward eternity (171); and the image of the clouded moon (222), which Southey had observed years before at Cintra, was noted down "with its application" even then (*Life*, IV, 107). Wordsworth, too, was fond of such emblemizing, as the somewhat similar passage from the *Excursion* which Southey chose as a motto for his own poem shows. But Wordsworth's emblems are also *seen* vividly; Southey's on the whole, are not.

At their best, however, Southey's descriptive passages are lively if conventional in technique, and what Taylor objected to as a Wordsworthian manner of inordinate "botanizing and pic-turesquizing" is in fact one of the poem's more pleasing aspects.

> Soon had the Prince
> Behind him left the farthest dwelling-place
> Of man: no fields of waving corn were here,
> Nor wicker storehouse for the autumnal grain,
> Vineyard, nor bowery fig, nor fruitful grove;
> Only the rocky vale, the mountain stream,

> Incumbent crags, and hills that over hills
> Arose on either hand, here hung with woods,
> Here rich with heath, that o'er some smooth ascent
> Its purple glory spread, or golden gorse;
> Bare here, and striated with many a hue,
> Scored by the wintry rain; by torrents here
> Riven, and with overhanging rocks abrupt. (160f.)

The scene is itemized rather than evoked, in language that is typically poor in active verbs. But its overall effect is graphic, and the austere northern mountain solitude contrasts pointedly with the earlier picture of Moorish Cordoba at sunset, with its gleaming "temples and towers," idyllic groves and hamlets, tiers of luminous hills, and "silent sky" (72f.). At times, moreover, particular settings have a symbolic appropriateness that enhances the action without appearing contrived. Such is the secluded valley head where Pelayo finds his family in safety and whence he launches the *Reconquista* in the name of domestic peace and independence. And such is the Horation glade, with its spring half in black shade, half shining "like a burnished mirror" in the moonlight, where Roderick, Julian, and Florinda try to sort out their checkered destinies.

Roderick is also distinguished from its predecessors by a greater restraint in the use of quaint detail: the "machinery" which Southey at one time planned to use—ruins, relics, images, and miraculous places—has been mostly relegated to the notes. These, indeed, are of formidable compensatory bulk. Almost as long as the poem itself, they amount to another "Omniana," in which Southey tilts against the windmills of Catholic superstition and intolerance, exhibits notable absurdities from the *Acta Sanctorum* and other lurid records of monkish devotion, and parades egregious examples of pseudo-learning "that may amuse [the] scholar" (283). Footnotes at times sprout secondary footnotes that have no longer any bearing on the text. Occasionally, also, the narrative is still used to introduce such antiquarian curiosities. But, on the whole, the poem itself is quite uncluttered. Machinery, so to speak, has finally gone underground and become pure apparatus. Unfortunately, the vacuum created by the relegation of machinery is promptly filled by a great deal of overt apologetics. What should have been a rich and stirring array of diverse values and conflicting sympathies—of Moslems, Catholics, and Mozarabs; of Jews, Arians, and Pelagians (Pelayo, as Southey notes, is named after the great Welsh heretic)—thus becomes yet another clash of absolutes masquerading as history.

The subject of the poem is the least far-fetched of Southey's epic matters and for once coincided with popular interest. The story of the struggle against the Moslem invaders was not only hallowed by Christian tradition but bore clear analogies to current events. Besides, the protagonists were Goths, who could not but appeal to an age enamored of its "Gothic" past. Above all, the story was one of a struggle for national independence; and nationalism was emerging as the leading political faith of Europe.

Southey takes some trouble to make *Roderick* a nationalist poem. The *Reconquista* had been fought, as Dryden's Ferdinand puts it in the *Conquest of Granada*, in the name of "Rodrique's . . . Gothic title." In Southey's narrative, on the contrary, the Goths are themselves usurpers and oppressors who are finally punished for their sins against the native population by the Moorish scourge. Conversely, the Asturian barons are said to be the native nobility who, amid their "rocks and glens and everlasting hills" (56), had retained much of their independence under successive occupations by "Punic and Roman, Kelt and Goth and Greek" (59). And Pelayo, the restorer of the monarchy, though Roderick's cousin, becomes king not by virtue of his "Gothic title" but as a native Spaniard in whom "the old Iberian blood / Of royal and remotest ancestry, / From undisputed sources flowed" (89f.).—"undefiled," Southey insists, albeit the claim derives, rather awkwardly, through Pelayo's degenerate mother! Accordingly, feudal allegiance to a "sovereign will" is replaced by "natural," that is, national obligation, to be honored in "free election." Since "Our portentous age, / As with an earthquake's desolating force, / Hath loosened and disjointed the whole frame / Of social order," the vassal no longer owes service "to the Lord / Who to his country doth acknowledge none" (183f.). Power, as in the Romanticized Robin Hood myth, passes from the feudal conqueror to the indigenous patriot.

Who or what the original "Iberians" were, Southey might have been hard put to say. But the idea of a nation's recovering its ancient rights and innate way of life in the midst of political diaster was far too intoxicating and immediately relevant to bear close analysis. Southey's Asturia might be quite different from Pelayo's; what mattered was that it resembled, say, the Tyrol of Andreas Hofer. *Roderick* is Southey's *Wilhelm Tell*.

Yet nationalism is, after all, but a secondary theme in the poem. While the Goths appear at first as usurpers brought to justice by other usurpers, Southey does not pursue this idea very consequentially; and the conflict of nationalities is superseded by the less ambiguous one between Cross and Crescent, sword and scimetar, the old theme of Tasso and Camoens, of the *Song of Roland* and the *Poema del Cid.* A generation that has seen the "glory" of Covadonga turn into holocaust at nearby Guernica may find nationalism as dubious an ideal as the zeal of the Crusades. Even so, we cannot but regret Southey's failure to probe more deeply what was then a new and powerful idea. His contemporaries, of course, could easily translate the struggle against the Moor into the struggle against Bonaparte and thus find it apt; *we* are left with a poem whose literal issue was dead long before its composition.

Besides, while Southey's view of Mohammed and his followers could not be *more* hostile than were his feelings about Napoleon, the use of the religious analogy did nothing to restrain those feelings or to render them more equitable. The Moors are depicted with far less sympathy than the Aztecs and have virtually no redeeming traits. They are a "dreadful brotherhood," "swarthy myriads," "misbelievers," who are licensed by their "impious creed accurst" to do "all bloody, all abominable things." Their banners are "blazoned scrolls of blasphemy" (16); their muezzins "pollute" Spain's towers with their call to the "Impostor's" "unhallowed prayer" (35, 233); their motives are Rapine and Lust; and what in the Christian is courage, is "pride" and "insolence" in the "lying Ishmaelite" and his "vicious," "sullen," "cruel and corrupt" confederates (132, 271f.). Of the brilliance and liberality of Omayyad Spain we hear nothing.

Conversely, the Christian cause is extolled as a "Holy War," and the defeat of the Moors is "due vengeance" from "the righteous, the immitigable sword" for "plunder, violation, massacre, / All hideous, all unutterable things" (272). Roderick swears that his soul will "efface her stain of mortal sin" in the "invader's blood" and "work out / Redemption for herself" by offering Moorish "carrion" as a sacrifice to "insulted Heaven" (50, 69); and Adosinda, who haunts the poem like a vindictive ghost of the gentle Joan of Arc, speaks of revenge as "the grace of God" (54). Throughout, man's most destructive instincts masquerade as heroic sentiment, "sublimed and sanctified" (ibid.) by religious metaphors of faith, devotion, and sacrifice. And the oratory is all the more provoking as it is nowhere balanced by a candid portrayal of the "Disasters of War": battles, Southey had come to feel, were "unfit for poetry" (*Letters*, III, 11).

Nor can we argue that Southey was simply depicting the manners of the time, for there is no sign that the poet had any reservations about the gory sentiments expressed. When Roderick reproaches Julian for having "turned away from Him, / Who saith, 'Forgive as ye would be forgiven' " to take his "fill of vengeance" (216), the irony is quite unconscious: the double standard is the poet's own. The only good Moor is a dead Moor; the only mercy he deserves, a *coup de grace*. One reviewer called *Roderick* the "expression of a deeply vindictive spirit" (Madden, 191). It is, at all events, the expression of a ferocious, resentful domesticity and xenophobia.

There is, indeed, one passage where Southey seems willing to give the devil his due, even to view Islam as a kind of reformed religion, a view that hearkens back to the days of *Thalaba* and the projected epic on Mohammed, days when he had at times had more sympathy with Moslems than with Christians. In this passage, Julian defends his apostasy as an honest revolt against the evils of Catholicism—"graven images, unnatural vows, / False records, fabling creeds, and juggling priests," and, above all, against the heresy hunting so contrary to "that liberty / Of faith . . . which the Prophet's law, / Liberal as Heaven from whence it came, to all / Indulges" (203 - 5). Evidently, Southey's anti-Moorish—that is, anti-French—sentiments here come at cross-purposes with his anti-Catholicism. Shortly afterwards, moreover, the Moorish chief issues an ultimatum to the Asturians which, though at variance with Julian's notions, does not lack loftiness of purpose and is couched in language more eloquent than any found elsewhere in the poem:

> 'Repent, and be forgiven!
> Nor think to stop the dreadful storm of war,
> Which, conquering and to conquer, must fulfill
> Its destined circle, rolling Eastward now,
> Back from the subjugated West, to sweep
> Thrones and dominions down, till in the bond
> Of unity all nations join, and Earth
> Acknowledge, as she sees one Sun in heaven,
> One God, one Chief, one Prophet, and one Law.
> Jerusalem, the holy City, bows
> To holier Mecca's creed; the Crescent shines
> Triumphant o'er the eternal pyramids;
> On the cold altars of the worshippers
> Of Fire, moss grows, and reptiles leave their slime;
> The African idolatries are fallen;
> And Europe's senseless gods of stone and wood
> Have had their day. . . . Is not the Earth the Lord's (206f.)

Perhaps Southey meant to suggest that Anti-Christ is most pernicious when he masquerades as Messiah, as Bonaparte masquerad-
ed as liberator and fulfiller of the Revolutionary cause. If so,
Southey makes a better devil's advocate than he does a crusader. At
any rate, no clear pattern emerges from these isolated instances.
While Southey is not above using a Moorish mouthpiece to vent his
spleen against Catholicism, the Moors are throughout imps of hell
to whom, therefore, applies what Southey said elsewhere of their
modern equivalent: "Force must be crushed by Force, / The power
of Evil by the power of Good, / Ere Order bless the suffering world
once more / Or Peace return again" (*Carmen Triumphale*, xviii).

Roderick is interesting as the only notable attempt of the period
to deal in epic form with the spirit of the Napoleonic wars; and, in-
sofar as it embodies that spirit in a complex, impersonal, genuinely
historical and therefore genuinely tragic and poetic vision of war as
a kind of cathartic upheaval in which an old order yields its place to
a newer and better one, it can still appeal to us. But Southey was
always more partisan than poet; and, since he remains too often
content with making propagandistic simplifications pass for poetic
truths, *Roderick* was bound to be forgotten, like the earlier *Joan of
Arc*, when it ceased to be politically relevant. It is thus perhaps a
deserved irony that, at the very moment when Southey was
publishing his epic of Spanish liberation, the treacherous and
degenerate Ferdinand, in whose name the Peninsular War had been
largely fought, abrogated the Constitution of Cadiz and annulled all
the progressive reforms that had resulted from the war and thereby
proved to be not only far worse than the liberal and beneficient
Joseph Bonaparte but the most oppressive and reactionary ruler
Spain had had in a century and a half. Pelayo was turning out to be
worse than either Goth or Moor.

Southey himself was at first bitterly disappointed at the turn of
events in Spain, and he never ceased to believe altogether that
republics were feasible once man was "advanced enough in civilisa-
tion for such a form of society" (*Life*, IV, 57). Soon, however, he
came to regard even Ferdinand's reactionary despotism as a
necessary bulwark against the "Jacobinical Atheists" (*Letters*, III,
14). *Roderick* thus marks pretty much the end of his career as a poet
of liberty and the beginning of his role as Poet Laureate and as
staunch supporter of the Establishment. Democracy might work
elsewhere or in the future; but as far as England and the present
were concerned, Southey now identified liberty with national in-

dependence and the British constitution. He was a "friend of the Church Establishment," he wrote, because "I am a heretic requiring toleration" (*Letters*, II, 108). If the Deluge was still inundating Europe, the Ark was no longer called Pantisocracy but Britannia and Ecclesia. Southey's career as epic poet had come full circle.

IV *Laureate Verse*

His career as a poet was, in fact, virtually at an end. Of Southey's post-laureate verse, though he professed great pride in the Laurel "which Dryden and diviner Spenser wore" and hoped to elevate the office to genuine national importance, very little deserves notice. Southey had entered upon the laureateship with the understanding that he would not be required to supply the traditional New Year's and Birthday Odes that his predecessor had still been obliged to produce; and eventually that tradition fell indeed into disuse, largely through Southey's influence. For a number of years, however, the "odious" task, as he called it, was still expected of him; and, after initial demurrals, he faithfully turned out annual odes, though without publishing them, and altogether wrote more official verse than any laureate before him except Ben Jonson.

Most of that output is quite unreadable. Writing Birthday Odes, Southey himself likened to making silk purses from sows' ears. The New Year's Ode he at first welcomed as an opportunity to sound off on public events, but that, too, soon became a chore. Even those poems on extraordinary occasions which he wrote unsolicitedly are pure fustian: Philippics against Bonaparte ("Remorseless, godless, full of fraud and lies / And black with murder and with perjuries . . . How long, O Lord! Holy and Just, how long!"); jeremiads against radicals and atheists; and fulsome Pindarics in praise of England, the Allies, and King George. In the *Carmina Aulica* ("court poems"), relentless panegyrics on the meeting of the Allied Sovereigns in England in 1814, Czar Alexander is hailed as "Conqueror, Deliverer, Friend of human-kind! . . . the Great, the Good, / The Glorious, the Beneficent, the Just." In "The Warning Voice," written in 1819, the year of Peterloo and Six Acts, the "multitude obscene" is shown to worship the great Whore Anarchy, and London appears as the modern Babylon, whence a Jacobinical ladder descends to Hell swarming with demons that carry "Horrors, obscenities, / Blasphemies, treasons, / And the seeds of strife and death" into the metropolis (III, 168f., 172, 227, 231). Written fre-

quently in the irregular, rhymeless *Thalaba* stanza—to the detri-
ment of the poetic quality and the despair of the Chief
Musician—the laureate poems radiate more heat than light; often,
they just merely smoulder. Only two deserve any consideration,
both of them dream visions, a mode Southey had been fond of since
the days of *Joan* and the earliest juvenilia: *The Poet's Pilgrimage to
Waterloo*, in a way Southey's poetic testament, and *A Vision of
Judgment*, his own poetic Waterloo.

The *Poet's Pilgrimage* (1816), Southey's commemoration of what
he regarded as the greatest event in British history, shows him at
both his best and his worst. It consists of two parts, one journalistic,
the other visionary. Part One describes the poet's autumnal barge
journey through the Flemish garden landscape in a "joyous company" of other Waterloo pilgrims,[11] surveys the "field of blood,"
and reviews the phases of the battle. Southey intersperses numerous
anecdotes and human touches, pores over war relics and over the
names and monuments of the dead, and poignantly contrasts
charred walls and rafters, old bloodstains, and "half-uncovered
graves" with the flowers and the grain that spring from the blood-
soaked ground, the "wrath and wreck" of human history with the
serene indifference of Nature's processes. But the naturalism of
"The Battle of Blenheim" is now largely replaced by nationalism;
and the language becomes increasingly rife with blood, duty, and
sacredness. Waterloo, now literally the "great victory" that
Blenheim had been only ironically in 1798, is compared not only to
Plataea, Tours, and the once detested Agincourt, but to Armageddon itself—the overthrow of Satan-Napoleon and of the Great
Whore of Revolution and Anarchy and her "fierce and many-
headed beast," (x, 15). Bonapartism, once deemed the betrayal of
the Revolution, now appears its damning natural consequence. And
the overriding feeling, as in *Roderick* and the Napoleonic odes, is
one of gloating satisfaction in the vengeance visited by the
"ministers of wrath divine" on the "lawless, faithless, godless foes"
(36, 50).

There is, to be sure, a larger perspective. In the dream vision that
forms Part Two, the poet describes himself as traveling over a vast
field full of folk symbolizing history. He passes through a corpse-
filled battle-ground and, following a mysterious call, comes to a
Babel-like tower, mighty but built on sand and crumbling at the
base. At its top he meets an Old Man, who calls himself "Wisdom,"
Earth's "noblest offspring," whom she "in her vigor self-

conceiving, bore" (59). This Nimrod and Worldly Wiseman, who represents both the "gross material philosophy" of the Revolution and the post-Revolutionary spirit of disillusionment and pessimism (3), first seeks to persuade the poet that "Pleasure is the aim, and Self the spring of all" and that, since there is no afterlife, men must rid themselves of "vain compunction" and "idle dreams" and create on earth the Heaven they find" (62): and then taunts him with his own youthful idealism. Did not "the Morning Star of Freedom," which rose so fair over the vine-clad hills of "rejoicing France," become a baleful influence until "on Waterloo it hath gone down in blood"? "Where now the reign of Liberty and Truth, / The Rights Omnipotent of Equal Man" that were to bring peace on earth? "Behold the Bourbon to that throne by force / Restored, from whence by fury he was cast! / Thus to the point where it began its course, / The melancholy circle comes at last; / And what are all the intermediate years? / What but a bootless waste of blood and tears." Germany, Italy, and Spain are as unfree as ever; England herself, threatened with ruin. Turn where we will, man's history is "but a thorny maze, without a plan"; winds, waves, and earthquakes "Are not more vague and purportless and blind / Than is the course of things among mankind!" (69 - 73).

The poet predictably rejects the crude pragmatism of the first argument by citing the superior pleasures of duty, virtue, and hope of heavenly reward. But he is fairly routed by the second, one that voices his own innermost anxieties and that contains poetry of a high order. Yet a real dialectic does not emerge here either. The Byronic gloom is evoked only to be ponderously exorcized: "Wisdom" dissolves into vapor, and the poet is taken over by a new mentor, a stern but motherly Muse and Beatrice, who guides him to an earthly paradise at the top of a specular mountain. Here he is commanded to eat from a scion of the Tree of Knowledge that grows from the grave of Adam; the bitter fruit almost kills him; but he clasps the Cross in time and is restored by a draught from the sweetening Water of Life that wells from the Rock of Ages—Southey's final version of the Bandusian fountain motif.

Thus symbolically renovated, the poet can now see the apparent gloom of existence irradiated—and its seeming chaos reduced to order—by the "plan" which vindicates the ways of God to man" (89). Predictably, Southey's theodicy is simple: *evil* and suffering are inevitable given man's *free will*, but ultimate *justice* is warranted by the *immortality* of the soul. To these tenets one must add the principle of *collective* retribution or "Divine vengeance" (*Letters*, II, 169): Africa's wretchedness is punishment for Africa's barbarity; Oriental slavery, the nemesis of Oriental vice; and so on. The only way out of the vicious cycle is the moral and intellectual progress that emanates from Europe, the spiritual "heart of earth." Napoleon's aim in striking at this heart was to "enslave" and "brutalize" mankind and to return the earth to such wickedness "as when / The Giantry of old their God defied." England, like a greater Noah, saved the world at Waterloo; and England will bring about its redemption and remake it in her image (93 - 5).

Three times in the poem Southey returns to the archetype and theme of his great unwritten epic, Noah's ark. The symbol of safety amid danger, of domestic peace amid universal turbulence, the ark epitomizes all of Southey's paradoxes, his Utopianism and his imperialism, his monkish domesticity and his hectic sense of duty, his encyclopedism and concurrent insularity. In the *Pilgrimage*, the image receives its final application. God's plan, for mankind, it appears now, is British hegemony and British colonialism. Herself the seat of Freedom, Science, and pure Religion, England is to bless the nations with her arts, her institutions, and her language; to abolish slavery, idolatry, and caste everywhere; to replenish, as God's chosen people, the earth with her increase; and to fulfill at last the millennial hope of the age through a *pax Britannica*.

There is much that is generous and genuinely progressive in these sentiments that also appear in the laureate odes and in the *Quarterly* essays written about this time. Yet it hardly requires the wisdom of hindsight to discern the dangers of this sort of secular millennialism in which nationalism, forgetful of its libertarian and pluralistic parentage, enters an unholy alliance with the totalitarian spirit of an older *Weltanschauung* and a flag presumes to offer "redemption to the groaning world" (III, 153). Even for its time, Southey's appeal to the nation to shoulder the White Man's Burden must appear tainted by political smugness or naivete, by its paternalism and ethnocentrism, and by that incorrigible dualism that divides the world into "good and evil principles" (X, 30), into Christians and barbarians—the empires, as the concurrently published *Lay of the Laureate* has it, "of Darkness and of Light" (156).

The *Pilgrimage* is in some ways poetically attractive, particularly Part I, as well as the Proem describing the poet's return to Keswick and his happy reunion with his children. The language, while at times redundant and prosy, is often simple and vivid; and the six-line stanza, adapted from Spenser's *Shepherds Calendar*, is handled with ease:

> In Cintra also have I dwelt erewhile,
>   That earthly Eden, and have seen at eve
> The sea-mists, gathering round its mountain pile,
>   Whelm with their billows all below, but leave
> One pinnacle sole seen, whereon it stood
> Like the Ark on Ararat, above the flood.
>
> And now I am a Cumbrian mountaineer;
>   Their wintry garments of unsullied snow
> The mountains have put on, the heavens are clear,
>   And yon dark lake spreads silently below;
> Who sees them only in their summer hour
> Sees but their beauties half, and knows not half their power. (16)

But the visionary scenario of Part II, partly borrowed from Camoens, appears antiquated and mechanical; and, after the moving lament of Wisdom, Southey relies on stock responses and conventional homiletics to drown out Wisdom's intolerable intimations of chance and futility. "To the Christian philosopher," the Argument of the poem states, "all things are clear and consistent"; and to that need for positive thinking our Noah piously sacrifices even the truth. No wonder the Hams of the age set about to uncover his nakedness.

They did so with the surreptitious publication of *Wat Tyler*; they did so again, more elegantly, after the appearance of *The Vision of Judgment* (1821). There is no space, or need, to discuss that unfortunate poem in detail or to rehearse the controversy with Byron that surrounds it.[12] It should be stressed, however, that, while a monumental instance of *poor* judgment, the *Vision* represents, in fact, some of the poet's earliest interests. Specifically, it realized Southey's long-standing ambition to re-introduce hexameter into English poetry, a medium which, despite the miscarriage of "Mohammed," always seemed to him ideally suited for "domestic poetry" and "pastoral epic" of the sort written by Voss and Goethe in Germany, and which he hoped would prove "full, stately, and sonorous, capable of great variety, great sweetness, and great strength" in English (*Letters*, III, 190). Whatever the poem's apparent political purpose, it is clear from the preface and from Southey's correspondence that he cared more about the meter than about the matter.

The *Vision* is thus Southey's final venture in the epic. Or rather, it is a final attempt to reconcile epic and romance by contemplating his age, the era of George III, not in the Classical manner of Virgil but in the "romantic" or "Gothic" one of Dante (cf. X, 204); that is, not by historical or legendary analogue but directly *sub specie aeternitatis*. This epic intention explains, in turn, the murderous and seemingly irrelevant attack on Byron and the Satanic School of Poetry. In *Don Juan*, as Southey saw it, Byron had launched a frontal attack, not merely against Southey himself, but against the entire epic tradition; and his infernal compound of "obscenity, sedition, and blasphemy" had imperiled the whole fabric of moral, political, and religious order for which that tradition stood. The *Vision of Judgment* is Southey's frantic attempt to prove that poets are not of the "Devil's party."

We cannot but admit that the attempt failed on all counts. The *oom-pah, oom-pa-pah* of the hexameter is often ponderous and monotone; the language, trite or prosy; and the visionary machinery, ludicrously obsolete, despite some memorable images and vivid light effects. Above all, we must wonder at the sheer folly of Southey's choosing the mad King George as his hero in this final poetic bout with the powers of hell. In the vision, the poet sees the "reverent form" of the king emerging from the burial vault to give thanks for his deliverance from the long night of his lunacy. George is met by the spirit of the assassinated Spencer Perceval and learns about England's heroic triumph (under the "wise" leadership of the Regent) over the "godless" Tyrant, as well as about her present renewed peril from the "Powers of Evil" and their "accursed conception of filth and of darkness" ([212] a reference to the imminent Cato-Street conspiracy). The poet presently finds himself at the pearly gates and is dazzled by the light streaming from golden towers and diamond pinnacles. An angel announces that "King George of England cometh to judgment" and summons his accusers. The souls of the wicked appear, shrouded in sulphurous clouds, and, led by the Prince of Darkness, range opposite the shimmering legions of the blest.

The "many-headed and monstrous Fiend" of sedition, whose numberless mouths hiss "watch-words of faction, / Freedom, Rights, Corruption, and War, and Oppression" (217), conducts the prosecution. But his witnesses, John Wilkes, "Lord of Misrule in his day" (218) and arch-Revolutionary, and Junius, the "nameless . . . libeller" who "shot his arrows in darkness" (220) and now wears an iron mask as punishment, are shamed into silence before the king's "clear conscience." Thereupon the whole infernal crew is hurled back to hell by a thunderstorm, and the "Absolvers" come forth—the spirits who had criticized the king on earth but who have since learned to "own the wrong they had offered." Among them, the "awful Spirit" of George Washington observes that, although they seemed Rebel and Tyrant to each other on earth, each in fact acted with "upright heart" and was "observant of duty, / Self-approved." The king agrees and blames the Revolutionary War on wicked fomenters of "faction and falsehood" (223 - 5). He then proceeds to plead his own cause by citing the difficulties of his of-fice and the goodness of his intentions. To err is human, he thinks, to forgive, divine. Omnipotence naturally rises to the occasion, utters a jovial "well done," and calls upon the king to enter into the Joy of the Lord. Amid great angelic applause, George puts on in-corruption at the Well of Life and enters through the gate, where he is received by a long pageant of English sovereigns and "worthies." While the king holds reunion with his deceased relatives, the poet, typically yearning for like bliss, tries to partake of the Water of Life but is overcome by darkness and falls headlong back to reality;

> Then I awoke, and beheld the mountains in twilight before me,
> Dark and distinct; and, instead of the rapturous sound of hosannas,
> Heard the bell from the tower, toll, toll through the silence of evening.

That heaven should thus become simply an extension of the Tory Establishment, where kings were apotheosized who would not have escaped censure elsewhere and where dissenters had to recant or be deported, naturally looked like the rankest sycophancy. The pachydermic George IV evidently thought the poem "very beautiful"; but even the pious Cuthbert Southey was dismayed by it; and William Taylor, after reading it "with peals of laughter," concluded that surely it must be a covert burlesque. Yet Southey meant neither to flatter nor to ridicule. But, while his conception of Heaven was always liberal in a theological regard, he was by now too thoroughly appalled by the specter of anarchy and cultural dis-integration to see anything funny in an attempt to enlist even an ecumenical God on the side of British law and order. Fortunately one of the "Devil's party" *did*!

CHAPTER 7

Days Among the Dead:
Prose Writings

BY common opinion, Southey's prose is greatly superior
to his poetry. Contemporaries deemed it exemplary, and more
recent critics have tended to agree. In fact, Southey did much to
free English prose from the labored solemnity of the school of John-
son, Gibbon, and Burke and to develop a medium suited to scholarly exposition, practical controversy, and unadorned narrative—a
style, as he put it, pregnant with meaning yet "plain as a Doric
building" (*Life*, II, 133). Plainness, however, is not always a virtue;
and, if Southey's prose is, as Coleridge said, a model of transparen-
cy and down-to-earth functionalism, it is also quite unpoetic and
justifies Byron's quip about the Laureate's "blank verse and blanker
prose": it is unfailingly discursive and denotative, often abstract
and Latinate in diction, rhythmical but not melodious, almost void
of metaphor, and frequently poor in active verbs and constructions.
Always richly informative, it seldom reaches beyond the merely
practical or commonplace in thought and feeling, seldom
transforms knowledge into power. It thus cannot, despite its vast
bulk, be said to occupy a prominent place in English letters. A brief
look at representative works in each of three main
categories—history and biography, essay and journal, anecdotal
miscellany—will, and must, suffice to round out our picture of
Southey the man and the poet.

I *History and Biography:* The Life of Nelson

Southey's historical writings do not repay extensive perusal today.
Immensely well read, Southey had a stupendous array of facts at his
command; but he lacked the political acumen and the interpretive
skill necessary to make history much more than a glossed chronicle

158

of events. His most ambitious project, the great "History of Portugal," was, indeed, to have been a work both encyclopedic and epic that would combine diversity of events and "manners" with unity of idea and design. But it was never completed, and the very vastness of Southey's plan suggests a fatal inability to select: the main opus was to be supplemented by additional volumes on the Portuguese empires in Asia and South America, on monasticism, on the Jesuits and Jesuit missions, and on Spanish and Portuguese literature. The only episode of the "History" ever to appear in print, *The Expedition of Orsua and the Crimes of Aguirre* (1821), is an extended article—it appeared originally in the *Edinburgh Annual Register*—that exhibits swift, economical narration. But, even at its best, Southey's historical writing is apt to tire the reader by a breathless hurry from detail to detail that leaves little room for any attempt to put things in perspective. Southey's main strength is his ability to crowd a great deal of information readably into a small space, to distill, in his own recurrent metaphor, "wine into alcohol." It is thus regrettable that his plan for a literary encyclopedia never came to fruition.[1]

Indiscriminate inclusiveness marks notably the three-volume colonial *History of Brazil*, the only completed portion of the great Portuguese scheme. Begun during the British South America venture of 1807, the work was soon disparaged by Southey himself, but was nonetheless doggedly continued and finished at last in 1819. The first Brazilian history ever written, it is at least a remarkable feat of research that is still authoritative today—it has recently been translated for the second time into Portuguese. By contrast, the *History of the Peninsular War* (1823 - 32) is vitiated by Southey's incompetence in military affairs and was handicapped from the outset by Wellington's refusal to make his papers available to Southey. It was thus speedily eclipsed by the authorized history published concurrently by Colonel Napier, who had the Duke's blessing and who had himself participated in the campaigns. However, Southey's work offers compact and graphic narrative, such as the moving account of the siege of Saragossa. Compactness is also the main virtue of the *Book of the Church* (1824), a popular and polemical religious history of England from the Druids to 1689.

Finer and more lasting fruits of Southey's historical researches are found in his biographies. Here, again, Southey tends to distill wine into alcohol, and his subjects rarely come fully alive. But the focus on the biography of a single man makes for a unity and a perspec-

tive not found in the histories. *The Life of Wesley* (1820) is a skillful
epitome of the entire Methodist movement. The *Lives of the British
Admirals* (1833 - 7), remarkable for its pioneering (if prolix) use of
Spanish sources, has been called the finest portrait gallery of
Elizabethan naval heroes in the language. Above all, the *Life of
Nelson* (1813) owes its continued popularity to its shapeliness and
perspicuity. Essentially an elaboration of Southey's review in the
Quarterly of the official Nelson biography published in 1806 by
James Stanier Clarke and John M'Arthur, the *Life* bears all the
traits of the review articles of the time—synopsis, glossed
paraphrase, frequent quotation—and has not inaccurately been
described as largely a "skillful literary abridgment" of the earlier
work.[2] There are instances of confused narrative and of stylistic un-
evenness that are due to a make-shift use of passages lifted from the
source—Southey was pressed for time. Moreover, the facts are not
always accurate by present standards of Nelson scholarship. But the
whole is a triumph of tidy epitomizing and a remarkably competent
work to come from a landlubber.

Southey's portrait of England's greatest naval hero is frank and
engaging. Southey does not have Carlyle's myth-making power, as
the feebleness of the attempt at apotheosis in the last sentence of
the *Life* makes plain. But neither does he indulge in headlong hero-
worship. While doing full justice to Nelson's naval genius, he
blames him severely, even unfairly, for the ruthless liquidation of
the Neapolitan revolutionaries and of their leader Carraciolo; he
repeatedly disparages Nelson's devotion to the degenerate
Neapolitan court; and, of course, he frowns upon Nelson's "in-
fatuated attachment," as he primly terms it, to Lady Hamilton to
whose influence he, in fact, ascribes all of Nelson's Neapolitan sins.

The limits of Southey's sympathy and candor appear in his treatment of the celebrated Emma. While, on the one hand, he palliates
Nelson's uncritical support of Naples' cowardly and remorseless
politics by simply blaming it on the "spell" which Lady Hamilton,
the close friend and confidante of the queen, had cast over him, he
does not, on the other hand, furnish any real insight into this "attachment" and Nelson's consequent separation from Lady
Nelson—a subject naturally shocking to Southey's prim and fervent
domesticity; nor does he render intelligible the continued close
friendship between Nelson and Sir William Hamilton. Although
many of the documents relating to the more Byronic aspects of
Nelson's life were then unavailable, and although it was scarcely ap-

propriate to dwell at length upon those aspects, we cannot help feeling that Southey's official reticence at times radiates the coldness of incomprehension and evasiveness.

For the most part, however, Southey found Nelson a man after his own heart. Nelson's boyishness, his love of children, the mixture of kindness and pugnacity in his actions and utterances were in fact traits of Southey's own personality, as was the self-righteousness versing on petulance that occasionally marked Nelson's dispatches. Southey himself was less vainglorious and did not have the soldier's obsession with honor, but he found personified in Nelson his own fanatical devotion to duty and what went with it: integrity, independence of mind, and a hearty jingoism.

"Duty is the great business of a sea officer," Nelson wrote to his bride; "all private considerations must give way to it, however painful" (37); "England expects every man to do his duty," was his famous last signal to his fleet before the battle of Trafalgar; and his last words—after he had bequeathed Lady Hamilton to his country—were a repeated "Thank God, I have done my duty" (284, 292f.). At the same time, he clearly did not interpret the term in a narrow regimental sense. Nelson's career, as Southey gleefully points out, was dotted with instances of his disregarding specific orders—usually with spectacular results, as in the battles of Cape St. Vincent and Copenhagen. But if he sometimes disobeyed for glory, "the last infirmity of this noble mind" (286), as he did notably at the unsuccessful storming of Santa Cruz when he lost two hundred and fifty men and his own right arm, he usually acted on what he considered higher imperatives than those issued by the admiralty—including, significantly, an almost idolatrous devotion to kings and an unqualified hatred and contempt of "the damned French villains" and everything French (183).

Above all, however, Southey admired Nelson's humane and kindly nature:

Never was any commander more beloved. He governed men by their reason and their affections; they knew that he was incapable of caprice or tyranny; and they obeyed him with alacrity and joy, because he possessed their confidence as well as their love. 'Our Nel,' they used to say, 'is as brave as a lion, and as gentle as a lamb.' Severe discipline he detested, though he had been bred in a severe school: he never inficted corporal punishment, if it were possible to avoid it, and when compelled to enforce it, he, who was familiar with wounds and death, suffered like a woman. . . . But in Nelson there was more than the easiness and humanity of a happy nature; he did not merely abstain from injury; his was an active and watchful benevolence, ever desirous not only to render justice, but to do good. (250f.)

This is eloquent praise; and, though the diction is typically abstract and colorless, with just a saving touch of synecdoche and simile, the passage sways us by the skill with which Southey amplifies and balances his statement.[3]

II   *Journalism:* Letters from England

The same qualitative difference that distinguishes Southey's biographies from his other historical writings also elevates a piece of journalism like the *Letters from England* above his formal essays and reviews. Reviewing, then a lucrative business, supplied a large part of Southey's livelihood; but, while his pieces have some historical weight in that they helped to bring about a more dispassionate, objective, and essentially synoptic and digestive type of reviewing, they are without critical significance and, for the most part, deal with ephemera.[4] His essays, often themselves based on reviews, are similarly limited in their merely topical concerns; and while they are sincere and vigorous, they are formless harangues, void of the sense of proportion and the ironic perspective that can turn even polemic into a thing of beauty. It is precisely a sense of form and esthetic detachment that makes the *Letters from England,* and even the *Colloquies,* still readable.

Southey had tried his hand successfully at the then-popular genre of epistolary journalism as early as 1797 when he published his *Letters Written During a Short Residence in Spain and Portugal,* a medley of anecdote, description, social comment, translations, original verse, historical information, and curious learning, that sold well and went through three editions. In the *Letters from England: by Don Manuel Alvares Espriella* (1807) he improved upon the type by combining travelogue, satire, and familiar essay in the manner of Voltaire's *Lettres Philosophiques* and Goldsmith's *Citizen of the World.* Planned as early as 1803 as an "omnium gatherum of the odd things I have seen in England" and written at intervals between then and 1807, the book was designed to set forth in an amusing way "all I know and much of what I think respecting this country and these times," and was published pseudonymously to promote sales and to throw off hostile reviewers.[5]

Though largely anecdotal and episodic, the *Letters* nonetheless exhibit a real cross section of life and "manners" in England at the end of the eighteenth century. Critical commentaries on political, economic, social, and religious affairs alternate with observations about modes of travel and transportation; countrysides and townscapes; cathedrals and antiquities; customs, styles, and fashions; foods and fads; sports and pastimes; all seasoned with local anecdotes and curiosities illustrative of human oddness in general and British spleen in particular. But what raises the work above the level of mere rhetoric and journalism is the use of a persona to veil the nakedness of Southey's biases. The choice of a young Spaniard as the pseudonymous author enabled Southey not only to hoodwink the critics but to counterpoint his critique of British abuses with a satiric portrait of Catholic and hidalgo mentality as he knew it and to create the amusing spectacle of a Papist ridiculing the English "heretics" for their superstitious enthusiasm!

Apart from such byplay, Southey's descriptions are often pedestrian. Don Manuel's journey through England naturally includes a survey of the Lake District. But that celebrated subject required far more of an imaginative synthesis than Southey's encyclopedic and miscellaneous approach could achieve. Scenes are described in picturesque detail and are said to be "lovely," "beautiful," "exquisite," and "grand"; but the account remains largely topographical, the scenic features are itemized rather than seen in perspective; and, while Don Manuel calls the experience unforgettable, he is confessedly unable to make it so for us.

In like manner, Southey vents his pity for the plight of the laboring poor in Birmingham and Manchester, but he does not evoke that plight in terms sufficiently compelling to elicit pity in the reader. Unlike Swift, whose artistry is directly proportionate to his sense of moral urgency, Southey all but drops his fictional character when his feelings are aroused. The result is a sentimental preachiness that is neither esthetically attractive nor rhetorically effective. What is most graphic and particular is rather the gay trivia scattered throughout, from Don Manuel's early description of the bustle in an English inn to the vivid sketches of Bath and Bristol, Southey's two hometowns, which conclude the book. The accounts of London, the "modern Tyre" (71), are particularly entertaining and informative. With its lamps and busy streets, its traffic and street cries, its theaters and shop-windows, London bursts upon the grave Spaniard as it must have burst upon the young Southey half a generation earlier.

Politically, the *Letters* represent a transition in Southey's thinking. The year of Don Manuel's visit is that of the Peace of Amiens
(1802), and Southey uses the occasion not only to record the il-
luminations and public rejoicings it called forth but to praise the
peace ministry and to denounce William Pitt's politics of "war-
mongering," crushing taxation, and anti-Jacobin hysteria. Francis
Burdett's agitation for Parliamentary reform is not yet the villainy it
became in the *Quarterly* essays. We hear of the evil of "retaining
institutions after their utility has ceased" (372). And, after criticiz-
ing the rotten boroughs and the fraud, bribery, and intimidation
rife at the hustings, Southey goes so far as to advocate the secret
ballot, a measure that was then regarded as radical and visionary
(286). Throughout, he pleads for more humane and civilized standards in public life. He deplores the barbarity of British martial law
and calls for military and naval reforms, including abolition of im-
pressment, limited service, and retirement pensions. He censures
Pitt's use of government informers and revenue spies as corrupting
public morals. He inveighs against cruel and lurid forms of punishment and against such things as boxing, bull and bear baiting, and
barbarous slaughter methods, emphasizing especially their brutaliz-
ing effect on the populace.

At the same time, Southey is already at variance with much of
what then passed for liberal philosophy. His plea for a reduction of
the number of capital offenses, for example, is not so much a plea
for greater leniency as it is an attack upon the penological
pragmatism which insists that prevention rather than retribution is
the end of punishment. "Vengeance," Southey maintains quite un-
fashionably, "is the foundation of all penal law, divine and
human," and punishments must, therefore, be exactly proportionate to the offenses and to the "degree of moral guilt which they
indicate in the offender" (124). The issue is not punitiveness as
such, but rather the materialism implicit in laws that, for example,
make forgery a capital offense. "More merciless than Draco," Don
Manuel observes, "or than those inquisitors who are never mentioned in this country without an abhorrent expression of real or
affected humanity, the commercial legislators of England are
satisfied with nothing but the life of the offender who sins against
the Bank, which is their Holy of Holies" (123). In fact, one of the
most prominent features of the *Letters* is their hostility to the commercialism of the English—their addiction to "getting and spending."

Commercialism, to Don Manuel, is the source of every social and economic evil; it is a poison that corrupts everything, "literature, arts, religion, government . . . a *lues* which has got into the system of the country, and is rotting flesh and bone" (368). It produces slavery in the colonies and child labor at home, pauperism in the country and untold misery in the new industrial towns. Southey particularly denounces the "manufacturing system," the most sinister progeny of the "commercial spirit":

I thought [Don Manuel writes from Manchester] of the cities in Arabian romance, where all the inhabitants were enchanted; here Commerce is the queen witch. . . . A happy country indeed it is for the higher orders; no where have the rich so many enjoyments, no where have the ambitious so fair a field, no where have the ingenious such encouragement, no where have the intellectual such advantages; but to talk of English happiness is like talking of Spartan freedom, the Helots are overlooked. In no other country can such riches be acquired by commerce, but it is the one who grows rich by the labor of the hundred. The hundred, human beings like himself, as wonderfully fashioned by Nature, gifted with like capacities, and equally made for immortality, are sacrificed body and soul. They are deprived in childhood of all instruction and all enjoyment; of the sports in which childhood instinctively indulges, of fresh air by day and of natural sleep by night. Their health physical and moral is alike destroyed; they die of diseases induced by unremitting task work, by confinement in the impure atmosphere of crowded rooms, by the particles of metallic or vegetable dust they are continually inhaling; or they live to grow up without decency, without comfort, and without hope, without morals, without religion, and without shame, and bring forth slaves like themselves to tread in the same path of misery. (209f.)

Like Blake, and later Dickens, Southey is particularly indignant about the callous disregard shown to the children of the poor, who are sold into the wage slavery of the factories, where, in Don Manuel's memorable phrase, they keep "the devil's *laus perennis*," or are forced to grow up in work houses where "there is none to love them, and consequently none whom they can love" (211). Southey was sufficiently old-fashioned to ascribe much of the profligacy of the poor—drunkenness among men and dissoluteness among women—to a mere lack of religious and moral instruction; but he had, like Wordsworth and Coleridge, an intuitive grasp of the vital importance of love and joy in the formation of character; and he passionately denounced a system that seemed calculated to stunt human growth.

Southey's nascent conservatism is apparent also in his fear that the new industrialism would impair the social order by eroding the middle ranks and by replacing the old graduated hierarchy with a two-caste system—in fact, Disraeli's "two nations"—of rich and poor, capitalist and proletariat, that could only end in revolution. The "manufacturing populace," destitute and lacking the "local attachments" of the peasantry, had nothing to lose but its chains. "Governments who found their prosperity upon manufactures," Don Manuel pithily writes, "sleep upon gunpowder" (375).

Southey's analysis of economic conditions in England is not rigorous or comprehensive. In his hands, industry is made the scapegoat for numerous and complex social and economic dislocations; and while his suggested remedies are generally sound—government regulation of industry and commerce, higher wages, reduction of the tax burden, stricter economy in government expenditures—they are often merely romantic, such as the proposal to turn back the clock and to reconvert "the poor into peasantry" and the towns into villages (379). Yet the *Letters* are remarkable for their articulate sensitivity to conditions wrought by the industrial revolution and for their early appeal to the social conscience in the face of radical change.

Finally, the *Letters* are also noteworthy for their "view of the different religious sects in the country"—an undertaking, Southey thought, equalled by "no former historian of heresies" (*Letters*, I, 407). The Catholic zeal of Don Manuel, if at times trying, is often put to good use, whether Don Manuel rejoices at the signs of Catholic resurgence in England, comments on the wordliness of the Establishment, deplores the "graceless and joyless system of manners" fostered by Calvinism, or pillories the day's *pseudodoxia epidemica*, from Methodism to Swedenborginanism and the lunatic fringe of a Thomas Taylor, Richard Brothers, or Joanna Southcott.

Much of Southey's commentary is superficial, and more has become obsolete; but some of it can still make us pause; and the rest remains at least a copious, readable source for the historian of manners, styles, and fashions, opinions, and institutions. Southey's satirical vein may not be gold or silver, and it disappears all too often (along with the fiction of Don Manuel) under the rubbish of tedious polemic and supernumerary detail. But, while it lasts, it yields a fine jovial tin, so to speak: something bright, flexible, and unpretentious.

III *Essays and Colloquies*

Little of that joviality survives in *Sir Thomas More: or, Colloquies on the Progress and Prospects of Society* (1829, 1831). By then, two intervening decades of social and political crisis and of personal losses had fostered a progressively anti-democratic, authoritarian viewpoint in Southey that left its imprint not only on the content but on the form of his writing. The growth of this outlook is most clearly traceable in the review essays which, written over a number of years, reappeared, revised and condensed, on the eve of the Reform Bill as *Essays Moral and Political* (1832). In them, Southey not only engages, at close quarters, the old bugbears of materialism, manufacturers, Malthus, Methodism, mobocracy, and Catholic Emancipation, but inveighs, in increasingly apocalyptic tones, against the monsters of disaffection, infidelity, and immortality by which he finds himself surrounded: the "un-English, un-Christian, inhuman spirit" growing in the populace; the "demoniacal" spirit of party among politicians; the "licentiousness" of the press; and a whole Domdaniel of disaffected literary men who, we learn, would publish any "scandal, sedition, obscenity, or blasphemy" to reduce the nation to their own depravity. The tendency towards dualism that once fed Southey's republican *Tyrannenhass* now recrudesces in behalf of law and order. "There are but two parties in this kingdom," Southey wrote in 1831, "the Revolutionists and the Loyalists." Two years later, he was even surer: "On our side we have God and the right."[6]

As many of the evils which Southey attacks were real enough, some of the remedies he proposes are sound: a system of universal education; a national works program to relieve unemployment and to develop natural resources; savings-banks; reforms of poor-laws and game-laws; laws to regulate working hours. But others now appear quaint or dubious such as the vociferous call for England to become the "hive" of nations"—Southey's smug insistence that, Robert Malthus notwithstanding, God clearly wished the English to be fruitful and multiply so that they could replenish the earth and subdue it. Increasingly, moreover, Southey's program appears not just conservative but repressive and reactionary and content to treat symptoms. If he favors the Bell system of national education, his purpose is not to raise an intelligent electorate but, in his favorite proverb, to "train up the people in the way they should go"—to instruct them in the moral and religious principles of the Established Church, and to disarm them by telling them to fear God, to honor the king, and to know their place. The answer to popular distress is not popular representation but moral rearmament; relief, not reform; charity, not change. Government should be left to gentlemen: governors, like poets, are evidently born, not made. *Vox populi* has never been *vox Dei*: "God is in the populace as he is in the hurricane, and the volcano, and the earthquake" (I, 421). Even rotten boroughs and government sinecures are necessary props of the Establishment; and Southey thinks that it might be wise not only to curb the press but to repair the stocks.

The picture is equally portentous and conspiratorial in the *Colloquies*, written between 1820 and 1829. England is swamped by commercial and philosophical materialism, scorched by religious and political fanaticism, poisoned by obscenity; and her only salvation from the blight of industry, the plague of revolution, and the "unholy alliance" of "Popery, Dissent, and Unbelief" (II, 43f.) lies in a frankly authoritarian and paternalistic government based on Anglican doctrine, social hierarchy, and a hereditary aristocracy, and supported by a system of national education—or, rather, indoctrination. To Southey, "Omnipresence to law, and omnipotence to order, this is indeed the fair ideal of commonwealth" (I, 105). "We shall get more Utopian," Southey wrote elsewhere "in having less liberty and more order" (*Letters*, IV, 252). Subjects cannot be guided by self-interest because, like children, they do not know where their true interests lie. The only effective "cement of political society" is thus the "principle of religious obedience"; "government by Public Opinion" is the beginning of anarchy (II, 197, 203).

Politics, like ethics, must be dictated, not by a utilitarian calculus, but by the consciousness of divine justice, that is, divine retribution, individual or collective. The only sure foundation of both morality and policy is a positive eschatological religion with its assertion of an ultimate and frankly vindictive *patria potestas* governing the universe. Infidels are therefore "engineers of evil" (109) who destroy the very foundations of the moral and political edifice. Even Dissent is a half-way station to disloyalty; and, while Southey concedes that sectarianism has its uses since, as he shrewdly observes, it "gratifies at once the social and the selfish feeling" (82), he rejects all forms of pluralism. He even welcomes the advent of technological warfare as enabling men to "act in masses as machines" rather than with "personal feeling" (I, 209f.).

Southey's critique of economic conditions and of the "trading spirit" often anticipates Carlyle's pungent invectives against Mammonism: "profit and loss became the rule of conduct; in came calculation, and out went feeling" (I, 79). In his analysis of the evils of capitalism—competition, exploitation, speculation, overproduction, unemployment, and alienation—he was ahead of his time; and his earnest and often eloquent concern about a divided nation—"the poor against the rich, the many against the few . . . youth against age" (31)—not only heralds a major Victorian theme but is not without relevance today. But here, too, his sympathies are too one-sided and his solutions largely romantic ones. Justly appalled by the inhuman mechanics of supply and demand and by the consequent emergence of an industrial proletariat, a "Helotry," poor, brutal, rootless, and disaffected, he sees in Medieval feudalism an alternative social structure in which the individual was neither a cog in a machine nor an atom in a void but a vital member of an organic body politic, whose station in a firm but subtly graduated hierarchy gave coherence to his life. While acknowledging the evils of actual feudal systems, as well as the "humanizing, civilizing, liberalizing" effects of commerce (197), Southey nevertheless insists that "a patriarchal state is better and happier than a commercial one" (II, 276). If villeins were in some respects like cattle, at least they were cared for. The way to help the laboring poor then was not to emancipate them to enable them to help themselves—that way lay anarchy and *jacquerie*—but to replace commercial exploitation by a benevolent despotism of god-fearing, incorruptible men like Robert Southey. Still dreaming of Utopia, Southey has come to the conclusion that Pantisocracy requires a Pantocrator.

What keeps the *Colloquies* alive—apart from Macaulay's famous review—is not only a fine prose style but its form for which Southey felt indebted to Boethius. By bringing more than one point of view to bear and by interspersing his social commentary with precise if not evocative descriptions of the Lake scenery and some vivid historical narrative, Southey relieves an otherwise formidable succession of homilies.

The idea of a dialogue with the ghost of Sir Thomas More is potentially a happy one. As a Catholic, Renaissance man, and arch-Utopian, More can not only function as a more enlightened Espriella but can provide instructive historical parallels—"it is your lot," he observes to his host, "as it was mine to live during one of the grand climacterics of the world"—and give perspective to Southey's own intellectual career: *"Et in Utopia Ego"* (I, 18). A sort of father-image (Southey identifies him with his uncle and "more than father" Herbert Hill and repeatedly alludes to Hamlet's encounter with the ghost), More is not only a figure of authority but at times a dark alter-ego whose stringent conservatism enables Southey to reserve for himself some of the optimism of his youth. Thus, while More prophesies "sedition, privy conspiracy and rebellion . . . false doctrine, heresy and schism," a second Wat Tyler (!), an English Jacquerie, and a worldwide Armageddon between the Holy Alliance and godless Democracy, Southey can, in his own character of "Montesinos," resurrect some of his early millennial dreams, defend Robert Owen's Socialism against More's objections to Owen's free-thinking, and affirm Immanuel Kant's faith in man's dialectical progress towards rationality and "a universal civil society, founded on the empire of political justice" (!) and "perpetual peace." "Rest there in full faith," More replies equivocally, "I leave you to your dream" (II, 410, 426).

Unfortunately, Southey's dialogue is too often a mere expository convenience, an excuse for discontinuity and expansiveness; and the discussion, while ranging and informed, is also diffuse, verbose, repetitive, and too biased to meet the highest standards of either fact or fiction. Always prone to reduce conflict of interest to a moral dualism, Southey does not create imaginary conversations with real dramatic substance and tension, but uses More as a mere mouthpiece, or *magister colloquii*, with whom he bandies lectures and swaps facts and quotations: the conversation, as Lamb remarked, might as well have passed between A and B. Mildly amusing at first, when Southey mistakes his visitor for an American by his quaint speech, the situation soon grows tedious; and Sir Thomas's behavior of vanishing and reappearing like the Cheshire Cat suits ill with the gravity, and length, of his discourse. At once too solid and too merely fictitious, Southey's More compels no suspension of disbelief, any more than Southey's calling himself "Montesinos," presumably with reference to Don Quixote's famous dream, signalizes any real self-parody. Ironically, Southey is at his best in his digressions when he evokes the view from Walla Crag; when he tells the legend of St. Kentigern, the patron of Crosthwaite Church at Keswick; or when he wistfully guides his ghostly visitor through his beloved library: "Ancient and Modern, Jew and Gentile, Mohammedan and Crusader, French and English, Spaniards and Portugueze, Dutch and Brazilians, fighting their old battles, silently now, upon the same shelf. . . . Here I possess these gathered treasures of time, the harvest of so many generations, laid up in my garners; and when I go to the window there is the lake, and the circle of the mountains, and the illimitable sky" (II, 342f.).

IV   The Doctor

From this library, rather than from the world beyond the window, Southey produced all his writings: his favorite occupation, he once said, was "to read and to compile" (*Memoir*, I, 429), to chronicle, epitomize, and moralize. No work is therefore more typical than the strange farrago of over six hundred closely printed, double-columned pages called *The Doctor* which Southey published—again anonymously—as his swansong towards the end of his life after he had worked on it at intervals for over two decades and to which he was still adding when his mind at last gave way. Ostensibly it tells the story of "Dr. Daniel Dove of Doncaster and his horse Nobs"—a yarn Coleridge used to spin, whose "humor lay in making it as long-winded as possible" and in never telling it the same way twice. In fact, however, the book, whose full title is *The Doctor, etc.*, comprises a Gargantuan mass of anecdotes, ruminations, homilies, curious learning, topography, genre sketches, extravagant fancies, chit-chat, plain nonsense, and innumerable synopses and excerpts from Southey's often recondite reading, all afloat on a mere trickle of narrative that often disappears for whole chapters and flows nowhere in particular. As Southey explained to Caroline Bowles, he intended "little more at first than to play the fool in a way that might amuse the wise" but soon "perceived that there was no way in which I could so conveniently dispose of some of my multifarious collections, nor so well send into the world some wholesome but unpalatable truths, nor advance speculations upon dark subjects, without giving offense or exciting animadversion. With something therefore of Tristram Shandy in its character, something of Rabelais, more of Montaigne, and a little of old Burton, the predominant character is still my own."[7]

In large portions, the work is in fact a glorified commonplace book. Southey liked to compare his researches to digging for pearls or precious stones in a dungheap; and one purpose of *The Doctor* was to mount these treasures and to offer them as a kind of literary rummage sale for the delight and instruction of posterity. As "quotationipotent mottocrat,"[8] he lords it over his readers in eight different languages. Virtually no chapter is without lengthy excerpts, some chapters are mere centos of quotations, each chapter has its motto, each volume an entire "prelude" of mottos. Many of these have little or nothing to do with the story, in spite of Southey's solemn protestations to the contrary; but, as in the *Omniana* or in the documentary undergirding of the epics, they exist for their own sake or serve as trappings for Southey's hobby-horses.

In particular, *The Doctor* also exhibits some of that packrat fascination for curious trivia, exploded opinions, weird superstitions, and morbid obsessions that makes parts of Southey's notebooks such bizarre reading. Ranging from reports about "that painter of great but insane genius" William Blake (clxxxi), through tales of gruesome or unscrupulous medical practices, to anecdotes about vampires, lycanthropes, and horned or oviparous women (cxxviii) and the belief that Eve was made from Adam's tail (ccviii), the book at times resembles Robert Burton's *Anatomy of Melancholy*, from which, indeed, it frequently quotes. Southey's attitude, however, while sometimes anatomical and pathological, is usually merely critical and homiletic—when not simply morbid—combining the complacence of hindsight with an anxious yet futile endeavor to separate "reasonable" belief from "unreasonable" credulity. As elsewhere, myth and religion, old miracle-mongers and new fanatics, monks and montebanks, Methodists, Mohammedans, and unclean spirits are judged at the bar of mere commonsense and "natural piety." There is some genuine criticism, as in the chapter on the persecution of the Jews and the superstitious calumnies that underlay them (cxx); but even in this case Southey does not see beyond "Popery" to the deeper causes of anti-Semitism. In another interesting chapter on fetishism and object-worship, Southey adopts the anthropological viewpoint of a de Brosses or Court de Gebelin, but only to discard it for a safe platitude about man's fallen condition (cxlvii). Southey's discourse on such matters is always but one part science and two parts apologetics.

Much of this gossip is in a spirit of fun. But, while the tone of *The Doctor* is temperate and whimsical, that does not bespeak a mellowing of Southey's opinions, but is due to the fact that he addresses himself throughout to the "Ladies," whom he assumes to be sympathetic to his fogyish views. When occasion serves, he attacks the Reform Bill as a "mass of crudities"; parades his contempt for all Whigs; scourges Catholic Emancipation, the manufacturing system, and democracy; and fires broadsides at "the race of Political Economists, our Malthusites, Benthamites, Utilitarians or Futilitarians" (xxxv). Conversely, while he is censuring the callousness of the Peers who defeated a bill against employment of children as chimney sweeps, he carefully pulls his punches, ostensibly lest "any irritation which [strong] language might excite should lessen the salutary effects of self-condemnation"—a scruple notably absent from his attacks on liberals and commoners—and hastens to add a caveat against "revolutionary schemes" and any inclination to substitute "political hopes" for "religious faith" (xvi).

With increasing bluntness, Southey insists that "sound" and "orthodox" are synonymous terms (ccxxxvi). "Knowledge" is good only if it leads to "wisdom," that is to say, to dutiful acquiescence is the *status quo* as the will of God. Duties, moreover, gain in moral value in proportion to their unpleasantness: to believe otherwise would be to sanction the nasty hedonism of the futilitarians. Needless to say, Southey merely raises eudaemonism to a higher level since he hinges his entire *Weltanschauung* on the concept of posthumous rewards and punishments, a concept to which even the existence of God seems at times merely a necessary presupposition. Christianity means essentially the guarantee of this metaphysical panacea; and Southey's reply to unbelief is the pragmatic one that only fools or knaves could want to demolish so priceless a comfort (ccxviiif.). Accordingly, he never tires of dwelling, sometimes casually, sometimes in full unction, upon the brevity of life; the vanity of earthly wishes; age, sorrow, and death; and their eventual redressal in a heaven of changeless order and *gemuetlichkeit*.

Better minds than Southey have held similar tenets. What estranges the modern reader is the defensive and commonplace character of Southey's reformulations; his refusal to engage in a real dialogue with the intellectual forces that were fast rendering such tenets obsolete; his futile attempt to turn back the clock to the time of the judicious Hooker and Robert South, favorite authors of his, and to drown out, with endless citations and iterations and name-calling, the new voices that he could not silence with more original arguments. Montaigne once said that he liked better to forge his mind than to furnish it: Southey openly prefers furnishing to forging (cxxiii). Too fragile to be broken, blown, burned, and made new, his mind grows merely by accretion—by his discovering ever new corroborations of what he already believes.

Yet therein lies also the charm of *The Doctor*—a charm that

makes the work something more than a mere monument of an exploded theology, philosophy, and psychology that is useful only to
the historian of opinions. In a ceaseless search for reassurance about
the enigma of death and for a "golden mean between superstition
and impiety" (clxxx), Southey ranges not only through Christian
theology and devotional writing but into remotest regions, from the
Institutions of Menu to the "Bardic System," from ruminations concerning ghosts and spirits to amused yet wistful anecdotes about the
searchers for the Elixir of Life and the Philosophers' Stone.
Moreover, under the protective persona of his fictitious hero,
Southey permits himself some unorthodox "speculations" about
pre-existence, metempsychosis, *karma*, and evolution—complete
with quotations from Wordsworth's "Immortality Ode"—which he
passes off as "the Columbian Philosophy," half in jest, half in
earnest, as his own yet not his own, comforting yet not committing.[9]
The spokesman of a kind of *Religio Medici*, Daniel Dove is also
Southey's Diogenes Teufelsdroeckh.

He does not, indeed, have the troubled Faustian nature of
Carlyle's hero. Physician, goodman, and rural "flossofer," he is
rather a sort of blend of Goldsmith's Dr. Primrose and Sterne's
Walter Shandy. But, like Teufelsdroeckh, he is a somewhat fantastic
alter-ego—he may even owe some of his later mystifications to
Carlyle's influence. The name Daniel, we are told, connotes both
the prophet and the patriarch Dan, as well as the river Don of Doncaster; Dove links the Doctor with Jonah, Joan of Arc, Columbus,
and the river Dove; and the letter D or Δ (blazoned in mystic triune
form on the title page) initials everything that is important, from
Danger, Doom, the Devil, and the Deity, to Duty, Devotion,
Domesticity, Drink, Dung, and Diarrhea (*sic*) (xxxiii, clxxvf.). Like
Wordsworth's Wanderer, moreover, the Doctor is represented as the
amiable mentor of the author's youth, his "guide, philosopher, and
friend," "teacher," and "moral physician"—an ideal elective father
figure (otherwise childless) who made him what he is and whose
confidant and apostolic disciple he became (clviii, cliii).

Like the Wanderer, Daniel also bears autobiographical traits. His
mother's name is Margaret; her aunt, the beautiful but cold,
shrewish, and overbearing Melicent Trewbody, seems to be a
caricature of Elizabeth Tyler; Daniel's "half-saved," quasi-Tobyish
uncle William Dove is clearly a portrait of Southey's uncle William
Tyler; and the famous "Story of the Three Bears," which Southey

introduces as one of William Dove's yarns was probably a story Southey had heard in childhood from the "Squire."[10]

These autobiographical elements are in fact among the most vivid and most truly narrative ones in the book. While plunging back into the "History of Portugal," Southey himself could sigh "how much more accurate, and perhaps a thousand years hence, more valuable, a book it would be were I to write the History of Wine Street below the Pump. . . . It almost startles me to see how the events of private life . . . equal or outdo novel and comedy [and] all that history offers" (*Life*, III, 32). If his letters are any indication, Southey might have done well with such personal narrative. With their steely cheerfulness; their puns and conundrums; their thousand projects and notices of, and responses to, everything from politics to poetry, and their "meipseads" and tattle about his children and his cats, the letters are among the most attractive of his prose writings. In this medium, even his fits of pharisaical self-righteousness are tolerable because they are manifestly subjective—the expressions, not of a spokesman, but of a character, who is truculent because vulnerable, and pugnacious from excessive tenderness. But Southey was too much the prisoner of his own defenses to be capable of the candor, or shamelessness, of his fellow-Romantics; and the masquerade of *Espriella* and the *Doctor* remained the only steps in this direction.

Characteristically, Daniel Dove is a figure of the past, the good old days. A coeval of Southey's grandparents, he represents an idyllic, pastoral interregnum of rural mirth and manners before materialism, manufacturing, Methodism, and Independence had reared their ugly heads: "We had our monarchy, our hierarchy, and our aristocracy,—God be praised for the benefits which have been derived from all three, and God in his mercy continue them to us!—but we had no plutarchy . . . no great capitalists. . . . Feudal tyranny had passed away, and moneyed tyranny had not yet arisen" (cii). A world of "local attachments," common decencies, and simple verities, it had few newspapers; no "pestiferous tracts, either seditious or sectarian" (cix); and no politics—Doncaster happily "sends no members to parliament" (xxxiv). Clouds of "Wilkes and liberty" brood distantly on the horizon—Southey makes his hero a contemporary of Wilkes at the University of Leyden—but only to set off the sunshine of this better day: Daniel, we are told, never associated with the reprobate Jack, "a man whose irreligion was of the worst kind, and who delighted in licentious conversation" (lxxxv). Utopia, too—for even Daniel dreams of Utopia—is now based on absolute monarchy, hereditary nobility, and an absolute constitution; Daniel's House of Commons is returned by universal suffrage but has no legislative power (ccxli)!

Southey populates this agrarian idyl with a variety of unexceptionable eighteenth-century characters. Mr. Allison, the retired tobacconist and local magnate, is a lesser Squire Allworthy, modeled, like the latter, on Ralph Allen of Bath; his residence, Thaxted Grange, owes much to Southey's memories of his grandmother's farm at Bedminster. Mr. Bacon, the widowed father of Deborah Dove, is a pastor and teacher of Goldsmithian purity. There is the elder Dove, "Flossofer Daniel," a fervent believer in white witchcraft who holds, with Kenelm Digby, that warts can be cured by washing the hands in moonshine—which, however, "must be caught in a bright silver basin" (vii). There is the childlike William Dove. Above all, there is Daniel, the Doctor and dreamer, Southey's embodiment of good-natured commonsense and a golden mean of innocent wisdom, prudent affection, and sensible piety. With a head well-furnished, if ill-forged; a heart affectionate, though neither spontaneous nor passionate; and a life of peaceful industry and domestic contentment, Daniel Dove is both an idealized portrait of Southey—we are told explicitly, in one of Southey's many coy self-references, that the Doctor was "like Southey" (xxxiv)—and a monument to a vanishing way of life.

It has been thought that Southey might have made a good novelist. *The Doctor* shows that Southey had an eye for settings and "manners" and could render an episode or dash off a portrait, at least of certain types of persons. But he lacked the psychological acumen and the moral sympathy required of a novelist and the ability to control and unify a broad array of characters and events. In several of the rather frequent bursts of unblushing self-praise that dot the book, Southey insists that the work has a unity all its own; and, in the Preface, he compares it rather preeningly to the peacock feather with which he is writing: "The combination of parts, each perfect in itself . . . yet all connected into one harmonious whole; the story running through like the stem or backbone, which the episodes and digressions fringe like so many featherlets, leading up to that catastrophe, the gem or eye-star, for which the whole was formed, and in which all terminate." What the "catastrophe" was to have been we shall never know; but, even if we did, the work would not evince the organic unity promised in the Preface. A later comparison to a musical suite (xciv) is more apt, but the book reminds us even more of a literary periodical like *The Spectator.*

Often, of course, the outrageous disproportion between story and detail is meant to be funny, as when Southey uses dozens of learned allusions and hundreds of equestrian terms to describe the Doctor's trusty steed Nobs (cxliiif.). More often, however, such detail is merely prolix, as when the narrative of Daniel's residence at Leyden is buried under numerous historical anecdotes, a list of things that might be described but won't be, and lengthy ruminations concerning the difference between falling and "getting" in love (xlix-liv). Even the most nearly sustained narrative, the love story of Mrs. Dove's parents, Leonard and Margaret, is thin in plot, notwithstanding its reliance on personal history, and it rarely rises above sentimental cliché: orphaned cousins, unfeeling relatives, wedded bliss of godliness and happy poverty, the girl's early death and enshrinement in the widower's worshipful memory, and so on. John Gibson Lockhart, reviewing *The Doctor* in the *Quarterly* (no. ci), deemed this "the sweetest Love-story that has been penned for many a day in the English tongue." Most people today will find it rather too sweet.

Some critics also have praised the humor in *The Doctor.* Southey's original intention had been, as he said, "to play the fool"; as early as 1805, in fact, he had dreamed of "out-Rabelaising Rabelais, out-Sternifying Sterne" (*New Letters,* I, 384) with a book of "sublime nonsense" such as "requires more wit, more sense, more reading, more knowledge, more learning, than go to the composition of half the wise ones of the world" (*Life,* II, 33). Southey can be charmingly whimsical, as in "The Three Bears," the accounts of the cats and the garden statues of Greta Hall, or the chapter concerning the elder Daniel's "Experiment upon Moonshine," a gem worthy of Sterne. But his attempts at "pantagruelism" are often overdone, and his "shandeizing" tends to decline into mawkishness and has little of Sterne's keen sense of the dubiousness of all things. Himself the melancholy buffoon whom he discusses in Chapter lxxi, Southey has the kind of wintry, inhibited humor that finds much mirth in fleas and flatulence but frowns on decolletages and that smirks about the conception and birth of Nobs but pretends that such things are confined to the animal kingdom. He can turn around to ridicule, in a "Chapter Extraordinaire," the

"Ultradelicates" and "Extrasuperfines" like Dr. Bowdler, whose
Family Shakespeare he calls (in roundabout terms) a gelding. In
general, however, *The Doctor* is an eminently Victorian book—one
repeatedly recommended for its impeccable morality and its
suitableness for reading in a "domestic circle."

Characteristically, Southey tries to compensate for his comic impotence by an immoderate amount of self-conscious ego-
tizing—what Lockhart, not realizing that he was excoriating his
own valued essayist and reviewer, called "the heavy magniloquence
of his own self-esteem." Throughout, Southey strives for comic
effect by turning the narrative upon itself; by chatting about its
genesis, profound purpose, and intricate method; by parrying
numerous thrusts from critics, real or imagined; by hinting that *The
Doctor* is the greatest book ever written; and by appealing to
posterity and the "Ladies" for their applause. Moreover, taking advantage of his anonymity, he coyly quotes from the writings of "Dr.
Southey," or otherwise refers to himself, rather more frequently
than anyone else would (or could) have done. At their best, these
"meipseads" and "tattle-de-moys" have a certain charm; but too
often they merely look puerile—as does the overuse of food
metaphors.

V *Epilogue*

"Scoff ye who will," Southey exclaimed in the Proem to *The
Poet's Pilgrimage*, "but let me, gracious Heaven, / Preserve this
boyish heart till life's last day." We have learned from Wordsworth
to admire such "natural piety"; and, thus taught, Edward Dowden
could speak of Southey as "one whose spirit, grave with a man's
wisdom, was pure as the spirit of a little child" (199). Yet I think it
would be more accurate to say that, unlike Wordsworth, Southey
never fully resolved the child's twofold need for dependence and
self-assertion into the "resolution and independence" of mature
adulthood. He himself cherished his boyishness as an "inward light
by nature given" to cheer him and to "shine forth with heavenly
radiance at the end" (X, 9). We hope that it did; but few readers
will find enough brilliance in "The Old Man's Comforts" (II, 171)
to lighten their own darkness.

Looking back, Southey also deemed it "the greatest of all advantages that I have passed more than half of my life in retirement,
conversing with books rather than men . . . communing with my

own heart, and taking that course which . . . seemed best to myself" (I, 6). The statement, typical in its somewhat bridling self-sufficiency, reveals the vicarious nature of Southey's literary life and bears out Coleridge's observation that "unceasing Authorship, never interrupted . . . but by sleep & eating," was Southey's way of compensating for the absence of fulfilling human relationships (*Coleridge*, III, 92). Southey's sketch of himself taking supper with a folio by his plate tells a similar story, as does Coleridge's reference to Southey's library as his "wife." To that library Southey retired not only to work and to feed his many charges "all from an ink-stand," but to seek refuge from the "aunt-hill" and, like the bears of his tale, from the intrusive world at large.

There he could relate to men from a distance by his writings and by his voluminous—and scrupulously punctual—correspondence. There, in particular, he communed with his soul-mate, the spinster and sentimental poetess Caroline Anne Bowles, who for many years provided an inspiration that Mrs. Southey, for all her wifely devotion, could not give; who sustained him especially in the difficult years of Edith's lunacy; and whom he married at last after Edith's death, shortly before his own lapse into senility.[11] Above all, however, Southey found joy and comfort in his "dear and noble books"—some fourteen thousand volumes—in arranging them, "worshipping" them daily, poring over them while light was left him, and patting them tenderly after his mind had at last worn itself out. His love for books, he told Caroline, never went past the honeymoon stage. Cutting the pages of a new volume was like exploring virgin land; opening a box of books, like stepping through the gate of heaven. To his books he felt beholden "for every blessing which I enjoy" (*Colloquies*, II, 346); without them, he must be looked after, "lest I should hang myself in a fit of despondency" (*Correspondence*, 117). "My days among the Dead are passed," he wrote in his best-known lyric: it is the truest line he penned.

As a result, Southey's writings inevitably breathe the spirit of museum and ivory tower, and few of them break through the charmed circle of folios and midnight oil to speak directly of the doubtful doom of human kind. His long poems command respect as valiant endeavors to revitalize epic and romance by supplying them with new subject matter and by adapting them to new themes. But all of them are vitiated by extravagance of incident, by a corresponding lack of metaphorical depth in the language, and above all by a fatal inability to create rounded and impressive characters. They

thus remained massive milestones on the road of a moribund tradition, influential only for the young Shelley.[12] Only *The Curse of
Kehama*, and perhaps *Roderick*, appeal to more than academic interest. Southey's lyrical poems, while again repeatedly innovative
and therefore of some historical significance, are even more severely
crippled by the dearth of metaphor in his language, as well as by
the absence of an ironic dimension. A few lyrics succeed by creating
expressive emblems, and a few ballads can still captivate us with
their quick-paced renditions of supernatural or otherwise pathetic
anecdote; the rest is negligible.

Of Southey's vast prose opus, his journalism, with its combination
of description, narration, and spry commentary, is most alive today,
including the *Life of Nelson* (which is really an extended review article); the *Letters from England;* and parts of the *Colloquies*, of the
Doctor, and of the private correspondence. Southey's prose style,
while no richer or more dynamic than his poetic language, is exemplary for its lucidity, amplitude, and literal precision. In his
larger historical works, however, Southey tends to bog down
because of his unworldly and compulsive ambition to chronicle
everything; his essays and polemical writings alienate us by their
humorless filibustering and their lack of dialectic; and the best
Southey can do in a work like *The Doctor* is to travesty his own
bookishness and garrulity and thus to turn it into a somewhat
ponderous joke. Among these impenetrable thickets, the spare grace
and patterned whimsy of the immortal "Story of the Three Bears"
seems almost magical.

If, despite all his eloquence, Southey very rarely speaks to us, if
his words seem apt but not inevitable, informative but seldom
irradiating, it is because in the final analysis he never fully faced
either the world or himself. Carlyle remembered him as "sharp,
almost fierce-looking . . . with very much of the militant in his
aspect" and having in his eyes "a mixture of sorrow and anger, or of
angry contempt, as if his indignant fight with the world had not yet
ended in victory, but also never should in defeat."[13] That is a telling
portrait, though a very Carlylean one. Equally telling is the "Portrait of the Author" that serves as the frontispiece to *The Doctor*. It
shows a curly-headed Southey seated at his writing-desk, with his
back to the viewer, facing a windowless wall lined solidly with
books. It sums up not only *The Doctor* but the life and work of its
author.

Notes and References

Chapter One

1. See *The Life and Correspondence of Robert Southey*, ed. Cuthbert Southey, 6 vols. (London, 1849 - 50), I, 1 · 157 (hereafter cited as *Life*): and Michael N. Stanton, "An Edition of the Autobiographical Letters of Robert Southey," University of Rochester doctoral dissertation (1972).

2. *New Letters of Robert Southey*, ed. Kenneth Curry, 2 vols. (New York, 1965), I, 150 (hereafter cited as *New Letters*).

3. *The Poetical Works of Robert Southey*, 10 vols. (Boston, 1878), II, 256f. (hereafter cited in the text in parentheses by volume and page and in the notes as *Works*).

4. *The Doctor* (London, 1848), ch. x. Cf. also Father William in "The Old Man's Comforts" (II, 171).

5. *Life*, IV, 186; *New Letters*, I, 10; *A Selection from the Letters of Robert Southey*, ed. J. W. Warter, 4 vols. (London, 1856), I, 4 (hereafter cited as *Letters*).

6. I quote from the original *and* the final version. The latter is more polished but also much tamer and rather verbose (e.g., ll. 19 - 35, added late); see *The Poetical Works of Robert Southey* (Paris, 1829), pp. 702f. (hereafter cited as *Works* [1829]).

7. *Life*, I, 186; *New Letters*, I, 17; *Essays, Moral and Political* (London, 1832), I, 299.

8. *The Correspondence of Robert Southey and Caroline Bowles*, ed. Edward Dowden (London, 1881), p. 52 (hereafter cited as *Correspondence*).

9. Cf. Mrs. H. Sandford, *Thomas Poole and His Friends* (London: Macmillan, 1888), I, 98; *New Letters*, II, 446; *The Collected Letters of S. T. Coleridge*, ed. E. L. Griggs, 6 vols. (Oxford: Clarendon Press, 1956 - 72), I, 114, 120 (hereafter cited as *Coleridge*).

10. *Coleridge*, I, 132, 120, 123, 114, 165, 171.

11. *Ibid.*, I, 586; II, 728; Jack Simmons, *Southey* (London, 1945), p. 65.

12. *The Notebooks of S. T. Coleridge*, I, ed. Kathleen Coburn (New York: Pantheon Books, 1957), no. 349 (hereafter *Notebooks*); *Coleridge*, III, 74; II, 1156, 1200.

13. E. L. Griggs, "Robert Southey's Estimate of Samuel Taylor Coleridge, A Study in Human Relations," *Huntington Library Quarterly*, IX (1945), 94.

14. J. W. Robberds, *Memoir of the Life and Writings of . . . William Taylor*, 2 vols. (London, 1843), I, 462, 455 (hereafter *Memoir*); *Life*, II, 277; *New Letters*, I, 261; Griggs, op. cit., p. 88.

Chapter Two

1. See Brian Wilkie, *Romantic Poets and Epic Tradition* (Madison: University of Wisconsin Press, 1965); also Karl Kroeber, *Romantic Narrative Art* (Madison, University of Wisconsin Press, 1960), and H. T. Swedenberg, Jr., *The Theory of Epic in England, 1650 - 1800* (Berkeley: University of California Press, 1944).

2. *Coleridge*, I, 320; the quote is from *Joan of Arc* (I, 42).

3. In some instances I have preferred to quote the text of the second edition, as reprinted in *Works* (1829).

4. Part of the description of the forest retreat was omitted from the final version for no evident reason: its omission undercuts Joan's recall of the scene in Book IV (I, 92).

5. *New Letters*, I, 29; *Works* (1829), 714, 30; *Life*, I, 269.

6. In the first edition, Joan is a war orphan who is raised by a hermit in the woods and receives her mission from an angel; she finds Dunois wounded and nurses him before setting out with him. The later version of Joan's childhood may have autobiographical overtones.

7. Cf. "Written on Sunday Morning" (II, 159). The historical Jehane, of course, was orthodox to a fault.

8. Southey considerably antedates Agnes Sorel's rule as the king's mistress.

9. See *Works*, I, 87f., 120f., 127f., 130, 143, 171, 173, 206, 209, 213, 215.

10. Cf. also the Tory diatribe against Paris as the modern Sodom (I, 60f.), replacing an earlier tribute to Brissot and the Girondists (*Works* [1829], 10).

11. See William Haller, *The Early Life of Robert Southey* (New York, 1917), pp. 170f.; Lionel Madden, ed., *Robert Southey* (London, 1972), pp. 40 - 50.

12. *Coleridge*, III, 510; *Collected Writings of Thomas De Quincey*, ed. David Masson (Edinburgh: Black, 1890), V, 241 - 2 (cf. *ibid.*, 384 ff.). In 1797, Southey did in fact sketch out "a tragedy on the martydom of Joan of Arc" (*Life*, I, 301), but he plainly could not come to terms with the subject. Cf. *Letters*, I, 62f.

13. Geoffrey Carnall, *Robert Southey and His Age* (Oxford, 1960), pp. 31f.

14. See *Southey's Commonplace Book*, ed. J. W. Warter, 4 vols. (London, 1849 - 51), IV, 189 - 91.

Chapter Three

1. *New Letters*, I, 511; *Letters*, I, 358; *Life*, I, 276, 317.

2. Originally entitled "The Devil's Thoughts" and published

anonymously in fourteen stanzas, of which all but four were by Coleridge, in the *Morning Post* (September 24, 1799). The greatly expanded version entitled "The Devil's Walk" was composed in 1827. Of this version, stanzas 1 - 5, 11 - 13, 15, and 20 - 57 are by Southey, but only 1 - 3, 15, and 17 are early. The original piece enjoyed a considerable underground fame and was both pirated and imitated, e. g., by Byron and Shelley.

3. *Life*, I, 35; Jack Simmons, *Southey* (London, 1945), pp. 52, 141.

4. Hazlitt, *The Spirit of the Age:* "Mr. Southey."

5. *Life*, I, 300 - 3; II, 239; *Correspondence*, 184; *Commonplace Book*, IV, 44, 195.

6. *Life*, II, 151, 267, 172; *Commonplace Book*, IV, 44.

7. Madden, p. 463. Southey once called himself "one of the most shame-faced of God's creatures" (*Correspondence*, 214).

8. *Letters*, I, 400; *The Letters of William and Dorothy Wordsworth: The Early Years*, ed. E. de Selincourt, rev. C. L. Shaver (Oxford: Clarendon, 1967), p. 223; *Correspondence*, 361; *Biographia Literaria*, ed. J. Shaw-cross (Oxford, 1907), I, 47; *Coleridge*, III, 316 (cf. I, 106, 175); *Notebooks*, I, no. 1815 (on "the character of Australis").

9. *Letters from Spain and Portugal* (1797), p. 272.

10. *Letters*, I, 21, 223 - 6, 378; *Essays*, II, 194f.; I, 246, 80f.; *Commonplace Book*, IV, 303f.

11. *Notebooks*, I, no. 1030; *Coleridge*, VI, 560 (1826).

12. *Life*, II, 83, 86, 132; *Letters*, I, 93, 104. *The Book of the Church* (1824) is especially virulent; Southey uses words like *abominable, ferocious, insane, loathsome, obscene*, etc., to describe idolatrous customs and beliefs.

13. *Letters*, I, 249, 268, 299, 371, 413, 416. In 1800, Southey called himself a Socinian; in 1808, something between a Socinian and an Arian.

14. *Life*, V, 49; *Letters*, I, 370, 356; *New Letters*, I, 474; *Colloquies*, I, 5.

15. *Works*, VI, 194; *Life*, II, 72f.; *Letters*, I, 63; *Letters from England*, ed. Jack Simmons (London, 1951), pp. 109 - 12, 432f.

16. *Letters*, I, 44; *Life*, I, 348, 278.

17. *Correspondence*, 366f. Cf. *ibid.*, 381f.: "I found myself naked [in] a catacomb, among the dust of the dead . . . clasped in the arms of a living skeleton, which endeavored to break in my ribs by its grasp. . . ."

18. See Geoffrey Grigson, *A Choice of Robert Southey's Verse* (London, 1970).

19. See my "The Epitaph and the Romantic Poets," *Huntington Library Quarterly*, XXX (1967), 113 - 46. Southey's estimate of his inscriptions was high.

20. See A. Dwight Culler, "Monodrama and Dramatic Monologue," *Publications of the Modern Language Association*, XC (1975), 366 - 85; and *Memoir*, I, 213.

21. A fifth, "Edward and Susan," appeared in the *Monthly Magazine* (1798) over the signature W. T. (for Wat Tyler) but was not republished.

22. *New Letters*, I, 45; *Memoir*, I, 461; *Commonplace Book*, IV, 258.

23. *Critical Review*, October 1798; cf. *Memoir*, I, 223.

24. See G. Carnall, " 'The Idiot Boy,' " *Notes & Queries*, III (1956), 81f.

25. Southey himself parodies the poem in "The Surgeon's Warning" about a surgeon who vainly tries to keep his corpse from the "resurrection man" and the scalpels of his own prentices.—For a kind of palinody, see the late, longish *All for Love* (1829), from the life of St. Basil, in which a Greek freedman sells his soul to the devil in order to obtain the daughter of his former master in marriage but is redeemed by the power of love.

Chapter Four

1. *Letters*, I, 46; *Memoir*, I, 304; *Works* (1829), 711; cf. *Commonplace Book*, IV, 11, 27, 31 - 7, and Southey's verses in Amos Cottle's *Edda* (1797).

2. Cf. Frank B. Manuel, *The Eighteenth Century Confronts the Gods* (1959; rpt. New York: Atheneum, 1967), pp. 210ff. On Romantic myth making, see also B. Feldman and R. D. Richardson, *The Rise of Modern Mythology* (Bloomington: Indiana University Press, 1972).

3. *Commonplace Book*, IV, 2f.; *Memoir*, I, 280; II, 96f.

4. *Commonplace Book*, IV, 11, 260; *Memoir*, I, 262f., 386.

5. See the MS. outline published by W. U. Ober, *Notes & Queries*, V (1958), 448; and cf. *Commonplace Book*, IV, 19f., 109 - 13, 117 - 9, 224f.

6. The plan for an "Oriental Poem" on the "Destruction of the Dom Daniel" existed as early as 1796. Composition began in 1799 and was completed in 1800 in Cintra. Some revisions were made in the second edition (1808).

7. See M. P. Conant, *The Oriental Tale in England* (New York, 1908).

8. See Robert Lowth, *De Sacra Poesia Hebraeorum* (1753, transl. 1794), which Southey knew. Southey was also influenced by "Ossian."

9. For a list of Southey's sources for *Thalaba*, see Haller, Appendix C.

10. Southey admitted that the episode bore no relation to the main story; he had once considered it as a subject for a separate poem.

11. *Memoir*, I, 502; II, 82; *Life*, II, 134; *Commonplace Book*, IV, 183.

12. For early plot sketches, see *Commonplace Book*, IV, 12-5. *Kehama* was appropriately dedicated to Landor, who also furnished much constructive criticism.—The friendship with Landor proved a lasting one. It had been preceded by years of mutual admiration. Southey, for example, had published a glowing and influential review of Landor's *Gebir* in 1799.

13. *Life*, II, 66f., 162, 283; *Letters*, I, 119, 231; see *Journal of a Residence in Portugal, 1800 - 1801*, ed. A. Cabral (Oxford, 1960), *passim*.

Chapter Five

1. Southey's main source for the Madoc legend was William Warrington, *The History of Wales* (London, 1786), p. 334. See also John Williams, *Enquiry Concerning the Discovery of America by Prince Madog* (London: B. White, 1791).

2. *Commonplace Book*, IV, 204 - 10; *Life*, II, 20f.; *Letters*, I, 243.

3. Cf. I, 85; and *Memoir*, I, 281, 499f., 517; *Life*, II, 7; *Letters*, I, 295f. In 1817 Southey edited a *Birth, Lyf and Actes of King Arthur. Robin Hood: A Fragment* (Edinburgh: Blackwood, 1847) appeared posthumously.

4. See, e. g., *Letters*, I, 166f., *New Letters*, I, 460; *Commonplace Book*, III, 804 - 6, 746 - 8. Most of Southey's "facts" about the Welsh bards are no longer accepted; cf. A. L. Owen, *The Famous Druids* (Oxford: Clarendon Press, 1962), pp. 194ff.

5. Carnall, 125; but cf. already *Life*, II, 52, 77, 243.

6. *Memoir*, I, 375; *New Letters*, I, 337; *Life*, II, 236; *The Lusiad*, tr. Julius Mickle, 3rd ed. (London: Cadell & Davies, 1798), I, cccxxiii; cf. *ibid.*, p. xxxvii: "No lesson can be of greater national importance than the history of the rise and fall of a commercial empire." Southey was also influenced by Alonzo de Ercilla's *La Araucana* (1590) and probably borrowed the name Lincoya from it.

7. Southey adapts his famous "Hirlas" from Evan Evans' *Specimens of the Poetry of the Ancient Welsh Bards* (1764).

8. The excommunication of Cyveilioc, which is historical, was actually pronounced by Giraldus Cambrensis, Baldwin's Welsh fellow-crusader!

9. As Southey, reviewing the Lewis and Clark Report in the *Quarterly* (no. 24), noted, the expedition disposed, *inter alia*, of the myth of "Welsh Indians" underlying *Madoc*. On the general subject, see Benjamin Bissell, *The American Indian in English Literature of the Eighteenth Century* (New Haven: Yale University Press, 1925); H. N. Fairchild, *The Noble Savage* (New York: Columbia University Press, 1928); R. H. Pearce, *Savagism and Civilization* (Baltimore: Johns Hopkins Press, 1967).

10. Huitzilopochtli, the proper tribal god of the Aztecs. For Southey's notes on the Mexican pantheon, see *Commonplace Book*, IV, 142 - 7.

11. Byron (*Don Juan*, I.cci) may be alluding directly to Southey's bumptious disclaimer, as also when he addresses him as "epic renegade" (Dedication).

12. *Memoir*, II, 80 - 94; *Letters*, I, 335f.; *New Letters*, I, 400.

13. The late *Tale of Paraguay* (1825), about a family of Mission Indians at one of the Jesuit reductions, completes the transformation of Pantisocracy into the missionary ideal; see my "Southey in the Tropics: A *Tale of Paraguay* and the Problem of Romantic Faith," *The Wordsworth Circle*, V (1974), 97 - 105.

Chapter Six

1. *Life*, II, 281. See L. Pfandl, "Robert Southey und Spanien," *Revue Hispanique*, XXVIII (1813), 1 - 315; A Cabral, *Southey e Portugal* (Lisbon, 1959).

2. *Amadis* is abridged from the Portuguese. *Palmerin* is a reworking of Anthony Munday's 1581 translation from the French in light of the Portuguese original. The *Cid* is, of course, from the Spanish.

3. *Chronicle of the Cid* (New York, n. d.), VI, xxii.

4. *Memoir*, II, 193; *Portuguese Journal*, 85; *Letters*, I, 99, 116; *Life*, VI, 192, II, 242; and cf. *Memoir*, I, 346.

5. The equivalent of three 500-page quarto volumes were completed by July 1804, and the entire work was more than once said to be ready, or almost ready, for the press. Ca. 550 MS. pages on the reign of Joao III and on the Portuguese in Asia are with the Hispanic Society of America.

6. *Life*, III, 283f., 98, 172, 155f.; *Letters*, II, 77, 338; Simmons, 127.

7. *Life*, III, 176, 151; *Letters*, II, 99.—Southey inspired both Landor and Scott to write poems on the same subject: Landor, a tragedy, *Count Julian* (1812); Scott, a piece of historical prophecy, the *Vision of Don Roderick* (1811), which is explicitly anti-Bonapartist. Cf. also Wordsworth's sonnet "Pelayo"; Byron's *Childe Harolds Pilgrimage*, I.xxxv; and Francisco Goya's painting "Dos de mayo," showing the knifing of French Moroccans by Spanish insurgents. There are numerous treatments of the Roderick-Pelayo theme in eighteenth and nineteenth-century Spanish literature.

8. In May, 1812. The event reduced Southey to "creeping fits," and he felt that only the army stood between the country and "the red sea of an English Jacquerie,—a Bellum Servile," and that a dictator was needed to "save the commonwealth." He urged suspension of *habeas corpus* and of freedom of press and debate, imprisonment of every "jacobin journalist," and hanging or transportation for the Luddites (*Life*, III, 334f., 342; *Letters*, II, 274). Coleridge urged Southey to warn the country "in your impressive way" of the "gigantic" menace (*Coleridge*, III, 410)—which Southey did, in the *Quarterly;* and Scott wrote to Southey: "You are quite right in apprehending a Jacquerie; the country is mined beneath our feet" (Simmons, 154).

9. In the *Chronica*, Roderick finally expiates his sin by having himself buried alive with a two-headed serpent that gnaws at his heart and genitals.

10. Originally she was identical with Pelayo's daughter Ormisinda.

11. Southey, his wife, and his daughter Edith May were in fact accompanying Southey's brother Henry, his bride, and his mother-in-law on a honeymoon journey. They fell in with other Englishmen on the way. See Southey's posthumously published *Journal of a Tour in the Netherlands* (Boston & New York: Houghton Mifflin, 1903).

12. See, e. g., Kenneth Curry, *Southey* (London, Boston, 1975), pp. 69, 172.

Chapter Seven

1. The "Bibliotheca Britannica"; cf. Simmons, 100; *Letters*, I, 219.

2. See the edition by Michael Macmillan (1892), p. 281n. I quote from the (excellently introduced) edition by E. R. H. Harvey (London, 1953).

3. Other biographical writings include the lives of Bunyan and Cowper prefixed to the editions of their works and the short lives of Cromwell and Wellington published in the *Quarterly* (nos. 26 - 7, 50).

4. Between 1797 and 1804, Southey wrote mostly for Arthur Aikin's liberal *Monthly Magazine* and for the more conservative *Critical Review*, including, for the latter, the reviews of *Lyrical Ballads* and *Gebir*. Between 1802 and 1808, he reviewed, for Aikin's *Annual Review*, (*inter alia*) Malthus's *Principles of Population*, Godwin's *Life of Chaucer*, Ritson's *Romances*, and Bruce's *Travels*. After 1808, he wrote mostly for the *Quarterly* (see *Life*, VI, 400 - 2; and K. Curry & R. Dedmon, "Southey's Contributions to *The Quarterly Review*," *The Wordsworth Circle*, VI [1975], 261 - 72).

5. *Life*, II, 231; *Letters*, I, 282; Simmons, *Letters from England*, p. xix.

6. *Essays*, I, 136; II, 84; *Life*, VI, 134, 222.

7. *Correspondence*, 326f.; cf. *Coleridge*, III, 391. The book was begun in 1813 as told in the opening chapter; vols. I & II appeared in 1834.

8. *The Doctor*, Interchapter xiii. I quote from J. W. Warter's one-volume edition (1848), using the numbering of chapters there given. M. H. FitzGerald's abridgment (London, 1930) omits much of the gay or extravagant trivia, thereby rendering the text more bland and solemn than it is.

9. *Ibid.*, Chs. ccxii-ccxxxvii. Early on he jestingly envisions his book as the future Bible of a new religion of "Dovery" (interch. ii). Cf. also *Colloquies*, II, 399, on the speculative uses of literature.

10. The discovery, in 1951, of an MS. version of this tale by one Eleanor Mure, which antedates Southey's version of 1837 by six years, has cast doubt upon Southey's authorship of this classic. The story, however, was current in the Southey household at least as early as 1813 (cf. *Letters*, II, 328). At the same time, Southey no doubt did not invent it but derived it from his uncle Tyler. Cf. *Times Literary Supplement*, November 23, 1951.

11. Southey's friendship with Caroline Bowles dates from 1818, when she wrote him for advice about publishing her first poem, *Ellen Fitzarthur*. Some dozen years younger than Southey, she had recently lost her mother and had gone into a severe emotional crisis, from which "abyss," she afterwards insisted, Southey had rescued her. They resembled each other remarkably.

12. See Warren U. Ober, "Lake Poet and Laureate: Southey's Significance to his own Generation," Indiana University doctoral dissertation (1958), pp. 357 - 65.

13. Madden, *Robert Southey*, p. 461

Selected Bibliography

PRIMARY SOURCES

The Poetical Works of Robert Southey, 10 vols, in 5. With a Memoir by H. T. Tuckerman. Boston: Houghton, Osgood, 1860, 1878. Reprinted by AMS Press.

Poems of Robert Southey. Ed. M. H. FitzGerald. Oxford University Press, 1909.

The Poetical Works of Robert Southey. Paris: Galignani, 1829.

A Choice of Robert Southey's Verse. Ed. Geoffrey Grigson. London: Faber, 1970.

Select Prose of Robert Southey. Ed. Jacob Zeitlin. New York: Macmillan. 1916.

The Chronicle of the Cid. Ed. V. S. Pritchett. New York: Heritage Press, 1958. Garden City: Doubleday, n. d. Paper.

The Life of Nelson. Ed. E. R. H. Harvey. London: MacDonald, 1953.

The Life of Wesley. Ed. M. H. FitzGerald, 2 vols. London: H. Mitford, 1925.

The History of Brazil, 3 vols. Ed. Herbert Cahn. New York: B. Franklin, 1971.

The Expedition of Orsua; And the Crimes of Aguirre. London: Longman, 1821.

The Book of the Church, 2 vols. London: J. Murray, 1824.

History of the Peninsular War, 3 vols. London: J. Murray, 1823 - 32.

Letters from England by Don Manuel Espriella. Ed. Jack Simmons. London: Cresset Press, 1951.

Essays, Moral and Political, 2 vols. 1832; rpt. New York: Barnes & Noble, 1972.

Sir Thomas More: or, Colloquies on the Progress and Prospects of Society, 2 vols. London: J. Murray, 1829, 1831.

The Doctor, etc. Ed. J. W. Warter. London: Longman, 1848. Ed. M. H. FitzGerald. London: Bell, 1930. Abridged.

Omniana, or Horae Otiosiores. Ed. Robert Gittings. Slough, Bucks.: Centaur, 1970.

Southey's Common-place Book, 4 vols. Ed. J. W. Water. London: Longman, 1850.

The Life and Correspondence of Robert Southey, 6 vols. Ed. Cuthbert C. Southey. London: Longman, 1849 - 50. Reprinted 1970.

A Selection from the Letters of Robert Southey, 4 vols. Ed. J. W. Warter. London: Longman, 1856. Reprinted by AMS Press.

New Letters of Robert Southey, 2 vols. Ed. Kenneth Curry. New York & London: Columbia University Press, 1965.

The Correspondence of Robert Southey and Caroline Bowles. Ed. Edward Dowden. Dublin: The University Press, 1881.

Memoir of the Life and Writings of the Late William Taylor, 2 vols. Ed. J. W. Robberds. London: J. Murray, 1843. Southey's correspondence with Taylor.

Letters of Robert Southey: A Selection. Ed. M. H. FitzGerald. London: Oxford University Press, 1912. Reprinted by AMS Press.

Journals of a Residence in Portugal, 1800 - 1801, and a Visit to France, 1838. Ed. Adolfo Cabral. Oxford: Clarendon Press, 1960.

SECONDARY SOURCES

ANONYMOUS. "Southey, A Problem of Romanticism: Poet Who Lost His Way," *Times Literary Supplement,* March 20, 1943. Centenary appraisal.

BERNHARDT-KABISH, ERNEST. "Southey in the Tropics: *A Tale of Paraguay* and the Problem of Romantic Faith," *The Wordsworth Circle,* V (1974), 97ff.

BRINTON, Crane. *The Political Ideas of the English Romanticists.* London: Oxford University Press, 1926. Southey's political common sense.

CABRAL, ADOLFO. *Southey e Portugal: 1774 - 1801.* Lisbon: P. Fernandez, 1959.

CARNALL, GEOFFREY. *Robert Southey and His Age: The Development of a Conservative Mind.* Oxford: Clarendon Press, 1960. Excellent study of the development of Southey's political and religious thought.

————. *Robert Southey.* London, New York: Longmans, 1964. Concise biography and criticism of Southey's major writings.

COBBAN, ALFRED. *Edmund Burke and the Revolt Against the Eighteenth Century: A Study of the Political and Social Thinking of Burke, Wordsworth, Coleridge, and Southey.* New York: Macmillan, 1929. Southey's conservatism.

COLERIDGE, SAMUEL TAYLOR. *Biographia Literaria,* 2 vols. Ed. J. Shawcross. London: Oxford University Press, 1907. Coleridge's estimate of Southey.

CURRY, KENNETH. *Southey.* London. Boston: Routledge & Kegan Paul, 1975. Comparable in scope to the present study, but stresses the prose.

DOWDEN, EDWARD. *Southey.* London: Macmillan, 1879. Hagiographical.

ELWIN, MALCOLM. *The First Romantics.* New York: Longmans, 1948. Relations between Southey, Coleridge, and Wordsworth.

GRIGGS, E. L. "Robert Southey's Estimate of Samuel Taylor Coleridge: A Study in Human Relations," *Huntington Library Quarterly,* IX (1945), 61 - 94.

HALLER, WILLIAM. *The Early Life of Robert Southey.* New York: Columbia University Press, 1917. The life and work to 1805. Of first importance.

HOFFPAUIR, RICHARD. "The Thematic Structure of Southey's Epic Poetry."
The Wordsworth Circle, VI (1975), 240 - 9; VII (1976), 109 - 16.

HOPKINS, KENNETH. *The Poets Laureate.* London: Bodley Head, 1954.
Southey's contribution to the Laureate office.

MADDEN, LIONEL. ed. *Robert Southey, the Critical Heritage.* London,
Boston: Routledge & Kegan Paul, 1972. Large selection of contemporary reviews.

PFANDL, L. "Southey und Spanien," *Revue Hispanique,* xxviii (1913), 1 -
315. Southey's relations to Spain and Spanish literature. Thorough.

RAIMOND, JEAN. *Robert Southey: L'homme et son temps; L'oeuvre; Le role.*
Paris: Didier, 1968. Broad descriptive and critical coverage.

SIMMONS, JACK. *Southey.* London: Collins, 1945. The best full biography.

WILKIE, BRIAN. *Romantic Poets and Epic Tradition.* Madison, Milwaukee:
Univ. of Wisconsin Press, 1965. Important chapter about *Joan of Arc.*

BIBLIOGRAPHY

BERNBAUM, ERNEST. *Guide through the Romantic Movement,* 2nd ed. New
York: Ronald Press, 1949. Includes a brief summary of Southey's work.

CURRY, KENNETH. "Southey." In *The English Romantic Poets and
Essayists, A Review of Research and Criticism,* rev. ed. Ed. C. W.
and L. H. Houtchens. New York: New York University Press, 1966.

Index

Akenside, Mark, 42, 63
Allen, Ralph, 176
Allen, Robert, 23 - 24
Annual Review, The, 187n4
Arabian Nights, The, 17, 85, 94
Ariosto, Ludovico, 17, 29, 41, 92; *Orlando Furioso*, 17, 85
Aristotle, 31, 123
Asiatic Researches, 98

Beaumont, Francis, and John Fletcher, 15
Beckford, William, *Vathek*, 85
Bedford, Grosvenor Charles, 18 - 19, 60
Berkeley, Bishop George, 111
Bhagavad-Gita, The, 98
Blake, William, 30, 58, 61, 172
Bodmer, Johann Jakob, 82
Boethius, Manlius Severinus, 169
Bonaparte. *See* Napoleon Bonaparte
Bowdler, Dr. Thomas, *The Family Shakespeare*, 178
Bowles, Caroline Anne (later Mrs. Southey), 55, 61 - 62, 179, 187n11
Bowles, William Lisle, 63, 66
Brosses, Charles de, 172
Brothers, Richard, 58 - 59, 166
Buerger, Gottfried August, *Lenore*, 73, 78, 90
Burdett, Sir Francis, 132, 164
Burnet, Thomas, *The Sacred Theory of the Earth*, 82
Burnett, George, 23
Burton, Robert, 171; *The Anatomy of Melancholy*, 172
Byron, George Gordon, Lord, 9, 29, 53, 57, 60, 77, 99, 123, 143, 155 - 57, 158, 186n7; *Don Juan*, 29, 53, 57, 123, 156; *The Vision of Judgment*, 53, 60, 157

Camoens, Luiz Vaz de, *The Lusiad*, 17, 46, 111, 116, 129, 148, 155

Canning, George, 64
Carlyle, Thomas, 54, 83, 160, 169, 180; *Sartor Resartus*, 174
Cervantes, Miguel de, 128, 131, 170
Chatterton, Thomas, 17
Chaucer, Geoffrey, 17
Chavis, Dom, and M. Cazotte, *Arabian Tales*, 94
Chronica del Rey Don Rodrigo, 133
Clarke, J. S., and John M'Arthur (Nelson biographers), 160
Coleridge, Samuel Taylor, 9, 23 - 28, 33, 45, 47, 51, 52 - 53, 54, 56 - 57, 60, 61, 66, 72 - 74, 97, 100, 109 - 10, 136 - 37, 143; "Kubla Khan," 77, 99, 107; "The Rime of the Ancient Mariner," 27, 45, 73, 74, 77, 90, 99
Coleridge, Sarah (nee Fricker), 22, 24, 27 - 28
Collier, Payne, 78
Collins, William, 63, 64
Corry, Isaac, 96
Cortez, Hernando, 122
Cottle, Joseph, 33, 53
Court de Gebelin, Antoine, 172
Cowper, William, 42
Crèvecoeur, St. John de, 23 - 24
Critical Review, The, 52, 187n4

Dante Alighieri, 39, 40, 156
D'Arc, Jeanne, 30 - 31
Davenant, William, 118
Davies, Edward, 110
Davy, Humphry, 53
De Quincey, Thomas, 45
Digby, Sir Kenelm, 176
Dryden, John, 64, 147, 151

Edinburgh Annual Register, The, 130, 159
Edinburgh, Review, The, 85
Enoch, The Book of, 82
Epictetus, 20, 44

Epicurus, 21
Ercilla, Alonzo de, *La Araucana*, 185n6
Euclid, 21

Fricker, Edith. *See* Southey, Edith
Fricker, Mary, 22, 24, 28
Fricker, Sarah. *See* Coleridge, Sarah

Gesner, Solomon, *The Death of Abel*, 17, 82
Gibbon, Edward, *The Decline and Fall of the Roman Empire*, 19, 129
Gifford, William, 18
Glover, Richard, *Leonidas*, 44
Godwin, William, 22, 24, 26, 48; *Political Justice*, 22
Goethe, Johann Wolfgang von, 70, 83, 155; *Faust*, 97; *The Sorrows of Young Werther*, 19
Goldsmith, Oliver, 68; *The Citizen of the World*, 162; *The Vicar of Wakefield*, 174
Goya, Francisco, 148, 186n7
Gray, Thomas, 16, 20, 63, 64, 81 - 82; *The Bard*, 111, 116, 141
Grimm, The Brothers, 17

Hamilton, Emma, 160 - 61
Hamilton, Sir William, 160
Herder, Johann Gottfried, 125
Herrick, Robert, 57
Hill, Herbert, 18, 21, 96, 170
Hill, Margaret, 96
Hofer, Andreas, 147
Hogg, James, 143
Homer, 17, 46, 109; *The Iliad*, 33, 109 - 10, 117; *The Odyssey*, 33, 110, 112, 117
Hooker, Richard, 173
Horace, 18, 139, 146, 153
Hucks, Joseph, 23
Hume, David, 125
Hurd, Richard, *Letters on Chivalry*, 29
Hutchinson, Sara, 136

Jeffrey, Francis, 70, 85, 143
Jones, Sir William, 83, 98
Jonson, Ben, 151
Junius, 157

Kant, Immanuel, 170
Keats, John, 85, 123, 127
Klopstock, Friedrich Gottlieb, 81, 82

Lamb, Charles, 73, 143, 170
Landor, Walter Savage, 55, 95, 143, 184n12, 186n7
L'Averdi, Clement, 31
Le Bossu, René, 31
Lewis, Matthew Gregory, 73
Lewis and Clark Expedition, The, 118
Lloyd, Charles, *Edmund Oliver*, 27
Lockhart, John Gibson, 177 - 78
Lovell, Robert, 24, 26, 28
Lowth, Robert, *De Sacra Poesia Hebraeorum*, 29, 86, 184n8
Lucan, *Pharsalia*, 30, 44
Luddite Riots, The, 132

Macaulay, Thomas Babington, 169
Malory, Sir Thomas, 129
Malthus, Robert, 57, 167, 173
Mandeville, Sir John, 88
Mason, William, 63, 81
Maurice, Thomas, 98
May, John, 13
Menu, Institutions of, 174
Mickle, Julius, 17, 111, 185n6
Milton, John, 17, 32, 42, 44, 61; *Paradise Lost*, 17, 109
Montaigne, Michel de, 171, 173
Monthly Magazine, The, 52, 187n4
More, Sir Thomas, 169

Napier, Sir William, 159
Napoleon Bonaparte, 31, 61, 97, 98, 130 - 31, 148, 150, 151 - 54, 156
Nelson, Horatio, Viscount, 160 - 62
Newbery, John, 14
Newman, John Henry, Cardinal, 84

Ossian, 19, 81, 93, 109, 110
Ovid, *Metamorphoses*, 17 - 18
Owen, Robert, 170

Paine, Thomas, 45, 47, 48
Perceval, Spencer, 132, 156
Percy, Thomas, 17, 64, 72, 82; *Reliques of Ancient English Poetry*, 17, 72

Picart, Bernard, *Religious Ceremonies*, 19, 81
Pitt, William (the Younger), 50, 164
Poema del Cid, 128, 148
Pope, Alexander, 17, 69
Purchas, Samuel, 88

Quarles, Francis, 65
Quarterly Review, The, 18, 44, 47, 154, 164, 177
Quicherat, Jules, 31

Rabelais, François, 18, 171, 177
Rousseau, Jean-Jacques, 16, 19, 32, 64

Sakuntala, 98, 101
Sayers, Dr. Frank, *Dramatic Sketches of Northern Mythology*, 81, 83, 85
Schiller, Friedrich, 27; *Die Jungfrau von Orleans*, 31; *Wilhelm Tell*, 147
Scott, Sir Walter, 73, 143, 186n7, 186n8
Seward, Edmund, 20 - 21, 23, 25, 64
Shaftesbury, Anthony Ashley Cooper, Earl of, 32
Shakespeare, William, 15, 17, 21
Shaw, George Bernard, 45
Shelley, Percy Bysshe, 19, 48, 50, 56, 85, 93, 95, 107, 132, 180; *Prometheus Unbound*, 19, 99, 102, 105
Sheridan, Richard Brinsley, 118
Sidney, Sir Philip, 17
Song of Roland, The, 148
Sonnerat, Pierre, 98
South, Robert, 173
Southcott, Joanna, 58, 60, 61, 166
Southey, Caroline Anne. *See* Bowles, Caroline Anne
Southey, Charles Cuthbert (son), 157
Southey, Edith (nee Fricker), 22 - 24, 26, 28, 95 - 96, 179, 186n11
Southey, Edith May (daughter), 186n11
Southey, Herbert (son), 15, 62
Southey, Margaret (daughter), 15, 96 - 97
Southey, Margaret Hill (mother), 13, 22, 25, 96, 174
Southey, Robert (father), 13, 17, 20
Southey, Robert: and Arthurian legend, 30, 110, 114, 116, 185n3; author-itarianism, 132, 167 - 70; and Aztec religion, 112 - 13, 118 - 23, 125 - 26, 148, 185n10; and books, 14, 55, 128, 170 - 71, 179; and Catholicism, 50, 58 - 59, 125 - 26, 128, 132, 146, 149, 163, 166, 167, 172; and character, 44 - 46, 49, 69 - 72, 74 - 77, 79, 94 - 95, 104 - 105, 126 - 27, 136 - 37, 144 - 45, 170, 176, 179; childhood, 13 - 17, 54; and colonialism, 111, 117, 167; and commercialism, 164 - 65, 175; conservatism, 166, 167 - 68, 173, 175; at Corston, 15 - 16; and the Demonic, 15, 19, 60 - 61, 75 - 80; and Dissent, 168; domesticity, 24, 26, 33, 50 - 51, 55, 67, 94 - 95, 144, 149, 154; and drama, 14 - 15, 47 - 49, 183n17; and dreams, 15, 18 - 19, 28, 60; early literary attempts, 17 - 18, 22; early reading, 14 - 15, 17; economic criticism, 164 - 66, 169; encyclopedism, 42, 159, 162 - 63, 171; and epic, 28 - 33, 81 - 84, 110 - 11, 117, 123 - 24, 131, 143, 151, 155 - 56, 179; and Hinduism, 83, 97 - 98, 100 - 104, 106 - 107; humor, 18, 55, 66, 78 - 80, 177 - 78, 180; and Indians (American), 65, 69, 82, 109 - 10, 112 - 14, 117 - 27, 185n9; and industrialism, 61, 163, 165 - 66, 169, 172, 175; and Islam, 83 - 84, 94, 138 - 39, 147 - 50, 172; journalism, 162 - 63, 180; at Keswick, 27, 97, 109, 138; and the Lake District, 97, 163; and law, 26, 57, 96; lyricism, 52, 63 - 69, 72, 96, 107 - 108, 152, 180; Manicheism, 89, 94, 150, 154; marriage, 26; and Methodism, 58, 166 - 67, 172, 175; and myth, 19, 59, 62, 81 - 84, 109, 125 - 26, 132 - 33, 172; nationalism, 30, 97, 110 - 11, 147 - 48, 152, 154; and the Noachid, 51, 98, 154 - 55; at Oxford, 20 - 23; and Pantisocracy, 23 - 26, 33, 51, 62, 70, 82, 110 - 11, 128, 151, 169, 185n13; and the Peninsular War, 68, 130 - 31; and penology, 164; personality, 53 - 57, 148 - 49, 154, 175, 176, 183n7; as Poet Laureate, 150 -

57; political views, 47, *50 - 51*, 98,
111, 132, *164, 167 - 68*, 170, *186n8*;
and Portugal, 50 - 52, 58, *95 - 97*,
111, 128 - 31; prose style, *158*, 162 -
63, 180; and the Reform Bill, 167,
172; religious views, 19, 21 - 22, 32,
35, 40, 45 - 46, 50, *57 - 63*, 83 - 84,
98, 113 - 14, 122, 124 - 26, 139 - 40,
146, 148, 153 - 54, 157, 163, 166,
168, *172 - 74*, 183n12, 13; and
revolution, 20, *22*, 30, *33*, 98, 105,
131 - 32, 150, *152 - 53*, 156 - 57, 167,
170, 173, *186n8*; and the Satanic
School, 57, 61, 156; social criticism,
163 - 69; and Spain, 128 - 32, 150;
and utilitarianism, 173; and Utopia,
23, 25 - 26, 53, 111, 117, 126, 154,
170, 176; and Wales, 109 - 11, 114 -
17, 185n4; at Westbury, 51 - 53, 65 -
66, 70, 72, 109; at Westminster, 18 -
20, 95, 109; and Zoroasterism, 83, 94

WORKS - DRAMA:
Fall of Robespierre, The, 26, 43, *48 - 49*
Wat Tyler, 18, 26, *46 - 49*, 155, 170

WORKS - POETRY:
All for Love, 184n25
"Amatory Poems of Abel Shufflebottom,
The," 66
Annual Anthology, The, 52
"Autumn," 68
Ballads, *72 - 80*, 180
Battle of Blenheim, The," 73 - 74
"Bishop Bruno," 77
"Botany Bay Eclogues," 69 - 70
"Caba, La," 69
Carmen Triumphale, 130, 150
Carmina Aulica, 151
"Chapel Bell, The," 20
"College Cat, The," 21, 33, 65
"Complaints of the Poor, The," 73
"Cornelius Agrippa," 80
"Corston," 16, 66
"Cross-roads, The," 74
Curse of Kehama, The, 16, *83*, 95, *97 -
108*, 125, 180
"Dancing Bear, The," 65
"Dead Friend, The," 64
"Death of Odin, The," 63 - 64, 82
"Death of Wallace, The," 65

Deluge, Epic on the. *See* Noachid
"Destruction of Jerusalem, The," 65
Devil's Walk, The, 52, 182n2
"Donica," 75
"Edward and Susan," 183n21
"English Eclogues," 70 - 72
"Evening Rainbow, The," 66
"God's Judgment on a Wicked Bishop,"
77, 79
"Grandmother's Tale, The," 71
"Hannah," 72
"Henry the Hermit," 72
"Holly Tree, The," 65, 67
"Hymn to the Penates," 50, 67
"Idiot Boy, The," 73
"Inchcape Rock, The," 75 - 76
Inscriptions, 68 - 69
"Jaspar," 75
Joan of Arc, 22, *30 - 46*, 49, 84, 92, 109,
110, 115, 122, 124, 132, 139, 148,
150, 152, 174, 182n4, 6, 12,
"Last of the Family, The," 71
Laureate Verse, 151 - 57
Lay of the Laureate, The, 154
"Lord William," 76
"Lucretia," 69
"Mad Woman, The," 74
Madoc, 52, 58, 97, *109 - 27*, 131, 132,
184n1
Madoc in Aztlan, 110, *117 - 27*
Madoc in Wales, *110 - 17*, 123
"Mary, the Maid of the Inn," 74
"Mohammed," 53, 82, 83 - 84, 98, 149
Monodramas, 69
"My Days Among the Dead
Are Passed," 72, 179
Noachid, The, *82 - 83*, 98, 154
"Oak of Our Fathers, The," 65
"Old Man's Comforts, The," 65, 178,
181n4
"Old Mansion House, The," 71
"Old Woman of Berkley, The," 78 - 79
"On My Own Miniature Picture," 68
"Pig, The," 65 - 67
"Pious Painter, The," 79
Poems, 26
Poet's Pilgrimage to Waterloo, The,
152 - 55, 178
"Queen Orraca and the Five Martyrs,"
79
"Race of Odin, The," 63 - 64, 82

"Remembrance," 16
"Retrospect, The," 16, 68
"Robin Hood," 110, 185n3
Roderick, the Last of the Goths, 95, 131 - 50, 152, 180, 186n7
"Romance," 63 - 64
"Rudiger," 76 - 77, 125
"Ruined Cottage, The," 72
"Sailor's Mother, The," 71
"Sailor Who Had Served in the Slave Trade, The," 74 - 75
"St. Bartholomew's Day," 65
"St. Gualberto," 75, 80
"St. Patrick's Purgatory," 77
"St. Romuald," 79
"Songs of the American Indians, 65, 82
"Sonnets on the Slave Trade," 66
"Spanish Armada, The," 65
"Surgeon's Warning, The," 184n25
Tale of Paraguay, A, 85, 185n13
Thalaba the Destroyer, 52, 77, 84 - 95, 98, 100, 103, 104, 105, 106, 108, 126, 131, 149, 152, 184n6
"To a Spider," 65
"To Contemplation," 63
"To Horror," 63
"To Margaret Hill," 67
"To the Genius of Africa," 63
"To Winter," 66 - 67
"Triumph of Woman, The," 64
"Verses to Have Been Addressed to His Grace the Duke of Portland," 33
Vision of Judgment, The, 61, 152, 155 - 57
"Vision of the Maid of Orleans, The," 34
"Warning Voice, The," 151
"Wedding, The," 71
"Widow, The," 64
"Wife of Fergus, The," 69
"Witch, The," 71 - 72
"Ximalpoca," 69
"Young Dragon, The," 80

WORKS - PROSE:
Amadis of Gaul (tr.), 57, 128, 185n2
Autobiographical letters, 13, 175
Book of the Church, The, 159, 183n12
Chronicle of the Cid, The, (tr.), 128 - 29, 131, 185n2
Colloquies, 58, 61, 162, 167 - 71, 180

Commonplace Book, The, 60, 172
Doctor, etc., The, 17, 60, 171 - 78, 180
Essays, Moral and Political, 162, 164, 167, 180
Expedition of Orsua and the Crimes of Aguirre, The, 159
Flagellant, The, 19, 80
History of Brazil, The, 159
"History of Portugal, The," 50, 95, 111, 129 - 30, 159, 175, 186n5
History of the Peninsular War, 130, 159
Journal of a Tour of the Netherlands, 186n11
"Letter to William Smith, A," 47
Letters from England, 59, 162 - 66, 175, 180
Letters Written During a Short Residence in Spain and Portugal, 52, 162
Life of Bunyan, The, 186n3
Life of Cowper, The, 186n3
Life of Nelson, The, 160 - 62, 180
Life of Wesley, 60, 61, 160
Lives of the British Admirals, 160
Omniana, or Horae Otiosiores, 60, 146
Palmerin of England, (tr.), 57, 128, 185n2
Reviews, 52, 162; of "The Rime of the Ancient Mariner," 27, 73; of *Lyrical Ballads*, 52, 73
Sir Thomas More. See Colloquies
"Story of the Three Bears, The," 65, 174 - 75, 177, 179, 180, 187n10
Spectator, The, 17, 177
Spenser, Edmund, 17, 29, 31, 44, 64, 69, 92, 95, 151; *The Faerie Queene*, 17, 85; *The Shepherds Calendar*, 155
Sterne, Laurence, 177; *Tristram Shandy*, 171, 174
Stukeley, William, 110
Swift, Jonathan, 163

Tasso, Torquato, 17, 31, 115, 148; *Jerusalem Delivered*, 17, 109, 115
Taylor, Thomas, 166
Taylor, William, 73, 78, 98, 111, 126, 143, 145, 157
Tennyson, Alfred, 117
Tippoo Sahib, 130
Tyler, Elizabeth, 13 - 17, 22, 25, 57, 62, 105, 174

Tyler, William, 17, 67, 100, 174 - 75, 187n10

Vincent, Dr. William, 19 - 20, 95
Virgil, 18, 31, 44, 69, 156; *The Aeneid*, 33, 37, 46, 109, 111, 119, 123
Voltaire, 19, 57, 83; *Lettres Philosophiques*, 162; *La Pucelle*, 31
Voss, Johann Heinrich, 155

Wagner, Richard, 82, 93
Warton, Thomas, 63; *History of English Poetry*, 17
Washington, George, 157
Weeks, Shadrach, 16, 25
Wellington, Arthur Wellesley, Duke of, 159

Wilberforce, Bishop Samuel, 125
Wilkes, John, 156, 175 - 76
Williams, Edward, 110
Wiliams, Helen Maria, 118
Williams, William, 16
Wither, George, 65
Wollstonecraft, Mary, 31, 51
Wordsworth, Dorothy, 56
Wordsworth, William, 9, 27, 31, 32, 51, 61, 68, 71 - 75, 82, 93, 145, 174, 178, 186n7; *The Excursion*, 72, 145; *Lyrical Ballads*, 53, 70, 74
Wynn, Charles W. W., 18 - 19, 47, 99, 109 - 10

Zend Avesta, The, 83